敦煌文化·译丛（汉英对照）

Dunhuang Culture in Translation: A Series

主编 姜秋霞
副主编 [美]安瑞 柳菁

箫管霓裳

敦煌乐舞

Raiment of Rainbows and Feathers: Music and Dance from the Dunhuang Murals

王克芬 柴剑虹 著 崇天霖 译

甘肃教育出版社

图书在版编目（CIP）数据

箫管霓裳：敦煌乐舞 = Raiment of Rainbows and Feathers:Music and Dance from the Dunhuang Murals：汉英对照 / 王克芬，柴剑虹著；崇天霖译. -- 兰州：甘肃教育出版社，2021.11
（敦煌文化·译丛 / 姜秋霞主编）
ISBN 978-7-5423-5146-3

Ⅰ. ①箫… Ⅱ. ①王… ②柴… ③崇… Ⅲ. ①敦煌壁画一乐舞一介绍一汉、英 Ⅳ. ①K879.41

中国版本图书馆 CIP 数据核字(2021)第 133380 号

箫管霓裳——敦煌乐舞

Raiment of Rainbows and Feathers: Music and Dance from the Dunhuang Murals

王克芬　柴剑虹　著　　崇天霖　译

责任编辑　王露莹
封面设计　石　璞
内文设计　方　圆
图片支持　敦煌研究院

出　版　甘肃教育出版社
社　址　兰州市读者大道 568 号　730030
网　址　www.gseph.cn　　E-mail　gseph@duzhe.cn
电　话　0931-8436105（编辑部）　0931-8773056(发行部)
传　真　0931-8773056
淘宝官方旗舰店　http://shop111038270.taobao.com

发　行　甘肃教育出版社　　印　刷　山东新华印务有限公司
开　本　787 毫米 × 1092 毫米　1/16　　印　张　17　　字　数　220 千
版　次　2021 年 11 月第 1 版
印　次　2021 年 11 月第 1 次印刷
书　号　ISBN 978-7-5423-5146-3　定　价　68.00 元

“丝绸之路·敦煌文化翻译”工程

编 委 会

“丝绸之路·敦煌文化翻译”工程是甘肃文化翻译中心在甘肃省委宣传部的领导下所实施的文化翻译工程，旨在助力共建“一带一路”，弘扬丝路文化和敦煌文化，推进敦煌文化国际交流与传播，推动中国文化“走出去”。

“敦煌文化·译丛”为“丝绸之路·敦煌文化翻译”工程系列成果之一。

敦煌汉长城(范宏伟　摄)

The Great Wall Built in the Han Dynasty in Dunhuang (Photo by Fan Hongwei)

“敦煌文化·译丛”简介

近年来,在“中华文化走出去”“讲好中国故事”与共建“一带一路”的大背景下,充分展示了中华民族文化自信的敦煌文化,以其丰富的内涵和独特的魅力吸引着全世界的目光。越来越多的海内外人士渴望掀起敦煌文化神秘的面纱,走近敦煌,从而走进敦煌。“敦煌文化·译丛”的编纂,以“敦煌文化走出去”为目标,以“讲好敦煌故事”为原则,对外传播敦煌文化,交流敦煌学思想,传承敦煌精神。

一、丛书内容

“敦煌文化·译丛”在传播内容上重视知识的可接受度,甄选了既有学术价值,又便于普及的敦煌学著作和敦煌文化读物进行翻译。所选书籍均为敦煌学著名专家所著,集学术性与科普性于一体,且呈现出一定的系统性,主题逐步涵盖敦煌文化完整版图,着力打造出相对全面的敦煌文化外宣丛书体系。本系列译丛采用中外语言对照的编纂方式,传播敦煌文化,交流敦煌学研究思想等。

“敦煌文化·译丛”以开放的模式分期分批编辑出版。第一辑包含《丝路明珠:敦煌》《艺苑瑰宝:莫高窟壁画与彩塑》《箫管霓裳:敦煌乐舞》及《遗响千年:敦煌的影响》四部作品的汉英对照读本。

《丝路明珠:敦煌》(郑炳林、李军著)以敦煌的历史、地位和周边名胜古迹为主题,分别讲述了从新石器时代、两汉、魏晋南北朝到西夏、元、明、清各个不同朝代历史背景下敦煌的发展和变迁;论述了丝绸之路开通后,敦煌作为中西交通线路上的重要枢纽、中西贸易的中转站和中央王朝经营西域的军事重镇的历史地位；介绍了包括莫高窟、榆林窟等佛教石窟，玉门关、阳关等城池关隘，及鸣沙山、月牙泉等自然景观在内的敦煌周边历史文化名胜和古迹。全书脉络清晰，语言生动，集资料性、故事性和知识性于一体，既突出了敦煌的地域文化特点，又展现了敦煌厚重的历史内涵，使这颗沉睡在茫茫大漠之中的璀璨明珠在世人面前焕发出夺目的光华。

《艺苑瑰宝：莫高窟壁画与彩塑》（赵声良著）概括介绍了敦煌彩塑和壁画的基本风貌，包括塑像、佛像画、飞天、故事画、经变画、山水画、装饰画等单元，并阐述了包含其中的文化价值、历史价值、艺术价值，展示出千年中国美术的脉络。这本书还对古代印度、中亚艺术与中国艺术的交流与融合作了分析，全书浸透着作者全方位学术研究的成果，以及自豪自信的文化情怀。文笔流畅，深入浅出，图文并茂，雅俗共赏，把博大精深的敦煌艺术成功地传达给了读者。

《箫管霓裳：敦煌乐舞》（王克芬、柴剑虹著）以敦煌莫高窟为主题，分别介绍了敦煌乐舞的人文背景及源流、经变画中的天宫乐舞、世俗画里的歌舞、特色鲜明的民族舞蹈、生动活泼的童子舞姿、敦煌乐舞的文化特征等内容。作者用凝练、简洁、流畅的笔触，以敦煌莫高窟壁画、彩塑为着眼点，文解图义，栩栩如生地展示了敦煌莫高窟壁画中丰富多彩的佛国乐舞形象。全书凝练紧凑，主题鲜明，语言流畅，专业性与普及性兼顾，为中外读者了解与欣赏敦煌乐舞打开了一扇大门。

《遗响千年：敦煌的影响》（刘进宝著）以敦煌文献的整理刊布与敦煌艺术探索和文艺创作为主题，分别介绍了敦煌学的产生背景、敦煌文献在各国的研究概况、中外文化艺术名人与敦煌的故事、敦煌艺术光辉照耀下的文学艺术创作成果、敦煌文物的保护及研究等内容。作者用通俗易懂、生动活泼的语言，将专业性与普及性融为一体，让读者与敦煌渐行渐近，相知相亲，向世人展现了敦煌文化在中国和世界所产生的深远影响。全书图文并茂、材料翔实、叙述生动，吸引中外读者走进敦煌辉煌灿烂的文化圣殿与艺术宝库。

这四部作品涵盖了敦煌文化中的重要板块，系统阐释了敦煌文化的历史发展、艺术价值与人文精神。一方面，从本体视角出发介绍敦煌的历史地理知识；另一方面，从认识视角出发展示敦煌文化艺术中最为人感知的两张名片——壁画雕塑与音乐舞蹈；最终，从价值视角出发凸显敦煌文化及敦煌学在全世界产生的影响。本系列译丛将促进敦煌艺术之美的国际化交流，补充与敦煌乐舞相关的深度双语语料，拓展敦煌历史地理相关的系统语言资料，为“敦煌在中国、敦煌学在世界”这一国际化命题提供了必要参考。

二、译介特点

“敦煌文化·译丛”以“传播敦煌文化，交流敦煌学思想”为主旨，采用“中英对照”的形式讲述敦煌故事、阐释敦煌精神。在译介方式上，运用多元的翻译策略和方法，进行文本对比与转换。在原文阐释上，一方面通过系统查阅历史文献、背景资料、中外敦煌学研究成果等，深刻理解原文语义；另一方面通过译者与原作者的对话与沟通，精准把握敦煌文化的精髓要义。在外文表达上，注重信息的有效表达，通过“中西合璧”的模式展开翻译，由中外译者通力合作，以“读者接受”为主导，运用适切的话语方式，综合的翻译方法，进行语言转换。译文尽可能贴近英语读者的表达习惯、思维模式、语言风格和理解能力，使所译作品不仅在文字上实现了“走出去”，同时使其文化内涵真正能够“走进去”，力图实现文化的深度传播。

“敦煌文化·译丛”的总体翻译原则：在充分理解和尊重原文的基础上，对于汉英语言文化中存在对应概念和表达的内容，尽量忠实于原文的内容和风格，力求准确再现原文的语言和文化信息。在遵循翻译基本原理的前提下，根据汉英两种语言和文化之间的差异，综合运用“归化”“异化”“融合化”等翻译策略，对原文部分内容进行适度的增减编改，灵活采用节译、概译、编译和解释性翻译等方法进行语言文本的转换。

“敦煌文化·译丛”的基本翻译方法：

1. 对于原文中文化概念和术语的翻译，一般采用我国官方出版物和官方网站中已有的外文表达。

2. 对于中国的历史朝代，在外文文本中补充了公元纪年法中的年份信息。但对于个别年代信息有争议的历史朝代，则不再标注年份。

3. 对于历史官衔名称，以“传播历史文化，兼顾读者理解”为目的，采用

“音译+名词”“音译+释义”等方法，一方面保留原有的文化特质，另一方面使读者易于接受；对于官衔、官职修饰词语过多的情况，则采用意译或概译的方法进行语义对应；对于官职官衔名在不同历史时期，虽名称未变，但语义内涵发生变化的，根据其语境中相应的含义进行转换。

4. 对于原文中出现的书籍名称，首先遵循“名从历史”“名从主人”的原则，沿用已有的译名。如果已有译名为汉语拼音，则在保留原有名称的基础上，增补英文译名；无英译文的书籍名称，则采用常规翻译方法进行文本对应。

5. 对于原文中的引文（如诗词、古籍文献），根据引文的作用进行有选择性的转换。若引文为核心论点，或用于描写相应的文化内容，且上下文未对引文内容进行解释或重述，则全文翻译；若引文仅用于衬托或强化相应的文化内容，且相关内容已在上下文说明或提及，则进行概译或省译。

6. 对于一些描写壁画形象的直白语言，为提升其艺术美感，采用“优化”的策略和“解释性翻译”的方法，进行语篇结构的扩充对应。

7. 对于宗教文化概念，首先采用已有的英文表达；对于有固定梵语表达的佛教概念，则采用“回译法”进行转换；没有约定俗成表达的宗教概念、中国本土宗教概念及其他宗教与中国文化相融合后产生的概念，则根据情况采用音译、直译或意译进行文本对应。

8. 对于需要补充文化背景信息的内容，一般采用“译者注”的方式进行补充说明，以便更有效地提高阅读理解力。包括但不限于下列情况：一是对于一些在历史演变过程中语义发生变化的文化名称，采用“译者注”的方式加以说明，如“刺史”这一官职名称，分别译为Inspector / Governor / Prefect，并通过“译者注”说明同一名称在不同历史时期因其职责发生变化采用不同译文的背景信息。二是对于一些特殊地名，为避免产生阅读障碍，在翻译的同时加“译者注”进行说明，如不以行政区划命名的大地区概念（中原、西域等），翻译的同时，通过“译者注”明确其内涵和范围；含有古代行政区划“州”“郡”“府”“县”“道”等的地名，在翻译行政区划词的同时适当增加“译者注”解释其含义；由于历史原因更改地名的，亦通过“译者注”加以阐明。三是当同音异义词音译后在译文中无法分辨时，也采用“译者注”的方式加以区分。

9. 本译丛遵循一致性原则，运用统一的翻译策略和方法，但同时也存在一些体现译者个体风格的差异化表达。

三、几点说明

1. 中文文本之外附加的内容，如附录等，经与中文作者沟通，不再收录。

2. 中文文本中个别问题需要进行勘误时，英译文转换正确的语义内容，同时增加必要的说明。

3. 本译丛在翻译过程中参考了大量国内外相关著作、辞典、图册、音像资料、网络资料及数据库等，具体参考目录将在每本书后单另列出。

最后需要说明的是，敦煌文化翻译是一项十分具有挑战性的工作，难点很多，难度很大。因此，作为"丝绸之路·敦煌文化翻译"工程的第一辑译丛，在翻译中难免存在许多不足之处，甚至可能有误译和错译之处。我们真诚期待广大读者、专家学者批评指正！

致　谢

"敦煌文化·译丛"在策划、翻译、出版过程中得到甘肃省委宣传部、中国外文局、兰州大学敦煌学研究所等单位的大力支持；在翻译过程中得到了著作者的翻译授权和学术指导；同时得到了甘肃省人民政府新闻办、兰州城市学院等单位的支持，在此一并感谢。

"敦煌文化·译丛"编委会

An Introduction to *Dunhuang Culture in Translation: A Series*

In recent years, Dunhuang culture—an emblem of the pride of Chinese civilization—has increasingly attracted the world's attention with its profound significance and unique charms. This has taken place against the backdrop of "Chinese culture going global," "telling China's story to the world," and the joint pursuit of the Belt and Road Initiative. Ever-increasing numbers of people both internationally and domestically want Dunhuang's veil of mystery to be lifted. Through reading this series, people can become more familiar with Dunhuang, paving the way to really "get into" Dunhuang. Thus, along the principles of "Dunhuang culture going forth into the world," as well as "telling Dunhuang's story," the *Dunhuang Culture in Translation* series has been compiled with the goal of communicating the concepts of Dunhuang culture, carrying on the spirit of Dunhuang, and promoting Dunhuang to an international audience.

Series Content

The *Dunhuang Culture in Translation: A Series* emphasizes appropriateness for its readers, selecting works in the field of Dunhuang studies which embody academic value and also can be made accessible to a general audience. All the books in this series were written by well-known experts in the field of Dunhuang studies, blending academic knowledge with popular science and presenting information in a systematic way, and using a compilation method in both Chinese and English. The topics cover the essential part of Dunhuang culture, resulting in a relatively comprehensive framework for disseminating this subject to the world. The translated volumes in this series use a Chinese-English format to promote Dunhuang culture and academic exchanges of Dunhuang studies.

Dunhuang Culture in Translation is a multi-volumed, inclusive series published in sets. The first set in the series includes four bilingual volumes: *Dunhuang: Pearl of the Silk Road*; *Art Treasures: Murals and Painted Sculptures in Mogao Caves*; *Raiment of Rainbows and Feathers: Music and Dance from the Dunhuang Murals*; and *Dunhuang: Its Everlasting Impact.*

Dunhuang: Pearl of the Silk Road (by Zheng Binglin and Li Jun) takes as its subject matter the history of Dunhuang as well as its surrounding attractions. It traces Dunhuang's development and changes against the historical background of different periods, from the Neolithic Age, the Han Dynasty, Wei, Jin, Northern and Southern dynasties to the Western Xia, Yuan, Ming, and Qing dynasties. This volume explores the opening of the Silk Road and Dunhuang's historical status as an important crossroads for Sino-Western exchanges, the part it played as an important hub for Sino-Western trade, and its role as a military center for the Central Plains' operations in the Western Regions. It introduces the Buddhist rock-cut cave temples of the Mogao Caves and the Yulin Caves, historical and cultural sites such as the Yangguan and Yumen passes, and surrounding natural scenic spots including the Mingsha Mountain and the Crescent Moon Spring. The whole book is presented with clear ideas and vivid language, integrating factual data, literary narrative, and scholarly expertise. It not only highlights the regional cultural characteristics of Dunhuang, but also reveals its profound historical connotations as well, making this bright pearl, sleeping in the vast desert, glow with its brilliance for the world to see.

Art Treasures: Murals and Painted Sculptures in Mogao Caves (by Zhao Shengliang) outlines the basic features of Dunhuang sculptures and murals, including polychromed statues, Buddhist iconography, apsaras, narrative paintings, sutra illustrations, landscape paintings, decorative motifs, and other elements, expounding their cultural, historical, and artistic value in addition to tracing the course of Chinese art for thousands of years. This volume, steeped in Dr. Zhao's comprehensive academic research and brimming with pride in Chinese culture, also analyzes the exchange and synthesis of visual arts from ancient India, Central Asia, and China. The writing is fluent and easy to understand, with copious illustrations accompanying the text. Sharing an appreciation of both the sophisticated and the popular, it successfully conveys Dunhuang's broad and profound art to its readers.

Raiment of Rainbows and Feathers: Music and Dance from the Dunhuang Murals (by Wang Kefen and Chai Jianhong) takes the Mogao Caves as its subject, introducing the cultural background and origins of Dunhuang music and dance, images of palace entertainment depicted in sutra illustrations, singing and dancing as found in secular paintings, distinctive ethnic dances, the lively lotus child dance, and more. The authors use concise and natural language to discuss the murals and the painted sculptures of the Mogao Caves, explaining the meaning of the images and vividly revealing the rich Buddhist and Chinese music and dance images found in Dunhuang wall paintings. Compact and concise, the book's themes are clear and the language is articulate, with an emphasis on balancing professional scholarship with accessibility to the public, opening the door for readers at home and abroad to understand and appreciate the performing arts of Dunhuang.

Dunhuang: Its Everlasting Impact (by Liu Jinbao) takes the compilation and classification of Dunhuang manuscripts, the exploration of Dunhuang art, and Dunhuang literary creation as its themes. It introduces the background of Dunhuang studies as a field, the research overview of Dunhuang manuscripts in various countries, the famous names behind Dunhuang studies both in China and around the world, and the literary and creative achievements in Dunhuang art, as well as the research, and conservation of Dunhuang relics. The author uses easy-to-understand, lively and dynamic language to integrate scholarship with mass-market appeal, allowing readers to "get closer" to Dunhuang, showing the profound influence of Dunhuang culture in China and internationally. The book's pictures and texts, informative materials, and vivid narrative style encourage both Chinese and English-speaking audiences to truly enter the brilliant cultural temples and treasure houses of Dunhuang.

The four works in this set form a system of their own, covering important areas of the Dunhuang cultural sphere, and systematically explaining the historical development, artistic value, and humanistic spirit of Dunhuang culture. On the one hand, the main objective of the books sets out to introduce the history and geography of Dunhuang, while on the other hand, it explores two of the most well-known aspects of Dunhuang arts: the visual arts and the performing arts. Finally, judging from its value, the set highlights the influence of Dunhuang culture and Dunhuang studies around the world. This collection of translations aims to promote international understanding of the aesthetics of Dunhuang art, supplement in-depth bilingual works related to Dunhuang music and dance, expand systematic language materials related to Dunhuang history and geography, and provide a must-have language reference for researchers of Dunhuang studies both in China and overseas.

Special Features of the Translation

Dunhuang Culture in Translation is organized around the themes of promoting Dunhuang culture and transmitting Dunhuang thought, telling the stories of Dunhuang, and expounding the spirit of Dunhuang in a Chinese-English format. In terms of translation methods, this series uses multiple strategies and methods to compare and translate texts. In terms of the interpretation of the original text, on the one hand, we can deeply understand the semantics of the original text through systematic review of historical documents, background materials, and research results in Dunhuang studies in China as well as internationally; on the other hand, we can accurately grasp the essence of Dunhuang culture through dialogue and communication between the translators and the original authors. In terms of foreign language expression, special attention has been paid to the effective expression of information. The translation has been done according to a Sino-Western model. The Chinese and English language translators have closely cooperated with one other, with reader accessibility as their primary consideration, using appropriate discourse modes and comprehensive translation methods to exchange languages. The translation is as close as possible to the idiomatic expression, modes of thought, language style, and reading comprehension of English-language readers, so that the translated text of the works not only achieves a "going out" in a literary sense, but simultaneously also allows the cultural connotations to truly "go in" and achieve a deep transmission into the readers' conceptualization.

The overarching translation principles of the *Dunhuang Culture in Translation: A Series* are as follows: on the basis of understanding and respecting the original text, for those expressions which have a corresponding concept and expression in English language and culture, the translation strives to accurately reproduce the original language and cultural information, faithful to the content and style of the original Chinese text. Moreover, on the premise of following standard principles of translation, according to differences between Chinese and English languages and cultures we have comprehensively employed translation strategies such as domestication, foreignization, and fusion to appropriately add, delete, edit, and modify the original content. We have adopted a flexible mixture of approaches such as abridged translation, generalized translation, compilation, and interpretative translation for language and text conversion.

The basic translation methods for the *Dunhuang Culture in Translation: A Series* are as follows:

1. For the translation of cultural concepts and terminology in the original text, foreign language expressions found in official publications and official websites of China have generally been used.

2. For historical dynasties, information for the dates using AD and BC has been added to the foreign language text. However, for historical dynasties with dates in dispute, the year is not noted.

3. For the translations of historical titles of official rank, our purpose is to enhance exchanges of history and culture, taking into account the readers' understanding. Thus, we have employed methods such as "*pinyin* transliteration + nouns," and "*pinyin* transliteration + gloss," on the one hand, retaining the original cultural characteristics of the titles, and, on the other hand, allowing readers to easily accept the title names. For official titles with multiple versions or modifiers, free translation or generalized translation methods have been used for semantic correspondence; for official titles from different historical periods, when the name has remained unchanged, but the semantic connotation has changed, the meaning has been conveyed according to the appropriate context.

4. For the titles of Chinese books, the principles of "using historical names" and "using names created by the original parties" have been followed. If an existing title is in *pinyin*, the English translation has been added on the basis of keeping the original name; if there is no English translation of the name of the classic text, conventional translation methods have been applied.

5. For citations or quotations in the original text (such as poems, classics), selective conversion has been carried out according to the function of the citation. If a quotation or citation functions as a core idea or is used to describe corresponding cultural content, and the context does not explain or restate the citation content, the full text is translated; if the quotation is only used to highlight or strengthen the corresponding cultural content, and the relevant content has been explained or mentioned in the context, general translation or deletion has been applied.

6. For certain basic, straightforward language describing mural imagery, in order to enhance their artistic beauty, "optimization" strategies and interpretative translation methods have been applied to expand the text.

7. For religious and cultural concepts, we have first adopted existing English terms and expressions where they exist; for Buddhist concepts with fixed, conventional Sanskrit names, we have used the back translation method to convert the terms from Chinese back into their original Sanskrit again. Religious concepts that are not expressed by conventional usage or fixed terms, native Chinese religious concepts, and concepts arising from the fusion of other religions and Chinese culture have been rendered by transliteration, literal translation or free translation based on the situation or context.

8. For the content that needs to be supplemented with cultural background information, we have generally used footnotes as supplementary explanations, in order to more effectively improve the readers' comprehension. This includes but is not limited to the following situations: First, for some cultural names whose semantics have changed in the course of historical evolution, we have used footnotes to explain them. For example, the official title of "*cishi*" is translated variously as Inspector, Governor, or Prefect, and a footnote is used to explain that the title for this post was modified over time due to changes in the position's responsibilities in

different historical periods. Second, for special place names, footnotes have been added to avoid confusion. For example, the concept of large geographical regions such as the Central Plains, the Western Regions, and so forth, was provided with footnotes to clarify their meaning and scope. Footnotes have been provided for place names with ancient administrative divisions such as "*zhou*" "*jun*" "*fu*" "*xian*" "*dao*" etc., where necessary or appropriate. Changes in place names due to historical reasons have also been clarified through the addition of footnotes. Third, when homophones cannot be distinguished in the translation after transliteration, footnotes or annotations have also been used to distinguish them.

9. This translation series follows the principle of consistency and uses unified translation strategies and methods, but some terms and expressions may vary and reflect the individual style of the translators.

Special Points for the Readers' Consideration

1. Appendices, indices, and glossaries in the original Chinese versions are not included in the volumes of this set, which is permitted by the original authors.

2. Where individual issues in the Chinese text have required correction, the information in the English translation has been presented in the corrected, revised form, and explanations have been added where necessary.

3. This translation series relies on a large number of Chinese and English language reference works, dictionaries, atlases, audiovisual materials, internet resources, and databases during the translation process. A specific bibliography is listed separately at the back of each volume.

One final thing to be said is that Dunhuang culture translation is a very demanding task, with many difficulties and great challenges. Therefore, as the first series in the Silk Road Dunhuang Culture Translation Project, there are inevitably many shortcomings in the translation, and there may even be mistranslations and errors. We sincerely encourage criticism and correction from readers, experts, and scholars in the field.

Acknowledgements

The *Dunhuang Culture in Translation* : *A Series* received strong support from the Publicity Department of the Gansu Provincial Party Committee, China Foreign Languages Publishing Administration, Institute of Dunhuang Studies of Lanzhou University, and other governmental offices in the planning, translation, and publication process of this series. Throughout the translation process, permission, authorization, and guidance were granted by the authors of each volume. The Information Office of the People's Government of Gansu Province, Lanzhou City University as well as other governmental offices and leaders all gave their encouragement and support to this project. We extend our heartfelt thanks and gratitude to them all.

Editorial Committee of *Dunhuang Culture in Translation: A Series*

目 录

Contents

目 录

Contents

腰鼓舞　榆林窟第 25 窟南壁

Waist Drum Dance (South Wall, Yulin Cave 25)

序言一

1975年，中国与英国签订了教育交流协议，恢复了中断将近10年的留学生互换项目。我作为首批留学生之一，同14位同学到英国学习。与此同时，英国学生也到中国留学。很多年以后，我遇到其中一位当年曾经在北京大学留学的英国学者，那时她已经是大英图书馆的东亚部负责人。她告诉我正在做的一件事情就是和中国文物局合作，把大英图书馆收藏的来自敦煌的历史资料复制给中方，以此加深两国专家围绕敦煌学的研究活动。可见因为历史上的多种原因，大量敦煌资料流散在海外，这对中国是一种损失，但是也催化了国外对敦煌的关注。

然而，敦煌学不局限于仅仅流散在海外的史料研究，真正的研究中心永远在敦煌，永远在中国。比如石窟代表的敦煌文化就是搬不走的，敦煌背后的历史和哲学思想是搬不走的。近些年，中国学者对敦煌的研究成绩斐然，加之敦煌文化的博大精深，非常有必要通过翻译，把中国学者的研究成果，把敦煌文化的精华，大张旗鼓地传播出去。特别是"一带一路"倡议不仅强化了中国与沿线国家的经济活动，也拉近了文化上的联系。民心相通首先要以文明互鉴为依托，以文化传播为纽带，达到美美与共。敦煌文化重要，对外传播更为重要。然而，集历史、艺术、宗教为一体的敦煌学覆盖历史时段长，涉及艺术门类全，代表的宗教影响深，反映的社会发展广，要翻译成外文实在太难了。

令人欣喜的是，以甘肃文化翻译中心姜秋霞教授领衔的团队卧薪尝胆、呕心沥血达六年，终于把首批共四部中英文对照版的"敦煌文化·译丛"呈现给国内外的读者。这四部图书分别是《丝路明珠：敦煌》《艺苑瑰宝：莫高窟壁画与彩塑》《箫管霓裳：敦煌乐舞》和《遗响千年：敦煌的影响》。这套图书的出版标志着我国首次有计划、成规模地、系统地把敦煌文化最新的研究成果用英文对外介绍。四本书用当代的语言把一个中国故事的过去与现在讲述给国际受众。这个翻译出版项目成就有多大，其艰难历程就有多长。翻译难，中译外更难，敦煌文化的翻译难上加难。这六年来，姜教授的团队经历了多少艰辛，比如为寻找一个准确的词汇花费多少心血，为精准传达一个观点熬去多少时光，读者只需翻阅一下这四本书，就会一目了然。

既然难度这么大，为什么还要翻译？姜教授说："翻译，不仅仅是语言的转换，更是对文化的阐释。翻译敦煌文化，不是简单的话码转换，也不是单纯的信息传递，更重要的是解释和阐释敦煌文化和历史遗存蕴含的哲学思想、人文精神、价值理念、道德规范；弘扬和传承蕴含其中的中华民族的文化精神、文化胸怀和文化自信。"通过她的话我感到，敦煌文化翻译反映了译者的一种家国情怀、对外传播的理想抱负和迎难而上的治学精神。没有坚定的信念、远大的抱负和刻苦的工作干劲，译者早已在翻译任务的困难面前望而却步。所以，在向译者团队表示祝贺的同时，我更想向他们表示崇高的敬意。

一套丛书有那么大的意义吗？文明互鉴需要文化信息的交流，做好对外交流就是要拿出外国人读得懂、看得明白的作品来。展示文化自信，需要拿出难啃的硬骨头成果来。这套丛书就是文化自信的产物，敦煌文化对外传播的最新之作。

然而，"敦煌文化·译丛"的意义不仅仅在作品上。丛书的翻译还是翻译团队不断成熟的一个过程。"敦煌文化·译丛"是"丝绸之路·敦煌文化翻译工程"的第一期项目。启动后译者发现翻译的难度极大，文化概念的翻译难度尤其大。于是翻译团队又启动了"敦煌文化中英对照术语库"的编制工作，并在《敦煌文化关键词》完成后，再开始推进"敦煌文化·译丛"的工作。"敦煌文化·译丛"第一辑四部图书以及衍生作品的问世见证了一支年轻的翻译队伍从无到有、从小到大、从弱到强的发展壮大。而作为设在兰州城市学院的一个团队，译者们作为教师也在培育着更加年轻的译者。他们的精神和经验必然让他们带出一支对外传播的人才队伍。

"敦煌文化·译丛"的意义还在于填补了"一带一路"建设的一个空白。敦煌，曾经是古代丝绸之路的重镇，如今是"一带一路"建设的重要支点。丛书给敦煌乃至甘肃省的对外文化交流提供了精品之作，增添了灿烂的文化光彩。讲好中国故事，传播中国声音不是一句口号，需要一部部的作品来支撑和实现。“敦煌文化·译丛”不仅展示了一段辉煌的历史，更彰显了中国文化自信和文化繁荣在新时代的成果。四部作品宣扬的不仅仅是中国历史上的文化积累，它们所介绍的四个方面更是代表中国在文明互鉴过程中的四颗璀璨明星，反射中国文化发展的过去，照亮中国文化传承的当今，预示中国文化生生不息的未来。

也正因为如此，我们期待“丝绸之路·敦煌文化翻译工程”的下一个项目。

中国外文局原副局长
中国翻译协会常务副会长 黄友义

2020 年 10 月

Foreword I

In 1975, China and the United Kingdom signed an educational exchange agreement, resuming the exchange program for foreign students which had been suspended for nearly 10 years. I went to the UK to study with 14 classmates as part of the first group of these students. At the same time, British students also came to study in China. Some years later, I ran into one of the British scholars who had studied at Peking University when I was studying in the UK. At the time we met, she was already head of the Department of Oriental at the British Library. She told me that she was working on a joint project with the State Bureau of Cultural Relics, replicating historical documents and materials from Dunhuang held in the British Library, in order to facilitate Dunhuang research by experts from our two nations. Due to various historical reasons, a large amount of Dunhuang materials were scattered in various places overseas. This may have been a loss for China, but it also catalyzed foreigners' attention on Dunhuang.

However, Dunhuang studies is not limited merely to the study of historical materials scattered around the world. The real center of research has always been in Dunhuang and in China. For example, Dunhuang culture, as represented by its cave temples, is irremovable. Likewise, the history and philosophical thought behind Dunhuang is also deeply rooted here. In recent years, Chinese scholars have made outstanding achievements in the study of Dunhuang, and, coupled with the profundity of Dunhuang culture, it has become truly necessary to make these research findings—along with the essence of Dunhuang culture—widely known through their translation. In particular, the Belt and Road Initiative has not only strengthened the economic activity between China and the countries along the route, but has also brought closer cultural ties between them. People-to-people exchange must first rely on cultural communication and mutual learning among civilizations so as to uphold the beauty and diversity of civilizations in the world. Dunhuang culture is important, but communication with the international community is even more significant. However, Dunhuang studies, which integrates history, art, and religion, covers a long historical period of time, involves a full range of arts, represents deep religious influences, and reflects a wide range of social developments. It is thus an extremely challenging task to translate the achievements of Dunhuang studies into another language.

It is now gratifying to see that the team led by Professor Jiang Qiuxia of the Gansu Cultural Translation and Interpreting Center has, after six years of hard work, completed the first four volumes of the Chinese-English bilingual *Dunhuang Culture in Translation* series, now being presented to readers at home and abroad. The titles of these four books are *Dunhuang: Pearl of the Silk Road*; *Art Treasures: Murals and Painted Sculptures in Mogao Caves*; *Raiment of Rainbows and Feathers: Music and Dance from Dunhuang Murals*; and *Dunhuang: Its Everlasting Impact*. The publication of this set of books marks the first time that China has introduced the latest Dunhuang culture research in English and Chinese at the same time, and on a planned, large-scale, and systematic basis. The four books use contemporary language to convey the past and present of a Chinese story to an international audience. This translation and publishing project has been a great achievement, and the process has been long and arduous. Translation in general is not an easy job and it is even more difficult to translate Chinese into another language; the difficulty in translating Dunhuang culture lies even beyond all this. For the past six years, Professor Jiang's team has gone through many hardships, for example, expending great effort researching and finding the exact vocabulary and terminology, and considerable time spent on accurately and faithfully conveying each author's point of view. Readers only need to browse through these four books and the difficulties they had to overcome will be made immediately evident.

Since it is so difficult, then why translate? As Professor Jiang said, "Translation is not merely the conversion of language, but also the interpretation of culture. Translating Dunhuang culture is not a simple code conversion, nor is it purely the transmission of information. More importantly, translation reveals and interprets the philosophical thought, humanistic spirit, and values contained in Dunhuang culture and historical relics, which is imbued with the cultural spirit, mind, and confidence of the Chinese nation." Her words convince me that Dunhuang culture translation reflects the translators' deep love for their country and their ideals and determination for communicating with the world at large, as well as their devoted academic scholarship in the face of challenges. Unless translators have firm beliefs, lofty commitment, and a strong work ethic, they may easily pull back from the difficulties of translation work. While congratulating the team of translators, I would also like to express my highest respect for them.

Why does a series of books hold that much significance? Mutual learning between civilizations requires the interchange of cultural information, and doing a good job in communication involves producing works that people from other countries can readily understand. Conveying cultural confidece requires extremely hard and sophisticated work. This book series, the latest achievement in the introduction of Dunhuang culture, is a product of that cultural confidece.

The significance of *Dunhuang Culture in Translation* however is not only in the finished works. The translation of the series also represents a process of continuous maturity of the translation team. *Dunhuang Culture in Translation* marks the first phase of a much larger program—the Silk Road Dunhuang Culture Translation Project. After its launch, the translators found that the work was extremely challenging, especially the translation of cultural concepts. Thus, the translation team began by compiling the Dunhuang Culture Chinese-English Terminology Database, and after the completion of the bilingual *Key Concepts in Dunhuang Culture*, it began to focus on the work of the *Dunhuang Culture in Translation* series. The publication of these four books and their related works of the first series of *Dunhuang Culture in Translation* witnessed the development and growth of a team of young translators starting from scratch, growing from small to large, and from weak to strong. Based at Lanzhou City University, members of this translation team are also teachers who are bringing up even younger translators. Their spirit and experience will inevitably guide them in fostering the next generation of talent for presenting information and culture to the international community.

What is significant is that the *Dunhuang Culture in Translation* series has filled a gap in the promotion of the Belt and Road Initiative. Dunhuang was once an important town on the ancient Silk Road and now holds an important position in promoting the Belt and Road Initiative. This book series provides excellent works for not only Dunhuang but also Gansu Province to conduct exchanges with the world, adding a superb new dimension in cultural communication. Telling China's story and getting China's voice heard is not just a slogan: it needs a series of solid works to help make it happen. *Dunhuang Culture in Translation* not only reveals a glorious history, but also demonstrates the achievements of Chinese cultural confidece and cultural prosperity in our present era. These four works make known not only the formation of culture in Chinese history, but the four facets they introduce also represent four bright stars of China in the process of mutual learning between civilizations. Reflecting the past of China's cultural development and illuminating the heritage of Chinese civilization, they herald the limitless future of Chinese culture.

It is precisely because of this that we now look forward to the next installment in the Silk Road Dunhuang Culture Translation Project.

Huang Youyi

Former Deputy Director-General of China Foreign Languages Publishing Administration

Vice President of Translators Association of China

October 2020

序言二

敦煌文化是丝绸之路文明的精髓，是中外文化交流背景之下形成的哲学思想、人文精神、价值理念、道德规范等，而丝绸之路是连接古代中国与中亚、南亚、东欧的经济文化的交通要道，因其贩运的商品主要是丝绸，所以称之为丝绸之路。同时还因其贩运的物品和使用的货币而被称作为玉石之路、白银之路、香药之路、茶马之路等。

丝绸之路还是一条中外文化交流的重要通道，西方的先进科学技术和文化都是通过这条通道传入中国的，同时中国的先进文化和科学技术也是通过这条国际通道传播到世界各国，中西文化经过这条道路互相碰撞、交融和接纳，促进了汉唐帝国和学术文化的发展。通过这条道路，印度的佛教、欧洲的景教、中亚的祆教和摩尼教进入中国，并在中国迅速传播开来，由于佛教寺院的建造和石窟的开凿，佛教造像的兴盛，犍陀罗佛教艺术流传中国，影响了中国佛教艺术及中国道教艺术的发展。

因景教艺术传入，中亚艺术风格传入中国，并影响了中古时期中国社会生活的方方面面。通过这条道路，产生于印度的天竺乐和中亚的康国乐、安国乐和新疆地区龟兹乐、疏勒乐、高昌乐等的音乐舞蹈相继传入并迅速传播开来，由外来音乐舞蹈和中国古代清乐融合而产生的西凉乐，成为中古中国乐舞的重要组成部分，推进了中国文化艺术的发展。

通过这条道路，中亚西域的物种、医技医籍、饮食、服饰、生活习惯等都进入中国，影响中国古代社会生活的各个方面。汉唐文化就是在对外来文化包容接纳的基础之上产生的。中国古代儒家典籍和道教以及先进的科学技术也是通过这条道路传播到中亚和东欧地区，推动了世界文化和科学技术的发展。古代中国通过这条道路了解世界，而世界也通过这条道路接纳中国。

敦煌文化形成之地的敦煌是丝绸之路东段和中段的交汇之地，也是丝绸之路的必经之地。敦煌最早见载于中国历史典籍《山海经》，《山海经》北山经记载敦薨之山出敦薨之水，敦薨之水西流注入泑泽，是为河源。

敦薨就是敦煌，是历史典籍对敦煌的最早记载。后来张骞出使西域，被匈奴扣押在河西及蒙古高原十余年，对这里的地理地貌非常熟悉，后来又到中亚从大月氏人那里收集到他们在敦煌一带生活的信息，敦煌一词很可能首先是从张骞开始使用，实际上就是敦薨的音译。

根据《汉书》的记载，实际上在汉朝设置敦煌郡之前的元鼎四年，敦煌一词已经开始使用。而敦煌地区的三危山就见载于《尚书·禹贡篇》，记载导黑水经过三危山流入南海，三危山就是敦煌的三危山，而黑水经我们根据《太平广记》和敦煌文书《瓜沙两郡史事编年并序》研究，就是流经敦煌的疏勒河，疏勒河在汉唐间曾称之为冥水，疏勒河上的沼泽湖泊也叫作乌泽，沿着疏勒河修建的军事屏障称之为昆仑障，都与黑有密切关系。

敦煌也是古代中国领导人行经之地，根据《穆天子传》的记载穆天子即位十五年，曾巡游至泑泽，即今天的罗布泊，前往罗布泊必须经过敦煌，因此周穆王十五年就曾来到敦煌。如果这个记载不误的话，公元前 962 年中国领导人已经来到了敦煌，到了新疆的罗布泊地区或者更远的哈密或者帕米尔高原一带。敦煌的龙勒山就因周时有龙马朝出咸阳，暮至寿昌，遗其衔勒，故名龙勒山。就是说周穆王时中原王朝已经同西域地区进行玉石贸易和马种交换。

汉武帝击败匈奴取得河西地区，置敦煌等河西四郡而拥有二关，玉门关、阳关是汉唐通西域的主要关隘，敦煌是汉唐中央政府经营西域的军事基地，同时也是来往商贾的都会城市。阳关是出敦煌到西域的和亲通使关隘，而与阳关对应的玉门关是出敦煌经营西域的军事关隘，俗称阴关或者凶关，与玉石贸易没有任何关系。

出敦煌西行分别有三条道路，南道至鄯善，中道到高昌，北道经伊吾，总汇敦煌。这三条道路都必须穿越戈壁沙漠地带，“上无飞鸟，下无走兽，复无水草”；“行旅负水担粮，履践沙石，往来困弊”；“西路险恶，人行迷误，沙河阻道，鬼魅热风，遇无免者”。这种情况说明没有充分的准备绝不敢贸然进入沙碛西行。

这样一来，经过沙碛考验的人们才能顺利来到敦煌，他们的精神和灵魂都经过严酷的自然环境的洗礼，有了一个质的升华。汉代李广利征大宛两次都是从敦煌出兵，两汉敦煌太守都参与经营西域，吐蕃占领敦煌之前的唐代，沙州刺史或者敦煌太守，经常参与经营西域的事务。

汉唐的敦煌是一个都会城市，国际化程度非常高。从两汉时期敦煌就居住着很多西域质子和西域商贾，特别是粟特人经常见载于出土文献和典籍中，到唐代更是这样，敦煌的胡人在唐朝中央军队中任职的很多，有的晋升为中央禁军的首领，像曹怀直，祖上帮助唐朝建功立业，被赐姓为曹，历代担任禁军要职。

特别是唐中宗神龙年间石城镇康艳典后裔部落随戍守播仙镇的凉州兵迁居敦煌，唐朝政府为安置这些粟特人在敦煌城周围专门设置了从化乡，从化乡最少有两个里四个村落，粟特人控制敦煌的市场贸易，出任市壁师并管理敦煌市场贸易。直到吐蕃时期敦煌粟特人康秀华仍然担任部落使，而安景旻出任敦煌都督。

张氏归义军时期，安景旻出任归义军节度使副使，而康秀华出任瓜州刺史左威卫将军，到张承奉时期，粟特人安怀恩出任押衙。914 年粟特人曹议金出任归义军节度使，敦煌成了粟特人领导下的归义军政权。除了粟特人，敦煌外来居民很多，有达怛人、回鹘人、突厥人、吐蕃人、波斯人、印度人、鄯善人、于阗人等，他们开店经营商品，经营酒店出卖食品，很多行市的头目都是这些胡人担任，特别是前往各地的商业贸易团体的头目都是由粟特胡人担任，胡商是敦煌市场贸易的主体，因此敦煌市场贸易的商人具有很高程度的国际性。

敦煌市场的商品也具有很高的国际性，敦煌地不产珍，献无奇玩，是一个贫乏的地方。由于敦煌地处交通要道，敦煌市场上商品非常丰富，有西域地区贩运而来的西州布、安西氎，有龟兹出产的胡粉，有中亚来的金青和水银，吐蕃地区的颜料石青、石绿和毛织品，波斯等地出产的胡锦和珠宝，伊州出产的铁器，于阗出产的玉石，东罗马的银器，西域印度的药材和香料，高丽出产的高丽锦，达怛和吐蕃出产的畜牧产品和兵器等，商品来自相邻各个地区或者中亚、南亚和东亚及中国内地各个地方。

作为交换的等价物是银币。金银器皿作为流通货币在晚唐五代的敦煌贸易市场比较常见,有罗马银盏、银盘子、金花银瓶子、银碗等;这些银器标明重量,用于支付物价,其性质显然是货币,不是作为一般意义上的器皿,表明银碗是作为货币流通于敦煌等地的贸易市场中;在对外贸易中还使用丝绸支付物价;在对内或小宗贸易上多用实物特别是粮食支付物价,作为交换的等价物进行交换。因此货币也具有国际性。

敦煌是佛教最早进入的地区。敦煌文献是关于中国佛教最为详细和真实的记载。敦煌汉简中就已经记载了寺院,寺院内的一切均有助于重构中国寺院的面貌。敦煌文献中还保存有最早的汉文景教经典、摩尼教经典,虽然敦煌文献中没有袄教经典,但是作为官府主办袄教祭祀仪式足以看出袄教的影响力。在敦煌佛教、道教、袄教、景教、摩尼教以及儒教之间的和谐共处超过相互排斥和争斗。特别是西域地区的胡腾舞、胡旋舞在敦煌地区非常流行,敦煌人在重大节日都要踏苏幕遮,出现于龟兹的舞蹈成为敦煌的流行舞。这种局面的基础就是敦煌多民族和平共处,互相包容,互相借鉴,共同发展。敦煌作为丝绸之路上的明珠,他的魅力就在于此。

丝绸之路也可称之为科技之路。西域地区的科学技术如医学、医方、天文历法等都是通过这条道路传入中国,中国的科学技术也是通过这条道路传向西域地区。敦煌文献的记载就是很好的见证。我们要交代的是敦煌出产瓜得名称瓜州,传说狐狸吃瓜首尾俱入瓜中,表明敦煌出产的瓜很大。回鹘瓜和大食瓜,名见于敦煌文献中,回鹘瓜,又叫瓤桃,这些地方在晚唐五代时期属于回鹘统治地区,所谓伊州回鹘、西州回鹘,大概称之为回鹘瓜就是出产于回鹘地区。

大食瓜,就是出产在大食地区的瓜,这种瓜是什么瓜呢,我们认为是西瓜,西瓜原产地南非,后来传播到埃及,又从埃及传到中亚,金代陕西同州有个官员出使西域,从中亚引进并在中原地区大量传播开来,当时人对这种瓜没有统一的名称,所以按照以地命名的习惯,称之为西瓜,原意可能是西域的瓜、西方的瓜等。今天陕西大荔的瓜还是很有名的,个大皮厚瓤甜。

医学技术的交流通过丝绸之路也很明显,汉唐时期虽然中医学很发达,但有些医术还没有西域波斯、印度先进,比如眼科中的白内障手术,就是从西域传入，唐史将其作为特殊案例记载。敦煌当地医学家的造诣是学兼中西。

敦煌是丝绸之路上的一颗明珠，敦煌文化是丝绸之路文明精髓所在，而丝绸之路是中西交通文化交流永恒的通途。第一，政治稳定是丝绸之路顺畅的基本要素，这包括历史上中央政权和丝绸之路沿线民族和国家的稳定。先秦时期，由于中原地区文化经济的发展，与周边地区形成很大的社会差异，这种差异导致一种稳定的向心力，加上周边民族对中原政府还不能构成威胁，中原政权虽然没有鼓励也并没阻止中外交往，中西交往属于一种原始状态进行，很多西域地区的特产通过丝绸之路流入中原地区，而中国的产品也经过这条通道进入西域。关于穆天子与西王母的会面，《山海经》关于河源和丝绸之路沿线的地理地貌的记载就是这一背景下的产物。

汉武帝凭借强大的军事实力打败匈奴，重新开启丝绸之路，开始了利用军事政治力量维系丝绸之路安全的时期，汉唐时期都是由国家经营沿线交通设施配置、道路维护和安全保障等，丝绸之路的兴衰几乎与国家政权稳定一致。宋代以后陆路衰落与海路有很大关系，但是沿线政治环境的变化因素起了极大的作用。

第二，经济利益的互惠是丝绸之路发展的基础，维系丝绸之路经久不衰的经济因素是利益的互惠。丝绸之路贸易有几个层面：首先是贡赐贸易，这是一种严重的不对等贸易，中央政府承受非常大的经济压力，贡赐之间的比例 1∶10 到 1∶40 左右，这种贸易是国家政治利益为主的贸易活动。其次是一般性贸易，基本上是由地方政府控制的经济贸易，由政府管理的贸易使团进行的贸易活动，这种贸易活动的利润都在 100%以上，使用等价物以金银丝绸为主，多数进行以物易物贸易，中国的丝绸外销和西域的香料宝物内售，有相当一部分的商人是西域胡人，在中国内地经营。胡商在中国进行的对外贸易和对内贸易，促进了汉唐社会经济繁荣发展，同时由于经济贸易的带动，沿线各地的经济也发展起来。特别是丝绸之路沿线物产并不丰富但地位十分重要的地区，财富经丝绸之路贸易在这些地区得到重新分配。经济上互惠是丝绸之路保持畅通的经济因素。

第三，丝绸之路文化研究是重新发展丝绸之路经济带的先决条件。今天我们研究丝绸之路经济带,更应当重视丝绸之路文化的研究。古代丝绸之路将古代沿线不同地区不同文化连接起来，这些文化通过文物文献等形式在丝绸之路沿线各个地区保存了下来，研究这些文物文献对揭示这一地区古代文明十分重要，研究该地区历史上对丝绸之路经营的经验和教训对今天有十分重要的借鉴作用,只有将其远古文明研究清楚,才有利于丝绸之路的发展。丝绸之路沿线的敦煌、高昌、哈密、库车、于阗等都是丝绸之路上的明珠,因此研究这些地区的历史文化就是丝绸之路的个案研究,是一项十分有意义的工作。

甘肃文化翻译中心组织翻译的“敦煌文化·译丛”,就是响应习近平总书记敦煌讲话精神,弘扬传承敦煌文化,提高文化自信的一个有力举措。

兰州大学敦煌学研究所所长　郑炳林

2020 年 10 月

Foreword Ⅱ

Dunhuang Culture is the essence of Silk Road civilization, with philosophical ideas formed in the context of cultural exchange between China and the outside world. It also represents the spirit of humanism, the concept of values, and the code of ethics. The Silk Road was the major economic and cultural link connecting ancient China, the Central Asia, South Asia and Eastern Europe. The Silk Road is so-called because silk was the main commodity transported along the route. But the Silk Road was also known as the Jade Road, the Silver Road, the Spice Road, and the Tea and Horse Road, among others, because such goods and currencies were also transported and used along the route.

The Silk Road was also an important route for cultural exchange between China and the outside world. This international thoroughfare was the means by which the West's advanced science, technology, and culture reached China, and by which China's advanced culture, science, and technology spread to other nations of the world. Through the Silk Road, Chinese and Western cultures met, mingled, and accepted each other, bringing about developments of the Han and Tang empires as well as academic cultures that have influenced the world. It was via this route that India's Buddhism, Europe's Nestorianism, and Central Asia's Zoroastrianism and Manichaeism entered China and spread quickly. Buddhist temple construction and cave excavation, the rise of Buddhist iconography, and the spread of Gandharan Buddhist art into China all contributed to the proliferation of magnificent Chinese Buddhist art, facilitating the development of the Taoist art.

The presence of Nestorian art and Central Asian art styles in China influenced medieval Chinese society and lifestyles in a multitude of ways. The music and dance originated from Indian music, Central Asia music and music of Xinjiang region entered through the Silk Road and quickly spread. The mingling of foreign music and dance and ancient Chinese *Qingyue* music produced Xiliang music, which became an essential element of medieval Chinese music and dance, and furthered the development of Chinese culture and art.

Through the Silk Road, plant species, medical technology, diet, dress, and everyday habits all entered China, influencing the lifestyle of ancient Chinese society in various ways. The culture of the Han and Tang dynasties emerged on the basis of these outside influences. Ancient Chinese Confucian texts, Taoism and advanced science and technology also passed along the Silk Road on their way to Central Asia and Eastern Europe, promoting the development of culture, science, and technology throughout the world. Through the Silk Road, ancient China was able to understand the world, and the world was able to accept China.

Dunhuang, where Dunhuang culture emerged, is located at the crossroads of the eastern and central sections of the Silk Road; travelers had to pass through Dunhuang on their way. Among Chinese historical texts, Dunhuang was first mentioned in the *Classic of Mountains and Seas*, from which the *North Mountain Classic* records that the Dunhong river flowed down Dunhong Mountain, and then westward into Lop Nur, where it formed the source of the Yellow River.

Dunhong was thus the name for Dunhuang, and was the earliest reference to the site. Later, Zhang Qian had his mission to the Western Regions, but was detained by the Xiongnu for more than ten years in the west of the Hexi Corridor and on the Mongolian plateau, becoming very familiar with the geography and landforms of the area. Then he traveled to the Central Asia to gather information from the Greater Yuezhi people about their life in the Dunhuang area. It is very likely that the name Dunhuang originated with Zhang Qian; he actually transcribed "Dunhong" as Dunhuang.

According to the *Book of Han*, in the fourth year of the Yuanding Era, before the establishment of Dunhuang Prefecture in the Han dynasty, the name Dunhuang was in fact already in use. Moreover, the Sanwei Mountain, recorded in the *Book of Yugong*, through which the Heishui River flowed into the South China Sea was the one situated in Dunhuang, while according to our research into the *Extensive Records of the Taiping Era* and the Dunhuang document *Chronology and Preface of the History of Guazhou and Shazhou*, the Heishui River was the Shule River which flows through Dunhuang. In the Han and Tang dynasties, the Shule River was known as the Mingshui River ("Dark Water"). The marshy lakes on the Shule River were also called the Black Marsh. The military barriers built along the Shule River were called the Kunlun Barrier. All three have implications of "darkness" or "blackness."

In ancient China, Dunhuang was also a place which emperors and high-rank officials passed during their travel to the west. In his 15th year of regin, King Mu, once travelled to present-day Lop Nur according to the *Tale of King Mu*. To reach Lop Nur, one must pass through Dunhuang; that is to say, King Mu had been to Dunhuang. If this account is to be believed, then Chinese leaders had already been to Dunhuang by 962 BC, as well as to present-day Xinjiang's Lop Nur region, or even further to Hami or the Pamir Plateau. Dunhuang's Longle Mountain (*longle* meaning headstall of dragon horse) was so-named because during the Zhou Dynasty, a powerful steed known as "dragon horse" left its headstall there during its trip from Xianyang in the morning to Shouchang (part of Dunhuang) in the evening. That is to say, by the time of King Mu, the Kingdoms in the Central Plains had already exchanged jade and horse breeds with the Western Regions.

Emperor Wu of the Han Dynasty defeated the Xiongnu to gain control of the Hexi Corridor. He set up Dunhuang and three other prefectures on the western side with the Yumen Pass ("Jade Gate") and the Yangguan Pass, which were the main border controls in the western part of the Han and Tang dynasties. Dunhuang was a military base for the central governments of the Han and Tang dynasties, as well as a leading mercantile city. Yangguan Pass was for peace-making envoys from Dunhuang heading west, while Yumen Pass was a protected pass for merchants heading west. It was commonly known as the Yinguan Pass, and actually had nothing to do with the jade trade.

There were three routes heading west from Dunhuang: the southern road to

Shanshan; the central road to Gaochang; and the northern road going via Yiwu. These three routes all crossed the Gobi and desert. These western routes were treacherous: there were no birds above, no animals on the ground, and no succulent plants. Carrying water and grain, walking over sand and rocks, going to and fro, people got lost, and rivers of sand blocked the way while otherworldly hot winds inevitably blew. This indicated that travelers did not dare go to the western side of the moraine without adequate preparation.

Only people who knew the lay of the land were able to get to Dunhuang. Their spirits were baptized by the character–building harshness of such an environment. In the Han Dynasty, Li Guangli conquered Dayuan twice from his base in Dunhuang. The Dunhuang governors of the Eastern and Western Han dynasties were involved in the administration of the Western Regions; likewise, in the Tang dynasty before the occupation of Dunhuang by the Tubo, the Shazhou inspectors or governors were also often involved in running affairs in the Western Regions.

Dunhuang was a burgeoning international metropolis during the Han and Tang dynasties. From the time of the Eastern and Western Han dynasties, Dunhuang was home to descendants of hostages and merchants from the Western Regions. The Sogdians in particular are often mentioned in excavated documents and texts, even more so in those from the Tang Dynasty. Foreigners served in the Tang Imperial Army in large numbers. Some were even promoted to leadership roles, such as Cao Huaizhi, whose ancestors helped build the Tang Dynasty. They were granted the surname Cao, and successive generations of the family served important roles in the Imperial Army.

In particular, during the Shenlong Era of the Emperor Zhongzong in the Tang Dynasty, the descendants of Kang Yandian from the Shicheng Town moved to Dunhuang with the Liangzhou soldiers who guarded the Boxian town; the Tang government set up the Conghua township to house the Sogdians. Conghua was at least two *li* large and contained four villages. The Sogdians controlled and managed Dunhuang's market trade. When the Tubo took over Dunhuang, the Sogdian Kang Xiuhua served as a tribal commissioner, while An Jingmin was appointed governor.

During the *Guiyijun* period under the Zhang clan, An Jingmin served as deputy military commissioner of the *Guiyijun* Force, while Kang Xiuhua served as general of the prefect of Guazhou. In the Zhang Chengfeng period, the Sogdian An Huai'en was appointed to a position equal to the military commissioner. In 914, the Sogdian Cao Yijin was appointed as the *Guiyijun*'s military commissioner, and the Dunhuang *Guiyijun* Force came under Sogdian leadership. Apart from the Sogdians, there were considerable numbers of other foreign residents in Dunhuang, including Tartars, Uyghurs, Turkic people, Tubo people, Persians, Indians, Shanshan people and Khotanese. They set up shops and restaurants, with many business leaders of foreign origin. In particular, commercial and trade groups that traveled to various places were led by Sogdians. Foreign traders made up the majority of Dunhuang market traders. For this reason, Dunhuang's business community was strongly multinational.

The goods for sale in Dunhuang's markets also had a strongly international flavor. Dunhuang itself produced little, with no treasures or exotic goods to offer. But because of the city's location on a major transportation route, its markets offered a rich array of goods. There were textiles from the Western Regions, fine muslin from Anxi, *Hu* powder from Kucha (Qiuci), lapis lazuli and mercury from Central Asia, blue and green mineral pigments as well as woolen fabrics from Tubo, Persian brocade and jewelry, ironware from Yizhou, Khotanese jade, silverware from Byzantium, medicines and spices from western India, brocade from Korea, and livestock products and weapons from Tartary and Tubo. Merchandise arrived here from neighboring regions in Central, South, and East Asia as well as the interior of China.

Silver coins were the currency for trade. Gold and silverware were also used as common circulating currencies in the markets of Dunhuang in the Late Tang era. There were Roman silver chalices, silver plates, gold and silver bottles, silver bowls, and so on. The silverware with marked weight was used when paying for goods, so that its value was as a currency rather than as a functional utensil or vessel in the general sense, revealing that silverware was used as a currency in the markets of Dunhuang and other places. Silk was also used for payment in foreign trade, while in domestic or small-scale trade, goods—especially food or grain—were often paid in-kind. Goods were exchanged for equivalent value, so the currencies themselves were multinational.

Dunhuang was Buddhism's original point of entry into China. The Dunhuang manuscripts themselves offer the most detailed and accurate records of Chinese Buddhism and the monastery is mentioned in Han bamboo slips from Dunhuang. These records are helpful in reconstructing the architecture and appearance of ancient Chinese temples. Among the Dunhuang texts are also the earliest extant Nestorian and Manichaean scriptures in Chinese. Although the Dunhuang manuscripts do not include Zoroastrian classics, the influence of Zoroastrianism can be seen in the fact that Zoroastrian rituals enjoyed official sponsorship. In Dunhuang, the peaceful co-existence of Buddhism, Taoism, Zoroastrianism, Nestorianism, Manichaeism, and Confucianism overcame any mutual exclusion or contention. This is especially true of the *Huteng* dance from the Western Regions, which was extremely popular in Dunhuang. It was enjoyed on important festival days. This dance, which first appeared in Qiuci, became Dunhuang's favorite dance. The basis of this situation was the peaceful co-existence of the many ethnic groups in Dunhuang, as well as their mutual inclusiveness, mutual learning, and common development. Dunhuang was the pearl of the Silk Road, and therein lies its charm.

The Silk Road can also be called the Technology Road. Science and technology from the Western Regions, such as medicine, pharmacology, and the astronomical calendar, entered China via this route; Chinese science and technology, in turn, also flowed westward along the same route. The Dunhuang manuscripts provide historical evidence of this. Dunhuang produced so many melons that it was named Guazhou (land of melons). Legend had it that a fox could eat a Dunhuang melon with its head and tail in it, such was the size of the melons. Uyghur melons and Dashi melons are even mentioned in Dunhuang historical records, where Uyghur melons were also known as "*rangtao*." In the Late Tang period and Five Dynasties, the area was held by Uyghurs. Among the so-called Yizhou and Xizhou Uyghurs, Uyghur melons, as they were probably called, were those produced in Uyghur areas.

Dashi melons were those from Arabia. What type of melons were these? It is believed that they were watermelons, which were originally from South Africa, and later reached Egypt, and from there it was made into Central Asia. In the Jin Dynasty, an official from Tongzhou of Shaanxi travelled west as an envoy, and introduced watermelon, after which it became widespread. The people of the time did not have a uniform name for watermelons, so according to naming conventions, it became the *xigua*. This probably just meant "melon from the Western Regions" or "melon from the West." Today, the melons from the Dali county of Shaanxi are also very well-known, with a thick rind and sweet taste.

The exchange of medical technology along the Silk Road was evident. While traditional Chinese medicine was highly developed by the time of the Han and Tang dynasties, many medical skills were absent. Persia and India, however, was at the forefront in certain skills such as cataract surgery, and this was introduced via the West, with Tang dynasty historical records giving it a special mention. Dunhuang's local medical specialists were accomplished in both Chinese and Western methods.

Dunhuang was the Pearl of the Silk Road, the essence of Silk Road civilization, and an eternal thoroughfare for communication and cultural exchange between China and the West. First, political stability was a basic element for the smooth operation of the route. This included the stability of central political power throughout its history, as well as that of ethnic groups and nations along the route. In the pre-Qin period, owing to cultural and economic development of the Central Plains, great social differences took shape as compared with the surrounding areas. These differences led to a stable centripetal force, with the surrounding ethnic groups not having sufficient strength to threaten the government of the Central Plains. Although the Central Plains government did not encourage Chinese exchanges with foreigners, it is not known to have prevented them, either. Exchanges between China and the West were rudimentary. Many specialty goods from the Western Regions passed into the Central Plains via the Silk Road, and Chinese products also headed west via the same road. According to legend, King Mu and the Queen Mother of the West met in the area extending from the Shule River to Lop Nur; the *Classic of Mountains and Seas* which details the geography and landforms along the Yellow River and the Silk Road is a product of this background.

Emperor Wu of the Han Dynasty defeated the Xiongnu with his powerful military, opened up the Silk Road again, and started using the strength of his military government to sustain a period of peace along the Road. During the Han and Tang dynasties, the state operated transport facilities along the route, maintained roads, and guaranteed safety. The rise and fall of the Silk Road occurred almost in line with the stability of state power. After the Song Dynasty, the decline in overland routes was correlated to the rise of the maritime trade routes, but changes in the political environment along the Silk Road also played a major role.

Second, mutual economic benefit was the basis of development along the Silk Road. The reciprocity of benefits was the factor that sustained the Silk Road economically. There were several dimensions of trade on the Silk Road: foremost was tribute trade, which had serious disparities. The central government withstood enormous economic pressure, with the ratio between tributes roughly somewhere between 1 ∶ 10 to 1 ∶ 40. This kind of trade asserted national political interest above all else. This was followed by general trade, which was basically controlled by regional authorities with government–managed trade envoys conducting trade. Profits from this trading activity exceeded 100%. Gold, silver, and silk were the primary mediums of exchange used, with many traders also engaged in bartering. Quite a few of the merchants engaged in China's silk exports and the sale of the Western Regions' treasured spices within China were foreigners from the West. China's foreign–led exports and domestic trade boosted the economic fortunes of Han and Tang society. Driven by trade, places all along the Silk Road also received an economic boost. For Silk Road areas that were not very productive but were nonetheless in important locations, wealth was distributed thanks to trade along the route. Economic reciprocity was the key factor that kept the Silk Road running smoothly.

Third, research into Silk Road culture is a prerequisite for an economic revival along this route. Today, when we research the Silk Road economic belt, we should pay more attention to the culture that developed there. The ancient Silk Road brought together disparate regions and cultures along the route. These cultures have been preserved in forms of artifacts and other material in different regions along the Silk Road. Researching these artifacts is extremely important if we want to learn more of the ancient civilizations of this area. Researching the historical experiences and lessons from the Silk Road trade is a vital reference point for today. Only careful study of its ancient civilizations will benefit future Silk Road development. Places such as Dunhuang, Gaochang, Hami, Kucha, and Khotan are all "pearls of the Silk Road." For that reason, research into the historical culture of these regions amounts to a special case study. It is an immensely significant work.

The *Dunhuang Culture in Translation* series, organized by the Gansu Cultural Translation and Interpreting Center, is a powerful initiative with which to respond to the spirit of General Secretary Xi Jinping's Dunhuang speech, promoting Dunhuang culture and enhancing cultural confidece.

Zheng Binglin

Head of Institute of Dunhuang Studies of Lanzhou University

October 2020

序言三

翻译，让敦煌文化走向世界

敦煌文化是中华文明几千年不断融会贯通的典范，是中国文化精神的重要代表。曾经，敦煌文化经历“敦煌在中国，敦煌学在国外”的历史。诚然，自20世纪初，敦煌藏经洞的发现、敦煌部分文献流失海外，引发世界各国敦煌学者对敦煌文化的关注，在国外产生了众多敦煌学研究成果。但敦煌文化的“根”在中国，对敦煌文化的认识与理解，源于中国。敦煌学的国际化发展，则需要通过文化的传播与学术的交流形成共识、共知与共享。翻译，无疑是使敦煌文化走向世界、敦煌精神被全人类共享的重要途径。

一、翻译是敦煌文化对外传播的“言说者”

文化对外传播、交流与沟通的重要途径是翻译。翻译敦煌文化，就是对外“言说”敦煌文化，传播敦煌文化的各个方面、各种内容。敦煌文化是包括宗教、艺术、科技、文学、医药、农业、建筑、民俗等内容的综合文化体系。翻译敦煌文化，就是对外讲述敦煌开放交流的文明历史，展示敦煌在中西互学互鉴中形成的艺术，介绍敦煌的科技医药，以及讲述融合发展的宗教文化思想等。通过系统翻译，让世界认识敦煌文化，了解全面的敦煌文化、真正的敦煌文化。

翻译敦煌文化，就是言说和表达最具代表性的、最能体现敦煌文化之源流的优秀文化。就其文化内容而言，一方面转换语言为载体的文化内容，如敦煌文献、敦煌学研究成果、敦煌学术思想等；另一方面转换艺术为载体的文化信息。敦煌文化，就其文化载体而言，具有多元的符号形式。语言载体包含写经、变文、宝卷、简牍等文学与非文学形态；艺术载体包含石窟建筑、雕塑、壁画等。翻译敦煌文化，即对敦煌文化各种载体所蕴含的历史、宗教、文学、艺术等文化内容,及其文化思想和文化精神进行语言转换,精确表达。以翻译言说敦煌文化,既要用语言讲述语言文化,还要用语言讲述非语言文化。一般而言,翻译是语言文本的转换。但在敦煌文化翻译中,除了常规的语际翻译,还存在符际转换方式,即对艺术文化的翻译,运用语言进行"互文性"表达。通过语际与符际双重转换,构建敦煌文化对外传播的系统体系。作为敦煌文化对外传播言说者的翻译,需要注重"言说"的方式,构建有效的话语体系。翻译,在传播文化中,表达文化,沟通文化,协调不同语言之间的文化理解。话语方式、话语风格决定文化元素的显现方式,决定文化内容的接受度,从而决定文化传播的效果和效力,是实现文化传播与交流的基础。翻译敦煌文化,要协调"异化""归化"转换策略,在尊重文化、名从历史的基础上,运用恰当适切的对外言说话语方式,针对文化内容、受众接受等用国际化语言表达方式,准确言说和表达敦煌文化,构建敦煌文化对外传播的完整叙事。

以翻译言说文化,不仅使敦煌文化充分"走出去",更使敦煌精神深入"走进去",有效实现敦煌文化的国际性传播与世界认同。

二、翻译是敦煌文化学术交流的"互动者"

翻译敦煌文化,就是搭建中外敦煌学术交流的互动平台,开展中外敦煌学研究的学术对话。20 世纪初以来,国内外学者对敦煌文化的研究,产生了众多研究成果,建树颇丰。通过对中外敦煌学研究成果的互译,对话学术,交流思想,从而深化对敦煌文化的认识。诚然,博大精深的敦煌文化及其精神价值,依旧存在有待认识与研究的极大空间,但交流已有的学术思想,无疑对进一步研究敦煌文化、认识敦煌文化具有重要的意义。互译,为搭建互动机制、建构交互认知,提供必要的路径。

一是开展敦煌文献的互译,通过对各国拥有的敦煌文献进行翻译转换,补充因文献缺省造成的"认识差",化解研究上的局限。敦煌莫高窟藏经洞发现的文献(包括写本、简牍),涉及佛教经典、道教经典、儒家典籍以及(敦煌)佛教文学、俗文学等文化内容,语言包含除汉文之外的藏文、回鹘文、于阗文、龟兹文、突厥文、粟特文和梵文等。敦煌文献是丝绸之路上中西文明交流的历史书写，是研究敦煌文化，以及其中蕴含的中国文化思想的重要文献资料。但敦煌文献因特殊的历史遭遇，一大部分遗书被劫掠至海外(如英国近万卷，法国五千余卷)，有关同一文化内容的文献资料散藏于中、英、法、日、俄等不同的国家，造成各国对敦煌文化认识的支离破碎，导致敦煌学研究的片面性。通过文献资料的译入、译出，可以搭建国内、国外敦煌学的多维研究平台、系统认识平台，将历史片段缀合起来，将同一文化现象进行综合研究，从而形成世界范围内的"系统敦煌学"。

二是进行敦煌学研究成果的互译，通过互译，使学术思想产生碰撞、比较，从而打开各自封闭的敦煌学，经由"他者"的敦煌学术参照系，关照自身的研究，丰富自身的认识；在与"他者"的交流中、在思想碰撞中深化对敦煌文化的理解。

敦煌文化是在中西方文化交融中形成和发展的，具有综合的文化内容体系、多元的文化思想，以及多样的历史发展形态。它是一个内在结构相互作用的文化体系，存在各系统成分之间的内在关系，如敦煌艺术研究与宗教文化研究的互补，中西方文化交流与文化融合过程的历史关系，文化演变与朝代结构的互动等。对敦煌文化的认识，需要系统地研究，才能构成认识的互补体系；只有互为补充的认识，才能不断完善对敦煌文化认识体系的构建。不同国家、不同时代，基于各自专业领域的研究，难免存在"认识差"。通过中外敦煌学研究思想的双向翻译，进行学术交流与对话，在互动中学习，在交流中互鉴，不仅能够产生新思路和新成果，而且能够使各国学者更深刻地理解敦煌文化，一方面可以减少因文化差异造成的认识误差，减少误读与误解；另一方面通过不同时代、不同文化背景、不同信仰体系的学者对历史文明的学术对话，协调敦煌学研究中的审美心理和文化价值"差"，以便达成共识，形成对敦煌历史文化概念的共同解读，从而提升敦煌文化的交流深度，实现敦煌文化的高层次对话与互动传播。

三、翻译是敦煌文化精神的诠释者和世界传承者

翻译，不仅仅是语言的转换，更是对文化的阐释。翻译敦煌文化，不是简

单的语码转换，也不是单纯的信息传递，更重要的是揭示和阐释敦煌文化和历史遗存所蕴含的哲学思想、人文精神、价值理念、道德规范；弘扬和传承蕴含其中的中华民族的文化精神、文化胸怀和文化自信。敦煌文化是中西文化交流融合的典范，敦煌石窟建筑、壁画，以中原文化为基础，充分吸收了中亚、西亚佛教艺术思想内容，体现了多元文化交融互鉴的内在精神，是中华文明开放体系的重要代表。在综合、系统的翻译过程中，深刻阐释其文明历程、文化精髓，阐释敦煌文化文明交流融合的思想方法，诠释中华文明海纳百川、兼容并蓄、博采众长的文化精髓，挖掘世界文明共同的存在根源，以及人类共同的理想目标。

翻译是一种诠释，具有文化"阐释力"。翻译敦煌文化，就是在研究敦煌文化的前提下，诠释敦煌文化的深刻含义。翻译敦煌文化，是译者与敦煌文化思想、文化精神的交流和互动，是现代视域与历史精髓的互文。作为敦煌文化"诠释者"的翻译，是某种意义上的敦煌文化研究，是敦煌学的一种组成部分。但诠释不是自创性解读，正如孔子所言，文化的传承，要遵循"述而不作，信而好古"。真正的敦煌文化翻译，就是在精准理解与充分诠释的基础上向世界传播敦煌文化思想，传承敦煌文化精神。

敦煌文化是在中西文明的相遇、相识、相融中形成和发展的，是各种文明交流融汇的结晶，蕴含开放包容、互学互鉴的文化精神。翻译是文化的交流、思想的对话，其本身就是敦煌文化精神的"外显"形式。敦煌学研究成果的翻译，是学术思想的互学与互鉴，尤其建立在中外学者"中西合璧"方式上的合译，更是在互动的理解过程中实践敦煌精神，是传承与弘扬敦煌文化的又一种深化、物化、具象化的方式。敦煌文化翻译，以其特有的文化交流与对话方式，向世界讲述敦煌故事，传播敦煌思想，弘扬敦煌精神，让敦煌文化在交流中成为世界的文化，敦煌学研究成为"世界的敦煌学"，敦煌精神成为人类的思想精神。

兰州城市学院副校长　教授
甘肃文化翻译中心　主任　姜秋霞

2020年10月

Foreword Ⅲ

Translation Connects Dunhuang Culture with the World

Dunhuang culture is a model of the continuous amalgamation of Chinese civilization over a span of thousands of years, and an important representation of the essence of Chinese culture. There was a time when Dunhuang culture experienced a historical reality of "Dunhuang itself is in China, yet Dunhuang studies is in the West." Of course, the discovery of the Dunhuang manuscripts at the beginning of the 20th century—with many of them taken overseas—brought the attention of scholars from all over the world to Dunhuang culture, and produced a large corpus of research from Dunhuang studies abroad. But Dunhuang culture is rooted in China, and the knowledge and understanding of Dunhuang culture originated in China. The international development of Dunhuang studies requires consensus, common knowledge, and sharing through cultural dissemination and academic exchange. Thus, translation is undoubtedly an important way to bring Dunhuang culture out to the world and for the spirit of Dunhuang to be shared by all humankind.

1. Translation is the voice of Dunhuang culture for the world community

Translation is an important method of cultural dissemination and communication. To translate Dunhuang culture is to introduce Dunhuang to the outside world, in other words, to share all aspects and content of Dunhuang culture. Dunhuang culture is a comprehensive cultural system that integrates religion, art, technology, literature, medicine, agriculture, architecture, and folk customs. Translating Dunhuang culture informs the public about the history of Dunhuang's civilization and its open exchanges, reveals the art of Dunhuang as a reflection of the mutual learning between China and the West, introduces Dunhuang's science, technology, and medicine, and explains the integration and development of its religious culture. Thus, systematic translation allows the world to not only know about Dunhuang, but also understand the true, comprehensive culture of Dunhuang.

Translating Dunhuang culture is to relate and express that which is most quintessential, reflecting the pinnacle of culture emanating from its source in Dunhuang itself. As far as cultural content is concerned, on the one hand, Dunhuang translation converts language—that of the Dunhuang manuscripts, Dunhuang studies, and Dunhuang academic theories—as a carrier of cultural content; on the other hand, it converts art as a carrier of cultural information. Dunhuang culture is embodied in multiple symbolic and semiotic forms. Language carriers include literary and non-literary forms such as scripture, *bianwen* (transformation texts), *baojuan* (prosimetric narratives), and bamboo slip archives; artistic carriers include rock-cut architecture, sculpture, and murals. Translating Dunhuang culture entails language conversion and the precise expression of its historical, religious, literary, artistic, and other cultural content contained in various carriers, as well as its cultural values and cultural spirit. The expression of Dunhuang culture through translation requires the use of both linguistic and non-linguistic conversion. Generally speaking, translation is the conversion of language text. However, in Dunhuang culture translation, in addition to the conventional interlingual translation, there is also an intersemiotic transformation method, which is to say that translation of art and culture uses language to express intertextuality. Through this interlingual and intersemiotic conversion, a systematic method for the communication of Dunhuang culture can be constructed. When we translate as the "voice" of Dunhuang culture, it is necessary to pay attention to the manner of "speaking," in order to construct an effective discourse system. Translation, in disseminating, expressing, and communicating culture, must coordinate cultural understanding between different languages. The style and mode of discourse—the foundation for achieving cultural dissemination and communication—determine how cultural elements appear, determine the acceptability of cultural content, and thus determine the effect as well as effectiveness of cultural transmission. When translating Dunhuang culture, it is necessary to closely coordinate both foreignization and domestication conversion strategies, and, on the basis of respecting culture and history, use appropriate foreign language expressions as well as international expressions for cultural content and audience acceptance. To accurately express Dunhuang culture, a complete narrative must be constructed for communicating Dunhuang culture to the world outside China.

Speaking through the language of translation not only enables Dunhuang culture to fully "go forth" into the world, but also enables the essence of Dunhuang to "go in" deeply as well, effectively realizing the international spread and world recognition of Dunhuang culture.

2. Translation is the liaison for Dunhuang cultural and academic exchange

Translating Dunhuang culture creates an interactive platform for academic exchange between China and the rest of the international community, facilitating academic dialogue between Chinese and overseas Dunhuang scholars. Since the beginning of the 20th century, academics both within China and abroad have produced much research on Dunhuang culture, making considerable achievements in the field. The understanding of Dunhuang culture can be deepened through the mutual translation of research findings in Dunhuang studies both within China and overseas, as well as through academic dialogue and the exchanging of ideas. It is true that there is still a great deal to be learned about Dunhuang with its extensive, profound culture and spiritual value, but the exchange of existing academic theories is undoubtedly of great significance for the further research and understanding of Dunhuang. Mutual translation provides a necessary pathway for constructing an interactive mechanism for the field and for the interchange of expertise.

The first task is to carry out the mutual translation of Dunhuang documents. The translation and conversion of Dunhuang documents owned by various countries can help supplement the deficiencies in understanding caused by dispersed and fragmented manuscripts, and thus resolving the limitations of research. The documents, manuscripts, and bamboo slip found in the Dunhuang Mogao Caves include Buddhist, Taoist, and Confucian classics, Buddhist scriptures unique to Dunhuang, popular literature, and other cultural content. In addition to Chinese, the languages include Tibetan, Uyghur, Khotanese, Kuchean, Turkic, Sogdian, Sanskrit, and more. The Dunhuang manuscripts constitute historical written records of the cultural exchanges between China and the West along the Silk Road. They are important documents for studying Dunhuang culture and the Chinese cultural thought contained therein. However, due to the special history of the Dunhuang documents, a large part of the manuscripts was unlawfully removed overseas, including nearly 10,000 manuscripts now located in the United Kingdom, and more than 5,000 in France. As a result, various countries have a fragmented interpretation of Dunhuang culture, leading to one-sidedness in research. Through the translation of documents and materials, a multi-dimensional research platform and a systematic understanding for Dunhuang studies at home and abroad can be developed, with historical manuscript fragments recombined to allow comprehensive research on the same cultural phenomena, thereby forming a worldwide system for Dunhuang studies.

The second task is to carry out the mutual translation of research findings in Dunhuang studies. Through mutual translation, academic theories can interact and undergo comparison, thereby broadening researchers' own closed-off Dunhuang research. Through "other" Dunhuang research and reference, scholars can reflect on their own research, enrich their own expertise, exchange ideas with the "other," and deepen the understanding of Dunhuang culture through the interaction of different theories.

Dunhuang culture was formed and developed as a fusion of Chinese and Western cultures. It comprises a comprehensive system of cultural content, ideology, and historical development. It is a cultural system with interactive structures, and there are internal relationships between the components of the system, as well. For example, Dunhuang art research and religious cultural studies complement one another; there has been a historical connection between the exchange of Chinese and Western cultures and the process of cultural diffusion; and there has been an interrelationship between cultural evolution and dynastic structures. The understanding of Dunhuang culture requires systematic research in order to form an interrelated branch of knowledge; only when mutual understanding is complementary, can the knowledge of Dunhuang culture be continuously improved. Differences in interpretation have been inevitable amongst different countries and throughout different eras, based on research in their respective professional fields. The Sino-Western translation of Chinese and international Dunhuang research findings and theories, academic exchange and dialogue, and interchange of ideas can not only generate new ideas and new results, but can also enable scholars from all over the world to have a deeper understanding of Dunhuang culture. On the one hand, this can reduce errors from misreading as well as misunderstandings caused by cultural differences. On the other hand, academic dialogue between scholars from different eras, cultural backgrounds, and religious viewpoints on historical civilizations can redress the gaps in Dunhuang research regarding its artistic and cultural value. This will better form a consensus and a common interpretation of Dunhuang historical and cultural concepts, thereby enhancing the depth of Dunhuang cultural exchange as well as enabling high-level dialogue and interactive communication on Dunhuang culture.

3. Translation is the interpreter and world inheritor of the spirit of Dunhuang culture.

Translation is not merely the conversion of language, but also the interpretation of culture. Translating Dunhuang culture is not simple code conversion, nor is it purely the transmission of information. More importantly, translation reveals and interprets the philosophical thought, humanistic spirit, and values contained in Dunhuang culture and historical relics, which is imbued with the cultural spirit, mind, and confidence of the Chinese nation. Dunhuang culture stands as a model of Chinese and Western cultural exchange and diffusion. Dunhuang cave temple architecture and murals are based on the Central Plains culture, which also absorbed the content of Central and Western Asian Buddhist art aesthetics and ideals, reflecting the inherent spirit of multicultural synthesis and mutual learning. Dunhuang is an important representation of the openness and inclusiveness of Chinese civilization. Comprehensive, systematic translation can profoundly explain Dunhuang's historical development and its cultural essence, reveal the thinking behind Dunhuang cultural exchange and integration, interpret the cultural essence of Chinese civilization, explore the common roots of world civilizations, and even tap into the common ideals of the human race.

Translation is a type of interpretation, with cultural interpretative power. Translating Dunhuang culture is to interpret the profound meaning of Dunhuang culture under the auspices of researching it. The translation of Dunhuang culture is the exchange and interaction between the translator and Dunhuang cultural ideology and spirit, as well as the intertextuality of modern vision and historical essence. To engage in translation as the "interpreter" of Dunhuang culture is indeed the study of Dunhuang culture in a certain sense, and is a component of Dunhuang studies in and of itself. However, interpretation is never self-generated. As Confucius said, the inheritance of culture must follow the principle of "transmitting but not innovating, loving antiquity and having faith in it." Dunhuang culture translation means sharing and inheriting the essence of Dunhuang culture on the basis of accurate understanding and full interpretation.

We can conclude that Dunhuang culture has formed and developed from the encounter, acquaintance, and fusion of Chinese and Western civilizations. It is the crystallization of the exchange and synthesis of various civilizations, and contains a cultural spirit of openness, inclusiveness, and mutual learning. Translation is cultural exchange, a dialogue of ideas, and itself is the "external" form of Dunhuang's cultural essence. The translation of Dunhuang studies involves the interchange and mutual appraisal of academic ideas. In particular, co-translations based on the Sino-Western cooperation by Chinese and foreign scholars put the spirit of Dunhuang culture into action. Through the process of interactive understanding, the inheritance and promotion of Dunhuang culture is further deepened and substantiated. Dunhuang culture translation brings the story of Dunhuang to the world, shares Dunhuang thought, and promotes the essence of Dunhuang via its unique cultural exchange and methods of communication. Thus Dunhuang culture becomes the world's culture in the exchange, Dunhuang studies becomes the world's Dunhuang studies, and the spirit of Dunhuang culture becomes humankind's ideological spirit.

Jiang Qiuxia
Professor and Vice President of Lanzhou City University
Head of Gansu Cultural Translation and Interpreting Center
October 2020

晚唐时期的独舞舞伎
Solo Dancer from Late Tang

前　言

Introduction

隋朝大业五年（609年），因动用数百万民工开通大运河，御龙舟、幸江都（今扬州）、凿太行、筑长城、狩猎塞北而被后世责骂为“奢靡荒淫”的隋炀帝杨广，又做出了一个惊世骇俗之举——大驾西巡河西。炀帝一行西渡黄河，经大斗拔谷，翻越祁连山，到了张掖，召集“二十七国贸易大会”（一说“三十余国”），也许称得上是最早的世贸大会，会间“盛陈文物，奏九部乐，设鱼龙曼延”。拿今天一句流行的话来说，也就是“文化搭台，经济唱戏”了。应该说，隋炀帝还是推动丝绸之路商贸往来与文化艺术交流的“有功之帝”。20世纪80年代，人们在名扬四海的

During the year 609 of the Sui Dynasty (581–618), Emperor Yang Guang, sharply criticized as an extravagant and dissolute tyrant by later generations for his costly projects including grand palaces, the Great Canal, the Great Wall, and military campaigns, travelled west to the Hexi Corridor. During this trip, Emperor Yang and his entourage sailed west across the Yellow River, passing Dadou–Bagu, traversing the Qilian Mountains, and finally arriving at Zhangye, where they convened a trade conference with 26 nations from the Western Regions. This conference may indeed deserve to be called the world's first international summit, during which cultural relics were put on display, nine orchestras gave concerts, and various shows were performed onstage. People may say that "culture set the stage for economic development." To be fair, Emperor Yang had many merits, promoting commerce and trade along the Silk Road as well as cultural and artistic exchanges. In the 1980s, the world–renowned

大型舞剧《丝路花雨》中，仿佛也看到了炀帝君臣欢宴各国宾客的歌舞盛况。《隋书·音乐志》上说：“始开皇初定，令置‘七部乐’：一曰《国伎》，二曰《清商伎》，三曰《高丽伎》，四曰《天竺伎》，五曰《安国伎》，六曰《龟兹伎》，七曰《文康伎》。又杂有疏勒、扶南、康国、百济、突厥、新罗、倭国等伎。……及大业中，炀帝乃定《清乐》《西凉》《龟兹》《天竺》《康国》《疏勒》《安国》《高丽》《礼毕》，以为九部。”这异彩纷呈的“九部乐”，应该正是河西大会的积极成果之一，而且奠定了盛唐乐舞空前繁荣的基础。

崛起于陇西的李唐王朝，更在基本沿袭隋代乐舞体制的基础上开拓创新，将中原、东北、西南乐舞与西域乐舞的交融推向高潮。唐太宗贞观年间废除《礼毕》，创制《燕乐》，又添上《高昌乐》，成为“十部乐”。到了“开

full-length dance drama “Rain of Flowers Along the Silk Road” vividly depicted the grand occasion where Emperor Yang and his ministers served a feast for guests from all around the known world. According to *The Book of Sui: Treaties on Music*, “During the Kaihuang Period (581–600), Yang, first Emperor of the Sui Dynasty, cataloged various popular music and dance from outside China into the *Seven Books of Music*, including National music, Qingshang music, Gaoli music, Tianzhu music, Anguo music, Qiuci music and Wenkang music ensembles. The music of Shule, Funan, Kangguo, Baiji, Tujue, Xinluo, and Japan were also included. Until the Daye Period, Emperor Yang had collected *Nine Books of Music* for Qingyue music, Xiliang (Western Liang) music, Qiuci music, Tianzhu music, Kangguo music, Shule music, Anguo music, Gaoli music and Libi music.” The *Nine Books of Music* were one of the positive achievements of the Hexi summit, and, with its emphasis on music from foreign lands, helped to lay the foundation for the flourishing music and dance scene of the Tang Dynasty (618–907).

The Tang imperial court, with its roots in the Longxi Prefecture, predominantly continued the performing arts styles of the Sui Dynasty with its own innovations, blending music and dance of the Central Plains, the northeast, and the southeast with that of the Western Regions, pushing it to a new high. During the Zhenguan Period (627–649), Emperor Taizong of the Tang Dynasty abolished Libi music,

（元）天（宝）盛世”，酷爱乐舞的风流天子唐明皇，身体力行，不仅亲临教坊演习歌舞杂戏，而且宠信乐舞伎人，点缀太平。于是，无论宫廷、民间，京城、边陲，歌舞活动遂蔚为大观。尤其是在丝绸之路的要冲河西地区，成为各民族舞乐繁茂的大舞台，诚如盛唐边塞诗人岑参所咏：“凉州七城十万家，胡人半解弹琵琶”（《凉州馆中与诸判官夜集》）、“琵琶长笛曲相和，羌儿胡雏齐唱歌”（《酒泉太守席上醉后作》）。后来，尽管安史之乱的“渔阳鼙鼓”，惊破了唐明皇与杨贵妃的“霓裳羽衣”，河西十余州一度和中原隔断，而丝路沿途的歌舞活动仍绵延不绝，到晚唐五代及宋初又增添若干新的色彩。这些乐舞盛景，自然也同魏晋南北朝及隋代的乐舞一样，成为地处丝

created *yanyue* music (banquet music), and added Gaochang music to create the *Ten Books of Music*. In the prosperous Kaiyuan and Tianbao periods, Emperor Xuanzong of the Tang Dynasty, a romantic monarch who had a deep love of music and dance, earnestly practiced what he advocated. He not only visited imperial music conservatories in person to learn and perform songs, dances, and dramas, but also gave royal patronage to musicians and dancers in the performing arts. As a result, whether in the royal court or among the common people, in the capital city of Chang'an or the surrounding border areas, singing and dancing activities frequently presented a dazzling sight, particularly in the Hexi Corridor. As a communication center of the Silk Road, Hexi became a grand stage for the dynamic development of music and dance from various nations. As poet Cen Shen wrote in his frontier poem "An Evening Gathering in Liangzhou with Assistants to the Local Leaders", "There are a hundred thousand households throughout the seven towns of Liangzhou / And half the Hu people are proficient in playing the *pipa*," and in his another poem "Written After the Jiuquan Prefect Got Drunk at the Banquet", "The voice of *pipa* and flute are harmonious with each other/As the Qiang and Hu people sing together." Later, the An Lushan Rebellion resulted in cutting off the prefectures in the Hexi Corridor from the Central Plains of China. However, singing and dancing activities along the Silk Road continued uninterrupted, with new elements introduced during the Late Tang Dynasty, the Five

路咽喉的敦煌艺术的重要内容，并且直接或间接地反映到敦煌壁画雕塑和相关写本之中。

以莫高窟为代表的敦煌石窟群，虽历经千年沧桑，留存至今的 700 余个洞窟仍然保存了大约近 5 万平方米的壁画和近 4 千身彩塑，其中有非常丰富的魏晋南北朝、隋唐五代、西夏与宋元时代的舞蹈形象；在 1900 年发现的藏经洞（莫高窟第 17 窟）的约 5 万卷（号）古代写本中，也存有曲谱、舞谱等珍贵的乐舞资料。我们这本小册子，就是希望主要通过敦煌壁画里乐舞形象的介绍与赏析，使广大读者对传承有绪、多姿多彩的敦煌舞蹈有更多感性的认识与理性的思索。至于敦煌乐曲及相关的乐器，则略有涉及，并不列在本书要详细介绍的范围之内。

在本书写作的过程中，我们除了运用对敦煌石窟实地考察踏查所得的

Dynasties (907–960), and the beginning of the Song Dynasty (960–1279). The same trend continued during the Wei, Jin, Northern and Southern Dynasties, and Sui Dynasty. Spectacular styles of dance became an important part of the performing arts in Dunhuang, due to its role as a major crossroads of the Silk Road. These dances were directly or indirectly reflected in Dunhuang murals, sculptures, and manuscripts.

Dunhuang, represented by the Mogao Caves, experienced many vicissitudes over a thousand–year period, but the remaining 700–plus cave temples contain more than 45,000 square meters of preserved murals and approximately 4,000 painted sculptures. They abound with dancing figures in different periods from the Wei, Jin, Northern and Southern Dynasties, Sui Dynasty, Tang Dynasty, the Five Dynasties, the Western Xia (1038 – 1227), Song Dynasty and Yuan Dynasty (1206 – 1368). The 50,000 ancient manuscripts found in the Library Cave (Cave 17) at Mogao also contain various records of rare music and dance materials such as musical scores and choreography notations. The aim of this book is to help readers increase their understanding and appreciation of the heritage and splendor of dance history in Dunhuang, by introducing music and dance images found in the Dunhuang murals. As for music and musical instruments, they are

第一手资料外，主要参考了公元2000年以前国内外出版的有关图录本，凡转载或复制图片，使用临摹图、线描图的，均经敦煌研究院或原作者同意授权，并将通过出版者为他们支付一定的报酬。这些临摹者有段文杰、霍熙亮、史苇湘、欧阳琳、吴荣鉴、万庚育、何治赵、范兴儒、娄婕、赵蓉、史敦宇、吴曼英等，谨向他们为此付出的辛勤劳动致以谢忱。笔者同时申明，也将继续欢迎研究者引述我们对中国舞蹈史、敦煌乐舞及敦煌舞谱研究已发表的成果并提出宝贵的批评意见。

referred to briefly, but are not covered in extensive detail.

For the writing of this book, besides using primary sources obtained at Dunhuang, we generally relied on literature and works published both in China and abroad before the year 2000. All reprinted or copied pictures, replicas, and line drawings were used by permission of the Dunhuang Academy or the original authors and were paid through their respective publishers. The illustrators for this publication include Duan Wenjie, Huo Xiliang, Shi Weixiang, Ouyang Lin, Wu Rongjian, Wan Gengyu, He Zhizhao, Fan Xingru, Lou Jie, Zhao Rong, Shi Dunyu, and Wu Manying. We would like to extend heartfelt gratitude for their great diligence. We also welcome researchers to quote, make critical comments on, or give feedback about our published research on the history of Chinese dance, Dunhuang music and dance, and Dunhuang choreography notation.

敦煌乐舞的人文背景及源流

Cultural Background and Origin of Dunhuang Music and Dance

华戎所交一都会

A Metropolis Where East and West Converged

汉武帝派霍去病率大军击败匈奴、开通河西走廊后，于公元前111年置敦煌郡，完成了“列四郡，据两关（玉门、阳关）”的战略部署。自此，汉朝多次从内地移民敦煌，同戍卒一道屯垦戍边；曹魏时代，两任敦煌太守仓慈、皇甫隆提倡百姓垦荒，推广使用耧耕与“衍溉法”，并鼓励胡汉通婚，增产粮食，繁衍人口；其后，两晋时期大量中原地区的移民进入敦煌，不仅大规模兴修水利，而且开办官学、私学，传播儒家学

During the Han Dynasty, Emperor Wu (140 BC–87 BC) appointed Huo Qubing to lead his army to fight the Xiongnu and open up the Hexi Corridor in present-day Gansu Province. Having succeeded, Emperor Wu established Dunhuang Prefecture in 111 BC and completed the strategic deployment by establishing the four prefectures of Wuwei, Zhangye, Jiuquan and Dunhuang in Hexi, and occupying the two passes of Yumen and Yangguan. After that, over times, civilians were ordered to migrate from China's Central Plains① to Dunhuang, to settle land and guard the border areas together with garrison soldiers. During the Wei Dynasty (220–265), the prefecture chiefs Cang Ci and Huangfu Long called for common people to reclaim land and settle the frontier in this area. They also promoted the use of drill barrows and flood irrigation methods to expand grain production, and encouraged intermarriage between the Hu and Han people to increase the population. Later, during the Jin Dynasty (265–420), large amounts of migrants from the China's Central Plains poured into Dunhuang. They not only undertook water conservation projects on a large scale,

① The Central Plains (*Zhongyuan*) refers to both a geographical area of China as well as the historical center of its political power and culture. The area in present-day Henan Province was originally China's cradle of civilization, particularly the regions in the Yellow River Valley. Later the term "Central Plains" was used to signify this area, and also included parts of the nearby provinces of Shandong, Shanxi, Hebei and Shaanxi. Generally speaking, it can be interpreted as "interior China" or "inland China" and the succession of imperial dynasties located there.

说，同时还建寺庙、开佛窟，翻译佛经，为东来西去的僧人与商旅提供各种便利，使这个地广民稀之地，逐渐开拓成文化发展、交通繁忙、“晏然富殖”的塞外绿洲。隋代，炀帝亲驾张掖，召开二十七国贸易大会，努力经营河西的政策取得积极成果，据《隋书·裴矩传》引《西域图记·序》云：此时的丝绸之路基本通行无阻，“发自敦煌，至于西海，凡为三道，各有襟带”。敦煌成为丝路南、中北三道的“咽喉之地”(图1)。

but also opened both government-sponsored and private schools to propagate Confucianism. In addition, they built temples, carved Buddhist niches and cave shrines, and translated Buddhist texts, for the convenience of monks and travelling merchants from around the world. As a result, this vast territory with a sparse population gradually was transformed into a peaceful, prosperous borderland oasis—a busy hub promoting cultural development. During the Sui Dynasty, Emperor Yang visited Zhangye in person, hosting a twenty-seven nation trade conference, and his efforts in the Hexi Corridor achieved positive results. According to *The Book of Sui: Biography of Pei Ju*, cited from preface to *The Illustrated Book of the Western Regions*, the Silk Road during this time could be travelled

图1 丝路三道示意图

Fig.1 Map of Three Routes Comprising the Silk Road

唐代，敦煌地区人文荟萃、商贸发达、民族交融，与我国新疆地区一道成为世界上历史悠久、地域广阔、自成体系、影响深远的四大文化体系（中国、印度、希腊、伊斯兰）的汇流地。当时，敦煌十三个乡聚居着汉、藏、印度、粟特、波斯、回鹘、朝鲜及康、安、曹、石等昭武九姓的数万居民，这些百姓宗教信仰不同、风俗各异而和睦共处，儒家学说与佛、道、摩尼、祆、景教兼容互补。据史籍与敦煌出土文书记载，自西晋至五代宋初，敦煌地区的佛寺、道观及各种祠庙总数近百座，仅归义军时期就有寺院 17 所、僧尼 1100 多人。以节日赛神、佛道仪式与各类庆典为中心的岁时民俗活动贯穿一年始终。盛唐时期，敦煌已经形成三河、百渠、八泉、十池的水利灌溉系统，仅党河干、支渠道的总长度就超过了 700 华

without hindrance: "From Dunhuang to the Mediterranean Sea, the three roads were all under control." Dunhuang thus became a vital hub for the northern, southern, and middle routes along the Silk Road (Fig.1).

During the Tang Dynasty, Dunhuang, with its broad gathering of talent, development of commerce and trade, and mingling of ethnic groups, became an area where the four great cultures of China, India, Greece, and Islam converged. With a long history and vast territory, this area established its own system of far-reaching influence. At that time, the thirteen townships of Dunhuang were home to thousands of residents of the Han and the Tibetans, and from countries of India, Sogdia, Persia, the Uyghur Khaganate, and Korea (Silla), as well as people from the influential Kang, An, Cao, Shi and other families belonging to the Nine Zhaowu Clans. People with different religious beliefs and customs lived side-by-side in harmony, and Confucianism coexisted with Buddhism, Daoism (Taoism), Manicheism, Zoroastrianism, and Nestorianism. According to historical records and unearthed relics, there were nearly one hundred Buddhist, Daoist, and ancestral temples in Dunhuang from the Western Jin Dynasty (265-317) to the Five Dynasties and early Song period. During the Guiyijun period alone, there were 17 temples housing over 1,100 ordained monks and nuns. Folk activities featuring festivals for deities, Buddhist and Daoist rituals, and various ceremonies were held throughout the year. By the Tang Dynasty, Dunhuang had developed an irrigation system of

里，不仅畜牧业稳定发展，而且人均耕地超过十亩，绿地占城区总面积的71%，果木成林，粮食生产不仅自给充裕，还“余粟转输灵州，漕下黄河，入太原仓，备关中凶年”（见《太平广记》卷四八五引《东城老父传》）。作为人文修养的重要基础，敦煌地区的学校教育令人瞩目。当地的官学（州郡县学）不仅是宣教儒家经典的讲堂，而且举办了医学院、阴阳学、道学、伎术院等各类专业训练机构；官学之外，私学（义学）按照开元二十一年（733年）诏令，“每乡之内，各里置一学”，每每由世家大儒授课，生徒济济一堂；更加突出的是敦煌地区的寺院学校，由于得到当地政权的大力支持，寺学的师资、课程开设等办学条件常常优于官学，所教授的“外学”知识也较为宽博扎实，许多重要的官宦子弟均进入寺学接受启蒙教育。以上种种，构成敦煌地

three rivers, 100 canals, eight springs and 10 pools. For the Danghe River alone, the total length of its main stream and branches exceeded 350 kilometers. The agriculture of Dunhuang maintained stable development and cultivated land reached over ten *mu* (0.67 hectares) per capita. Green spaces made up 71% of the urban area with fruit orchards and self-sufficient food production. According to the 485th volume of the *Extensive Records of the Taiping Era*, cited from the *Biography of Jia Chang*, Dunhuang even had so much grain that “surplus grains were transported to Lingzhou and sent to Taiyuan by water transportation on the Yellow River to prepare for the impending famine in Guanzhong.”

As an important foundation for literary achievements, Dunhuang had a remarkable educational system. Local government-sponsored schools—district, prefecture, and county schools—not only propagated and taught Confucian classics, but also set up professional training institutions for medicine, *yin-yang* theory, Daoism, and various other skills. Moreover, as for private schools, according to an imperial edict in 733, “There shall be one school within each township.”Lessons were given by well-known Confucian teachers with an enrollment of many students. Monastic schools were even more prominent because of the strong support from local authorities. The faculty and curriculum were often superior to those of government-sponsored schools, and Confucianism taught at these schools was broader and more profound. Therefore, many children of government

区独具特色的人文环境，再加上敦煌地区商旅往来频繁，手工业发达，店铺林立，寺院殷实，富足的经济也为文化艺术活动创造了条件，使得敦煌成为"华戎所交"的著名的国际文化都会。

officials were sent into monastic schools for their elementary education. All of these contributed to the unique cultural environment of Dunhuang. In addition, with advanced handicraft industries, large amounts of commerce, substantial numbers of temples, and frequent visits from caravans of travelling merchants, the financial prosperity of Dunhuang also created ripe conditions for its cultural and artistic activities, making it a well-known international metropolis where East and West converged.

刚柔兼济大舞台

Hard and Soft Combined on One Stage

敦煌地区独特的人文与地理环境，为中原与西域的乐舞交融提供了广阔的大舞台。从魏晋南北朝时代开始，中原江南地区轻歌曼舞的柔美，北方西域一带马背民族狂放豪迈的刚健，在敦煌地区兼收并蓄，开出绚丽之花。

南北朝时期政权更迭频繁，民族迁徙规模浩大，内地居民大量进入河西地区，乐舞交流亦掀起高潮，汇通东西南北各地区舞蹈艺术，上承秦汉舞蹈余韵，下开

The unique cultural and geographical environment of Dunhuang also provided a grand stage for the blending of music and dance from the Central Plains and the Western Regions①. During the Wei, Jin, and Northern and Southern Dynasties, Dunhuang absorbed both the softness of the southern area of the Central Plains, which featured soft music and graceful dancing, and the explosive energy of the tribal Western Regions which featured wild and heroic people on horseback—resulting in a magnificent cultural flowering.

Frequent regime changes during the Northern and Southern Dynasties (420–589) led to large-scale ethnic migration as well as residents from the inland China pouring into Dunhuang in huge numbers, as a result of which exchanges of music and dance reached a high point. Performing arts around the world co-mingled here, inheriting the charming style of dance of the Qin (221 BC–206 BC) and Han dynasties, and later assimilating the music and dance of the Sui and Tang dynasties. At that time, the northern and southern areas not only absorbed *qingshang* music, a type of folk music and dance popular in the Han Dynasty, but also integrated it with local and regional folk dance forms. As for dances of

---

① The Western Regions (*Xiyu*) was a historical name used by China to refer to areas west of the Yumen Pass. Although the specific areas changed over time, it primarily referred to Central Asia, but could also include the Tarim Basin in present-day Xinjiang, as well as other regions to the west of China, including India. The Western Regions were an important part of the Silk Road and also played an important role in the transmission of Buddhism into China.

隋唐乐舞先河。当时,南北两地除各自吸取汉朝改编自民间的清商乐舞外,也各自融合当地的民族舞蹈,尤其是北方北周时期的舞蹈,既是西域、西凉、高丽、鲜卑等民族民间舞蹈交融的结晶,又大大丰富了以中原传统乐舞为基础的宫廷雅乐。在这场乐舞大交流中,敦煌所在的河西及临近的新疆地区,地位格外重要——既是龟兹、高昌、疏勒、安国等西域诸国伎乐在此融合后传入内地的通道,又是因吸取西域舞蹈营养而大大丰富了的中原乐舞回流西返展示新丰采的舞台。成为“九部乐”之一的西凉乐,就是直接在河西地区融合产生而传入中原的新乐舞。《旧唐书·音乐志》上说它是“凉人所传中国旧乐而杂以羌胡之声”,实际上它是以“特善诸国”的新疆龟兹乐为主的西域各族乐舞与中原汉民族乐舞融合后的新型乐舞,十六国时期产生于河西的凉州(今甘肃武威),后来逐渐演变成型,又被北魏政权吸收为宫廷乐舞。从敦

the northern areas and in the Northern Zhou in particular, it was not only the result of the integration of ethnic dances of the Western Regions, including Xiliang, Gaoli and Xianbei, but was also greatly enriched by the refined aristocratic music that was based on traditional music and dance of the Central Plains. The Hexi Corridor, where Dunhuang is located, and its neighboring area, Xinjiang, both played a fundamental role in this great exchange of music and dance. They were both the gateway for the amalgamated music of the Western Regions to be introduced to the interior China, and a stage where the performing arts of the Central Plains could be performed with influences from the Western Regions. An example of this was Xiliang (Western Liang) music of the *Nine Books of Music*. It was a new style of performing arts, synthesized in the Hexi region. *The Old Book of Tang: Treaties on Music* described it as "traditional Chinese music spread among the Liang people, mingled with Qiang and Hu music."However, it was actually a new kind of music and dance, combining together that of the Western Regions, which mainly featured Xinjiang Qiuci music, considered the best among all the ethnic music, and that of the Han people in the Central Plains. Xiliang music, generated during the Sixteen Kingdoms period at Liangzhou (present-day Wuwei in Gansu), gradually took shape and was finally adopted by the Northern Wei as its official court music and dance. From dancing images of the Northern Dynasties

图 2　舞姿刚劲的伎乐天(莫高窟第 272 窟窟顶东披)
Fig.2 Female Heavily Dancer in Lively Dance Pose (East Slope of the Ceiling, Mogao Cave 272)

图 3　药叉的刚健舞姿之一(莫高窟第 290 窟西壁)
Fig.3　Bold Dance Pose of a *Yakša*, 1(west wall, Mogao Cave 290)

煌壁画中展现的北朝舞蹈形象看,它们巧妙地结合了北方游牧民族雄健粗犷的气质与佛教发源地尼泊尔、印度一带婀娜多姿的舞风,豪放明快,具有特殊的艺术魅力(图 2~ 图 5)。

隋唐时期,国家统一,经济发达,文化交流盛况空前,也为乐舞艺术的发展与繁荣提供了最丰厚的土壤,迎来了中国各民族舞蹈最辉煌的黄金时代。唐代社会具有博采众长、兼收并蓄、为我所用的气度,因而能够融会贯通,创造出为民众喜闻乐见的新艺术。一方面,唐舞以华夏传

(386–581) displayed in the Dunhuang murals, it can be seen that they subtly combined the rough and bold temperament of tribal, nomadic peoples with the graceful and charming choreographic styles of Nepal and India where Buddhism originated. As a result, they are energetic and sprightly, with unique artistic charm (Figs.2–5).

The Sui and Tang dynasties enjoyed national unity, prosperous economies, and unprecedented cultural exchange, which provided rich soil for the development of the performing arts, thus becoming a golden age of ethnic dance. Tang society had a unique interest in outside cultures, incorporating diverse elements for its own benefit. As a result, it created innovative art for ms that

统舞蹈为基础，广泛吸纳东北、西南、西域各地区民族的舞蹈艺术精华，或原样搬演，或部分吸取，或融化再创；另一方面，随着佛教典籍与文化的传播，佛教中国化、世俗化进程的加速，源远流长、自成体系的佛教艺术也日益贴近民众生活，为发展唐代音乐、舞蹈、美术注入了新的活

people were delighted to see and hear. On the one hand, Tang period dance was based on traditional Chinese dance, but it extensively borrowed from and absorbed essential elements of other ethnic choreography from the northeast, southwest, and the Western Regions. It either used the original dances in their entirety, incorporated parts of them, or created a new fusion from them. On the other hand, with the spread of Buddhist texts and culture, as well as the accelerating sinicization and secularization of Buddhism, other related arts with their own

图 4　药叉的刚健舞姿之二(莫高窟第 290 窟西壁)
Fig.4　Bold Dance Pose of a *Yakśa*, 2(West Wall, Mogao Cave 290)

图 5　药叉的刚健舞姿之三(莫高窟第 290 窟西壁)
Fig.5　Bold Dance Pose of a *Yakśa*, 3 (West Wall, Mogao Cave 290)

力。这就大大地丰富了唐代的舞蹈艺术，使其取得了辉煌的成就，而且成为当时社会生活不可或缺的组成部分。敦煌莫高窟作为丝路明珠、河西佛都，其僧俗舞蹈活动应当特别繁盛、精彩，以人间乐舞为基础的丰富多彩的佛国乐舞形象也在佛寺、石窟的经变画、伎乐图中栩栩如生地展示出来，敦煌石窟壁画、彩塑，遂成为荟萃唐舞形象的资料宝库。

long-standing aesthetics also became part of even ordinary people's lives. Thus a new energy was injected into the development of Tang Dynasty music, dance, and fine arts. This greatly enriched the dance arts of the Tang Dynasty, bringing it to a dazzling level of achievement, and making it an indispensable part of every level of society. As the pearl of the Silk Road and the Buddhist center of the Hexi Corridor, the Mogao Caves were full of thriving dance activities for monks and lay devotees. Murals of sutra illustrations and musical performances vividly depict a variety of Buddhist dancing figures, which were based on folk music and dance. As a result, today the murals and painted sculptures of Dunhuang form a valuable repository of Tang Dynasty dance images.

不绝如缕说渊源

Lingering Echoes of the Past: Tracing the Origins of Dunhuang Art

我们在具体介绍敦煌壁画中的舞蹈形象之前，还需要对它们的概貌与源流做些简要的说明。

敦煌莫高窟南区存有壁画的492个洞窟，几乎每个洞窟都有舞蹈形象。这些舞蹈形象可以分为人们臆想与传说中神佛世界的天宫乐舞与人世间的民俗乐舞两大类。天宫乐舞包括天宫伎乐、飞天伎乐、化生伎乐、经变画伎乐以及各种护法神（如金刚力士、药叉、迦陵频伽等）等具有舞蹈感的形象——有在窟顶、龛楣飞舞翱翔的飞天，在天宫凭栏奏乐、舞动的伎乐天，在经变画中有乐队伴奏的急速旋转腾踏的伎乐天与翩翩起舞的人首鸟身的迦陵频伽鸟(美音鸟)，还有塑像中那些具有舞蹈美感的菩萨、力士等(图6~图12)。民俗乐舞则

Before specifically introducing the images of music and dance depicted in the Mogao Caves at Dunhuang, we need to briefly explain their origin and general development.

Almost each of the 492 cave temples in the southern part of the Mogao Caves includes dancing figures. They can be divided into two types: music and dance of deities and Buddhas in heavenly realms as imagined by people or depicted in myths and legends, and folk music and dance from the secular world. Music and dance in celestial abodes include depictions of musical performers, flying *apsaras*, musicians in sutra illustrations, and other dancing figures of various Dharma protectors, including *lokapasns*, *yaksas*, and *kalavinkas*. There are supernatural female beings dancing and flying on the grotto ceilings and niche lintels, soaring performers playing music and dancing in heavenly palaces, entertainers twirling and dancing with musical accompaniment, fantastical *kalaviṅkas* with human heads and bird bodies dancing elegantly in sutra illustrations, as well as sculptures of bodhisattvas and Dharma protectors embodying the very beauty of dance and choreography (Figs.6–12). Folk music and dance include scenes with patrons and dance scenes based on narrative paintings of the Buddha's life, which include scenes of travel, farming, banquets, weddings, worship, and holiday celebrations. These types of

图 6　凌空吹笛的飞天(莫高窟第 249 窟西壁)
Fig.6　Image of an *Apsara* Playing a Flute (West Wall, Mogao Cave 249)

图 7　合乐歌唱的飞天之一(莫高窟第 285 窟南壁)
Fig.7　Image of an *Apsara* Dancing to Music, 1 (South Wall, Mogao Cave 285)

图 8　合乐歌唱的飞天之二(莫高窟第 285 窟南壁)
Fig.8　Image of an *Apsara* Dancing to Music, 2 (South Wall, Mogao Cave 285)

图 9　做弹指状的两伎乐(莫高窟第 251 窟南壁)
Fig.9　Images of Celestial Performers Playing Instruments (South Wall, Mogao Cave 251)

包括供养人行列中的乐舞场面和佛传故事画里生活气息浓厚的舞蹈画面——出行、农耕、宴饮、嫁娶、祭祀、节日庆典中的舞蹈形象。这类舞蹈壁画，直接而真实地反映了当时社会生活中的舞蹈形式。此外,安西榆林窟、东千佛洞、西千佛洞、水峡口、五个庙及莫高窟北区的少数洞窟也保存了相当丰富、生动

murals directly and realistically reflect the dance forms prevalent in society at that time. Moreover, several murals from the Yulin Caves, the Eastern Thousand Buddha Caves, the Western Thousand Buddha Caves at Dunhuang, the Shuixiakou Caves in Guazhou County, the Five Temple Caves in Subei County, and the northern side of the Mogao Caves also contain rich and vivid dance images. Zheng Ruzhong of the Dunhuang Academy has been committed to the research of *yueji* (performing musicians) and musical instruments in Dunhuang mural images and has made significant contributions

的舞蹈形象。敦煌研究院的郑汝中先生，多年来致力于敦煌壁画乐舞图像中乐伎与乐器的研究，贡献至巨。据他多年的深入调查统计，仅莫高窟绘有乐舞形象的洞窟就有240个，乐舞形象3400多身，其中以乐伎居多。因他的研究侧重于“乐”，故将“乐伎”与“舞伎”区别分类。我们这本书的主题虽然是“舞”，但因与音乐关系密切，所以在具体的介绍和分析中也还是要涉及为舞蹈伴奏的乐队。

敦煌壁画中的舞蹈形象源远流长，自先秦、两汉至隋、唐、五代，随时代变迁而风貌各异，代有奇葩，不绝如缕，承继与发展变化的脉络清晰。根据敦煌艺术史家的研究，敦煌壁画舞蹈图像大致可以分为早、中、晚三个阶段：早期——北凉及北朝时期。早期的舞蹈壁画构图比较单一，多为单身的乐舞动作再现，人物形

in this area. According to his investigation and statistics compiled over the years, there are 240 caves painted with musical dance images in the Mogao Caves alone, including more than 3, 400 musical dance images, most of which are of performing musicians. Because his research focused on music, he differentiated musical performers (*yueji*) from dancing performers (*wuji*). Although the subject of this book is primarily dance, which is closely associated with music, the detailed introduction and analysis also involve the musical groups which accompany the dancers.

The dance images in the Dunhuang murals have a long history and show various styles and features ranging from the pre-Qin period (Paleolithic period-221 BC), the Western Han (206 BC-AD 25), and Eastern Han (25-220) to the Sui, Tang, and Five Dynasties. They include wonderful works from each of these dynasties, and their transmission, development, and changes follow a clear thread. According to historical research, the dance images from the Dunhuang murals can be roughly divided into early, middle, and late stages. The early stage was during the Northern Dynasties and Northern Liang. The dance murals from this early stage are simple in composition and mostly appear as dancing by a single person, of which the characters are mostly plain and simple, with strong figures and bold, unrestrained movement, showing the distinct styles of the Western Regions, northern nomadic tribes, and India. The middle stage took place during the Sui and Tang dynasties, a period spanning over 300 years from 581 to 907. The dance murals of the middle stage are represented by

图 10　西域舞风格的天宫伎乐(莫高窟第 248 窟北壁)

Fig.10　Image of a Celestial Dancer in the Style of the Western Regions (North Wall, Mogao Cave 248)

象大都稚拙古朴，体态粗壮，动作刚健奔放，带有明显的西域及北方游牧民族的风格，也还有印度的风格。中期——隋、唐时期。中期的舞蹈壁画，以巨幅经变画为代表，大多气势恢弘，富丽堂皇，而且题材

huge, magnificent sutra illustrations (*jingbian*), depicting a wide range of subjects and colorful images, vividly reflecting various dances including multi-ethnic musical dance, as well as dances with rich local customs from the Hexi Corridor. The late stage occurred from the Five Dynasties to the Yuan Dynasty, roughly the period from 907 to 1368. The dance murals

图 11 飞天舞姿(莫高窟第 303 窟北壁)

Fig.11 Dance Image of an *Apsara* (North Wall, Mogao Cave 303)

图 12 经变画乐舞图(莫高窟第 331 窟舞伎摹本)
Fig.12 Musical Dance from a Sutra Illustration (Based on Image of Dancer in Mogao Cave 331)

大为拓展,形象丰富多彩,多民族交融的乐舞、各种类型及河西地区乡土风情浓郁的舞蹈都有生动的反映。晚期——五代、西夏、宋、元时期。晚期舞蹈壁画,总的呈衰微趋势,大多在构图、画技、形象描绘上沿袭前代,较少创新,艺术感染力降低,但榆林窟西夏时期和莫高窟第 465

of the late stage tend to reflect a decline in quality; most follow the former stages in composition, painting techniques, and execution. They lack innovation and exhibit a reduction in artistic appeal, with the exception of some excellent murals in the Yulin Caves painted during the Western Xia period, as well as Mogao Cave 465, painted sometime in the Yuan Dynasty, both of which exhibit strong lines and color for

窟元代的一些精彩壁画却是例外，在舞姿的线条勾勒与色彩描绘上都颇具功力，依然光彩熠熠，动人心魄。需要强调的是，上述三个阶段的划分，只是为了说明敦煌舞蹈壁画形象在历史发展长河中的演化轨迹和继承关系与时代特征，并不表明它们之间有截然不同的差异与隔断；恰恰相反，它们正可雄辩地证明我国古代舞蹈艺术是在各民族文化交融之中逐渐累积与丰富起来的，也证实了文化发展与政治、经济、文化交流的密切关联。

the dance poses and are splendid and attractive. It needs to be emphasized that the division of the above-mentioned three stages is to express the evolution, transmitted styles and motifs, and contemporary features in the images of the Dunhuang dance paintings in its long history. The intention is not to imply that there are distinct, abrupt differences between them; on the contrary, they eloquently prove that ancient Chinese performing arts gradually absorbed and synthesized various styles, reflecting deep ethnic cultural integration. They also demonstrate the close association between cultural development and political, economic, and sociocultural exchange.

箫管霓裳：敦煌乐舞

Raiment of Rainbows and Feathers: Music and Dance from the Dunhuang Murals

菩萨如宫娃
经变画中的天宫乐舞

Bodhisattvas as Celestial Palace Maidens: Music and Dance Images in Sutra Illustration Paintings

天宫伎乐形象在莫高窟现存最早的北凉时代的洞窟中已经出现，他们的基调豪放、刚健、粗犷、强壮，一般身披帛带，或手执各种乐器，或空手而舞，姿态各异。飞天形象源远流长，发展脉络清晰，时代特色鲜明，形态丰富多彩，被称作“敦煌壁画的灵魂”。北朝时期的飞天伎乐形象，则清瘦飘逸，动感强烈，或持花蕾、抛花瓣，或吹奏乐器，亦有空手者，均展示在天界急速飞翔的舞姿。因为飞天可单列专题介绍，其舞姿已融入各种壁画舞蹈的形象之中，本书不再具体叙述。早期敦煌壁画里天宫伎乐的动作特征是大幅度地扭腰出胯、伸臂扬掌，体态挺拔舒展，带有明显的尼泊尔、印度风格。例如莫高窟第251 窟北壁有一身北魏时期的天宫伎乐舞者，自左肩而下斜披宽薄巾帛，犹如印度妇女所穿的纱丽，身体向右微微挺胯，右手于胸前做“托掌”姿，左臂向下做“按掌”姿，颇具印度舞韵味，正反映了印度佛教艺术对敦煌的影响。

盛唐时期，揭开了中国古代舞蹈史上最为灿烂辉煌的篇章。唐舞形式多样，健舞、软舞风格各异，尤其是因为最高统治者的爱好与提倡，用于宫廷朝会、宴飨的宫廷宴乐舞蹈在很大程度上代表了唐代舞蹈的艺术风范和最高水准。从唐代开始，敦煌壁画中出现了大铺的

The images of performers in heavenly abodes first appeared in caves of the Northern Liang period, which constituted the earliest of the Mogao Caves. Their figures are bold, robust, unrestrained, and strong. They generally wear long silk sashes on their clothing, and some hold various musical instruments, whereas others dance empty-handed. But it is the images of flying *apsaras* (Chinese: *feitian*) that are familiar to most as the heart and soul of the Dunhuang murals due to their long history, clear developmental timeline, and distinctive, colorful appearance. The images of these supernatural flying musicians, which began to be painted during the Northern Dynasties, are slim, elegant, and dynamic. Some hold stalks with flower buds or toss flower petals, some play musical instruments, and some hold nothing at all. However, they all depict flying dance movements in heavenly abodes. Flying *apsaras* are so numerous and widespread in the murals of Dunhuang that they could constitute a volume all their own—this book merely introduces them briefly and does not go into elaborate detail. These heavenly musicians in the early-stage Dunhuang murals exhibit drastically twisting waists and extended arms. Their postures are tall and straight, showing obvious Nepalese and Indian influences. For example, there is a celestial musician painted on the north wall of Mogao Cave 251 wearing a broad silk sash extending down from the left shoulder. She moves her hips slightly to the right, lifts her right palm upward toward her chest, and presses her left arm and palm downward, showing the style of Indian dance and reflecting the influence of Indian Buddhist arts in Dunhuang.

Ancient Chinese dance achieved its zenith during the High Tang Dynasty. There were many types of choreography in the Tang Dynasty, such as *jianwu* ("energetic dance") and *ruanwu* ("soft dance"), each of which had their own style. Owing to royal patronage and sponsorship, the court dancing performed during occasions such as morning gatherings and banquets represented the

经变画，成为佛教及其艺术中国化、世俗化的集中体现。唐代壁画中的天宫乐舞形象来源于现实的舞蹈活动，经过艺术的加工创造，又得到升华，在服饰、体态上显得更美、更圣洁，与现实舞人有所不同。唐代经变画天宫乐舞中的菩萨形象体态丰腴，曲线圆润，服饰华美，温婉典丽，神情安详，正是宫廷及民间舞蹈活动的折射与提升，故而唐时即流行着“菩萨如宫娃”的说法。

五代时期敦煌壁画中的舞蹈形象，在舞姿、服饰、舞具的运用上均秉承唐代风范，舞蹈内容也与唐时相仿，包括长绸巾舞、腰鼓舞、琵琶舞等。引人注目的是五代壁画中又出现了久违的舞袖形象。“长袖善舞”本是自先秦以来中原的固有传统，在汉晋时代曾风靡不衰，唐以后的有关记载亦史不绝书，但在敦煌，长袖舞的图像却是在五代榆林窟的壁画中才出现的。虽然五代及宋、元时期的敦煌壁画是在唐代基础上延续的，但由于种种原因，艺术上创新因素不多，许多人物画不免流于板滞，舞蹈场景画面所表现的舞姿造型、风采神韵、动感意境均不如唐壁画丰富生动。因此，本书较少选用五代以后的乐舞壁画来举例鉴赏，但这并不说明这一时期舞蹈图像数量较少。

highest artistic achievement of Tang Dynasty dance to a large extent. From the Tang Dynasty onward, sutra illustrations (*jingbian*) appeared in Dunhuang murals and became the main embodiment of sinicization and secularization of Buddhism and its related arts. The Tang period mural images of musical dance in heavenly realms were based on real-life dance activities during this time; however, in these paintings they have undergone a process of innovation, improvement, and enhancement of the costumes and movements, making them different from dancers in ordinary life. These bodhisattva images from the Tang Dynasty are buxom, shapely, wear elegant and beautiful costumes, and bear serene expressions—both a reflection as well as a sublimation of court and folk dance activities. As a result, the saying "A bodhisattva is like a celestial maiden" became very popular during the Tang Dynasty.

The dance images in Dunhuang murals painted during the Five Dynasties period followed the style of the Tang Dynasty in terms of the poses, costumes and props, and the content was similar to that of the Tang, including the long ribbon dance, waist drum dance, *pipa* dance and so forth. One noteworthy development was that figures wearing long sleeves reappeared in the murals from the Five Dynasties. Dancing with long sleeves was a long-standing tradition in the Central Plains of China since the pre-Qin period and was popular during the Han and Jin dynasties as well. Although there had been records of this style of dance since the Tang Dynasty, it was not until the Five Dynasties that images of such dance first appeared in the nearby Yulin Caves, located approximately 100 km east of Mogao. The Dunhuang murals painted from the Five Dynasties through the Song and Yuan period were essentially a continuation of those of the Tang Dynasty. They are generally derivative and exhibit few innovative elements. Many of the figures are dull; the dance postures and artistic conception are less vivid and lack the same charm as their Tang counterparts. Because of this, the musical dance murals after the Five Dynasties constitute few of the examples used in this book; however, this does not mean there are fewer dance images from this period.

巾舞

Ribbon Dance

唐代经变画中的天宫伎乐场面，有一个最显著的特点，就是舞者双肩均披巾带，上下舞动。即使是手执琵琶、肩挂腰鼓的伎乐天，也同时身佩长巾而舞。在许多乐舞图中，长巾则不仅是舞者身上的装饰品，更是重要的舞具，成为今人研究与鉴赏古代《巾舞》的形象资料。

《巾舞》因舞者执巾舞蹈而得名，在我国中原地区有悠久的历史。相传在公元前 11 世纪的西周时代用于祭祀的《六小舞》中，就有《帗舞》，舞者手执五彩缯；汉代的《巾舞》由《公莫舞》发展演化而成，已用于宴飨，舞者所用巾帛最长的可达两丈多，其舞法与今天的《红绸舞》相同；唐朝妇女普遍使用披帛，舞女亦常执披帛而舞，而在宫廷与上层官宦

In sutra illustration paintings from the Tang Dynasty that feature flying *apsaras*, one of the most noticeable features of these images is that the dancers wear broad sashes or narrow shawls across both shoulders. They appear to move these ribbon-like sashes up and down. Even bodhisattvas playing the *pipa* with waist drums hanging from their shoulders dance with a long sash at the same time. In many musical dance scenes, these long sashes are not only a dancer's ornamental accessory, but also an important dance prop. They provide rich visual sources for scholars to research and appreciate this ancient dance form.

The ribbon dance got its name because of the ribbon-like sash held by dancers while dancing. It has a long history in Chinese civilization. According to legend, there had been a cape dance as part of the Six Minor Dances used for state rituals during the 11th century BC era of the Western Zhou Dynasty (1046 BC–771 BC), in which dancers performed with colorful silk fabrics in their hands. By the Han Dynasty, the ribbon dance was performed at banquets, having evolved and developed from an ancient dance called the *gongmo* dance. The long sashes that these dancers used could be more than six meters long. The choreography was similar to the *hongchou* (red silk) dance performed in China today. Women of the Tang Dynasty generally wore silk shawls or long scarves, the dancers of this era also

家庭的宴乐中巾舞更是盛行不衰,“敛翠凝歌黛,流香动舞巾”,大诗人白居易在《题周皓大夫新亭子二十二韵》中的诗句便是这种情景的生动写照。

敦煌壁画中姿态各异的披帛执巾而舞的伎乐天,虽然其功能是“娱佛”,并非全是实际生活中的舞蹈原型,但那些卷曲拂垂、流动飞扬的舞巾,无不折射出唐代舞蹈活动中舞巾的艺术形象。敦煌唐代壁画中巾舞的舞蹈造型众多,形式多样,让我们选择其中的佼佼者来逐一欣赏。

莫高窟第220窟南壁双人巾舞(图13),是绘于初唐时期的巾舞图像。二舞伎做“吸腿”姿势赤足立于小圆花毯(舞筵)上,双手上下对称挥巾而舞。二舞伎舞姿全同,整齐协调,只是左右相对而异,这正是双人舞常用的编排手法。唐代的编舞艺术已经达到相当高的水平,在双人舞的编排上,出现了多种处理方法。有时是

danced with narrow silk scarves, and the ribbon dance became popular at court and among nobles. The great Tang poet Bai Juyi's verse, "A Twenty-Two Line Ode to Senior Official Zhou Hao's New Pavilion, "captures such an image: "The lady frowns as she sings and dances with floweral headwears/Fragrance permeates the moving, dancing ribbons."

The flying *apsaras* as seen in the Dunhuang murals, with all kinds of poses, movements, and silk sashes, provided entertainment to the Buddhas in heavenly realms as devotional offerings and were not a reflection of dance in real life. However, the curling, flowing, flying sashes represented an idealized, artistic image of the ribbon dance. As there are myriad dance poses and scenes of ribbon dancing in the Dunhuang murals from the Tang Dynasty, it would do well to examine some of the more notable ones.

On the south wall of Mogao Cave 220 is an image of a ribbon dance performed by two people, painted in the Early Tang period (Fig.13). Two barefoot dancers lift their knees as they balance on small circular tapestries or mats, waving ribbons up and down in synchronized motions. The movements of the two performers are in mirror image, a common style of choreography at the time. Performing arts in the Tang Dynasty had reached an advanced level, and there was a variety of choreography designed for two performers. One style was for the two dancers to move in a unified, synchronized way. Often the dancers worked in concert together, with high and low or back and forth movements, back-to-back

图 13 双人巾舞(莫高窟第 220 窟南壁)
Fig.13 Ribbon Dance for Two Performers (South Wall, Mogao Cave 220)

二人动作一致,两两对称,即唐人诗所谓“鸾影乍回头并举,凤声初歇翅齐张”(卢肇《湖南观双柘枝舞赋》);也有的是高低前后,错落有致,或一张一收,或一背一面,对比性强,同时又相互呼应协调。前者最难之处就在于巾帛飘带动静感的协调统一与对称一致,而这幅双人巾舞恰恰在这一点上处理得当——上扬翻飞与下垂卷曲的飘带仿佛在一刹那间达到了动

or face-to-face, providing a striking echoing effect. The difficulty and skill lay in the coordination of the symmetry while at the same time maintaining the tension and dynamic movements of the sash-like ribbons. The mural from Mogao Cave 220 captures this style of dance perfectly, with its depiction of rising and falling ribbons flowing in unison.

Figure 14 reveals a Tang period ribbon dance for two performers, seen on the north wall in Cave 172 (Fig.14). The two dancers lift their ribbons as they dance

与静的完美结合。

莫高窟第172窟北壁正背两面双人巾舞(图14),是绘于盛唐时期经变图中的双人巾舞场面。二舞者在长方毯上举巾而舞,舞姿动态完全一致,却用了一正面、一背面的处理,使画面既富于变化,又能让观者同时清晰地观赏到同一舞姿的正背两面。那围绕舞者的长巾飘拂的动势,与画面中央似乎缠绕在一起又急速分离的带结,使人感到舞者正有力地挥动双臂而急步环行。

莫高窟第148窟东壁舞姿迥异的双人巾舞(图15),也是盛唐时期的壁画,二舞伎在梅花图案的长方舞筵上舞动长巾,虽然都是单足吸腿,却姿态迥异:一侧首,一平视;一背面,一正面;一收臂,一张臂;一屈身,一直立。一静一动,均在舞动卷曲的8字绸花中得到展现。画面处理既对比鲜明,又彼此呼应。即便是图中作为背景的水池里的两朵莲花,也是色彩一深一浅,一上涌,一下浮。唐代诗人李群玉的《长沙九日登东楼观舞》诗有“低回莲破

on a rectangular carpet. Their dance poses are identical, but one stands facing the viewer, while the other turns facing away, bringing variety to identical movements. The winding, twirling long ribbons seem to entwine and embrace the performers, giving the appearance of waving arms and quick, circular motions.

Another image of a ribbon dance for two performers, also from the Tang period, appears at Mogao on the east wall of Cave 148 (Fig.15). The two performers wave long sash-like ribbons on a rectangular dance mat or tapestry decorated with a plum blossom pattern. Although they both stand on single legs, their poses are completely different. One dancer tilts her head, while the other looks straight ahead; one dancer faces the viewer, while the other faces away. One dancer extends her arms, while the other keeps them close; one dancer bends downward, while the other stands upright. Static and dynamic beauty is shown in the waving and curling figure-eight shapes formed by the silk sashes. The images both complement and contrast with one another. Even the two lotuses in the background pool have contrasting colors—one is dark and the other light; one reaches upward, as the other floats downward. In this way, the artist's ingenuity in handling the composition of a ribbon dance for two performers is revealed.

The mural in Cave 205 depicts a ribbon dance for two performers in the “soft dance”

图 14　正背两面双人巾舞(莫高窟第 172 窟北壁)
Fig.14　Ribbon Dance for Two Performers (North Wall, Mogao Cave 172)

图 15　舞姿迥异的双人巾舞(莫高窟第 148 窟东壁)

Fig.15　Pair of Dancers Performing Ribbon Dance in Different Poses (East Wall, Mogao Cave 148)

浪，凌乱雪萦风”之句，颇合此图意境，亦可见画家在处理双人巾舞画面上的匠心。

莫高窟第 205 窟是软舞风格的双人巾舞(图 16)。如果说前面几幅舞图展现了唐人“健舞”的风格，那么这幅同样是盛唐时期的壁画表现的就是“软舞”的风貌。二舞伎单足立于方毯之上，一正面，一背向，面部内侧，相向而舞，手臂一抬举头顶，一斜垂腰下，手做“弹指”状；侧出胯，身体呈 S 形；巾带披肩绕臂，下垂卷曲，说明正在轻歌声中表演一段节奏舒缓、舞姿柔婉的曼舞。

莫高窟第 201 窟表现的是倾身低头的单人巾舞（图 17）。巾舞常为单人表演。这幅中唐时期的壁画描绘的正是属于软舞的单人巾舞。头戴花冠、上身赤裸的舞伎在方形舞筵上倾身低头，垂目凝神，舒展双臂挥动巾带而舞。长巾漫卷拂垂，舞姿柔曼，动势舒缓，同样给人以美的享受。

莫高窟第 358 窟南壁西

(*ruanwu*) style (Fig.16). If the previous dance images can be said to show a vigorous, energetic dance style from Tang society, then this image reflects a gentle, languid dance style and its characteristics. The two dancers stand with one leg on the carpet: one figure faces the viewer while the other has her back turned; simultaneously both are looking at each other. They both dance with one arm lifted overhead and the other arm pressing downward toward the floor, with accompanying hand positions. They move their hips in a sinuous S-shape, as flowing sashes encircle their arms. This type of dance was performed gracefully and slowly, accompanied by soft singing.

Mogao Cave 201 shows a single ribbon dancer, with the performer leaning to the side and lowering her head (Fig.17). Ribbon dancing was usually performed solo. This mural, painted during the Middle Tang, provides another example of “soft dancing.” The partially clothed dancer wears a coronet-style headdress, with eyelids lowered in fixed attention, arms outstretched and holding waving ribbons. Audiences took great enjoyment in watching these performances with fluttering, twining ribbons as dancers executed slow, graceful, and supple movements.

Another mural from Dunhuang depicting a single ribbon dancer appears on the south wall of Cave 358 (Fig.18). A special feature of this painting is the musical ensemble on both sides of the dancer: three people on the right play a *pipa* (a pear-shaped Chinese lute), a transverse

图 16 软舞风格的双人巾舞(莫高窟第 205 窟摹本)

Fig.16 Pair of Dancers Performing Ribbon Dance in the Style of Soft Dance (Replica of Mogao Cave 205)

域乐韵伴奏的单人巾舞（图18),是中唐时期的壁画。这幅壁画的单人巾舞的特点在于舞伎两侧的乐队：右边三人用琵琶、横笛、拍板伴奏，左侧三人用琴、筚篥和箜篌伴奏,除横笛、琴外,其余四种均是西域的龟兹乐器。在这充满西域乐韵的混合乐队的伴奏中，舞伎两手执巾上扬,扭胯踏足,神情安详。中原传统舞蹈与西域音乐的这

flute, and wooden clappers; on the left, three musicians play a harp, a *bili* pipe, and a *konghou*. Except for the transverse flute and harp, the other four musical instruments are all from Kucha (Chinese: Qiuci; present-day Kuche in Xinjiang). Accompanied by the ensemble, the dancer holds a ribbon with both hands, swaying her hips and moving her feet with a serene expression on her face. This combined form of traditional dance from the Central Plains of China and the music and tribal rhythms of the Western Regions is quite common in Tang period Dunhuang murals. In yet another mural from the same cave, located on the north side,

图 17　倾身低头的单人巾舞(莫高窟第 201 窟)
Fig.17　Single Ribbon Dance(Mogao Cave 201)

图 18　西域乐韵伴奏的单人巾舞(莫高窟第 358 窟南壁)
Fig.18　Single Ribbon Dance Accompanied by Kucha Music (South Wall, Mogao Cave 358)

种组合形式,在敦煌唐代壁画里屡见不鲜,在 358 窟北壁的另一幅八人伴奏的巾舞画面中，也有三人击腰鼓与横笛、筚篥、拍板、箜篌等一道伴奏的场面。而且特别有意思的是,这两幅画中舞者与伴奏者均做闭目状,仿佛全都沉浸在乐舞的仙境之中。类似的舞姿我们还可以举出莫高窟第 341 窟经变画里的图像,舞者两臂挂巾上扬,踏足于圆毯之上,扭胯吸腿的姿势都很突出(图 19)。

莫高窟第 112 窟南壁举

there is another image of a dancer with accompanying musicians, playing waist drums, transverse flutes, *bili* pipes, clappers and *konghhou*. A particularly interesting thing about this scene is that the dancers and accompanists all have their eyes closed, as if all are immersed in a sublime, heavenly realm of music and dance. The image in Cave 341 is similar. The dancer treads on a circular rug or mat, with broad ribbons hanging from her arms, once again with twisting waist and lifted knee in this distinctive hallmark pose (Fig.19).

The mural on the south wall of Mogao Cave 112 was also painted during the Middle Tang period (Fig.20). This single ribbon dance image portrays the dancer's pose of holding a long sash and lifting her foot to lunge forward. The

图 19　急舞旋巾(莫高窟第 341 窟摹本)

Fig.19　Single Ribbon Dance with Quick Steps (Replica of Mogao Cave 341)

步急行的单人巾舞(图 20),也是中唐时期的壁画。这幅巾舞画面特别细致地描绘了舞伎执巾前倾、举步急行的姿态。舞者细腰宽胸,在箜篌、笙、海螺等乐器的伴奏下,双臂所搭巾帛系连腰间,两手执双色巾带,左足踏毯翘指,右腿后掖在花裙

dancer has a slender waist and broad chest. She is accompanied by musical instruments including the *konghou*, *sheng* (a reed pipe wind instrument), and conch. The wide ribbons hanging from her arms are tied at the waist. As her hands grasp the two-tone ribbon, her left foot steps on the carpet, while the other leg is tucked into the *dhoti*-style skirt giving the impression of forward motion. When modern dancers perform the *changchou* (long silk) dance, they rush onto the stage waving

图 20　举步急行的单人巾舞(莫高窟第 112 窟南壁)
Fig.20　Single Ribbon Dance with Running Steps (South Wall, Mogao Cave 112)

内,有明显的欲举步前行的动姿。现在舞蹈家表演《长绸舞》时,也常采用这种长绸搭臂，急步出场，然后挥巾起舞的艺术处理,显示出古今传承的关系。

莫高窟第 286 窟南壁有一幅巾舞壁画,很可能绘于吐蕃占领敦煌的中唐时期。舞伎在方毯上踏足收腿执巾而舞,巾带翻卷成纹,似为舞巾动势造成的绸花,正与梅花图案的舞筵相映成趣。舞者左半身画面略有残缺,但其丰腴的面部十分清晰，既富有唐代标准美女的丰满,又具备吐蕃民族所欣赏的健壮。与此相近的是第 154 窟北壁的巾舞舞伎形象(图 21),同样绘于中唐时期。舞者头部略长而面部丰腴,体格健壮。发上花髻成蝴蝶形状，舞巾抖落成双色绸花。大概是因为场地比较局促的缘故,舞者的动势不大。

long silk ribbons hanging from their arms, demonstrating the relationship between dance of the past and present, the ancient and modern.

The ribbon dance mural on the south wall of Cave 286 in Mogao (not pictured) was probably painted in the Middle Tang era, when the Tubo Regime ruled Dunhuang. Again the performer stands on one leg on the dance carpet, with lifted knee. She holds a striped ribbon, which appears to form flowers made by its movement, contrasting with the floor tapestry decorated with a plum blossom motif. The left half of the dancer's body was slightly damaged, but her plump face remains clearly visible. This dancer's image reflects not only the facial beauty standards of the Tang, but the strong, shapely body that was also appreciated by the people of the Tubo Regime. A similar image exists of a ribbon dancer located on the north wall of Cave 154, again painted during the Middle Tang (Fig.21). The dancer has a slightly elongated head, a plump, pretty face, and a robust body. Her hair's chignons are butterfly-shaped and the silk sash forms double flower shapes. The performer's movements appear small and restricted, most likely because the artistic space for the composition was relatively tight and cramped.

A dance scene is depicted on the east wall of Cave 12 from the *Sutra of Requiting Blessings Received*, painted during the Late Tang Dynasty (Fig. 22). The dancer tilts her body and extends her arms outward, holding broad ribbons and rotating her hips as she moves. Unlike in most ribbon dancing, the narrow silk scarf or shawl wrapped around the dancer's shoulders and tied at the waist is fairly short. The ribbon the dancer holds is relatively short

图21　巾舞(莫高窟第 154 窟北壁)
Fig.21　Ribbon Dance (North Wall, Mogao Cave 154)

莫高窟第12窟东壁短巾单人巾舞(图22),是晚唐时期所绘的《报恩经》经变画中的单人巾舞场景。舞伎斜张双臂,执巾扭胯而舞。与一般巾舞不同的是舞伎肩上所披、腰间所系的绸巾均较短,手执的巾带也不长,与长巾飞扬或环绕卷曲不同。绸带的动势,反映出舞姿较舒缓沉稳。八人的伴奏乐队用的除拍板外,似乎都是箫、笛一类的管乐,也从一个侧面证明所强调的是中原的传统乐舞。

莫高窟第85窟南壁有大型乐队伴奏的巾舞(图23),这是晚唐时期所绘的大型乐舞场面,一舞伎在长方形舞筵上翩然起舞,两侧各有八人的伴奏乐队,演奏着十六种各不相同的民族乐器。舞者双臂挽搭长巾,右臂抬举,左臂侧展,戴"山"字形头饰,微侧脸,倾身扭腰,清晰地衬托出优美的S形体态,增添了舞巾的动势。舞者视线向下,更显出典丽妩媚的情态。据史料记载,

as well, unlike the typical long ribbons which float and curl about. The appearance of the ribbon indicates that the dance movements were slow and steady. The eight-musician ensemble which accompanies the dancer play wind instruments including the vertical bamboo flute, and transverse flute, demonstrating that traditional music and dance from the Central Plains was emphasized.

On the south wall of Mogao Cave 85 is another mural of a ribbon dance accompanied by a large ensemble of musicians (Fig.23). It is a large-scale music and dance scene painted in the Late Tang period. One dancer performs gracefully on a rectangular carpet or mat, flanked on each side by an accompanying orchestra each with eight people, playing 16 different kinds of ethnic musical instruments in total. The dancer holds a long silk sash, with her right arm and palm extended upward, and her left arm extending sideways. She wears a "mountain-style" crown, so-called not because the style comes from a mountainous region, but because the tripartite shape visually resembles the Chinese character for the word "mountain" (*shan*). Her face angles downward, which clearly serves as a foil to the graceful S-shaped pose, adding to the dynamic movements of the sash. The dancer's lowered gaze enhances the beautiful, enchanting mood. According to historical records, during the Tang period, court dancers and musicians numbered as many as several hundred people. The performing group in this mural represents the epitome of the integration of large-scale Tang court music and

图 22　短巾单人巾舞(莫高窟第 12 窟东壁)
Fig.22　Single Ribbon Dance (East Wall, Mogao Cave 12)

唐代有些大型宫廷乐舞，奏乐起舞者可多达几百人。这幅壁画里的乐舞组合，恰是唐代宫廷大型乐舞多民族乐舞汇合的缩影。

莫高窟第 197 窟北壁表现的是赤裸上身的巾舞（图 24）。作为佛教艺术中的形象，唐代经变画中的乐工舞伎常常赤裸上身，与当时的现实生活不同，可能是画工为了表现佛国世界的圣洁美好而特意描绘的。唐代现实生活中的舞蹈，演员的服饰特别讲究，“百宝装腰带，真珠络臂鞲”(杜甫《即事》);“宝钗新梳倭堕髻，锦带交垂连理襦”(许景先《折柳篇》)。因此，大多数伎乐形象均有明显而突出的头饰、项圈、臂钏、璎珞等装饰，冲淡了裸体的感觉。而这幅中唐时期的壁画由于所用颜料突出了身体上赭红色的线描，淡化了其他服饰的颜色，配以舞伎上方全裸的莲花童子图像，

dance with multi-ethnic performing arts.

Cave 197 at Mogao depicts partially-clothed dancers on its north wall mural (Fig.24). As figures in Buddhist visual arts, musicians and dancers in the Tang Dynasty sutra illustrations are often presented with unclothed upper torsos, as opposed to actual performers in daily life at the time. Perhaps it was the special intention of the artists to convey the holy, pure meaning of the Buddhist world by depicting the performers in this manner. In real life, dance in the Tang Dynasty focused heavily on the costumes of the performers. As the following verses of poetry illustrate: “Thousands of treasures decorate the waistband/While pearls are bunched on the sleeves”in “Impromptu” written by Tang poet Du Fu (712–770); and “Precious hairpins adorned her chignon/And beautiful ribbons dangled from her jacket” in “Broken Willow Branches” by Tang poet Xu Jingxian (677–730). Therefore, most female performers wear prominent accessories, such as headwear, wide necklaces, arm bands or armlets, jade and pearl necklaces and so forth, which somewhat cover the naked appearance. Thus, this mural from the Middle Tang Dynasty highlights the figure of the body by using charcoal-sketched outlines and desaturated pigments for the other colors of the costumes. The nude effect is further highlighted with a naked, cherubic lotus child image above the dancer. The *kalaviṅka* (a mythical double-winged, human-headed bird who preaches the Buddha's word in heavenly abodes) on the left of the dancer, and the double-headed bird dancing in front of the carpet form a delightful contrast with the dancer

图 23　大型乐队伴奏的巾舞(莫高窟第 85 窟南壁)
Fig.23　Ribbon Dance Accompanied by Large Orchestra (South Wall, Mogao Cave 85)

图 24　赤裸上身的巾舞(莫高窟第 197 窟北壁)
Fig.24　Ribbon Dance Performers with Nude Torsos (North Wall, Mogao Cave 197)

更突出了裸体的效果。舞伎左侧的双翼裸体飞天和舞筵前展翅踏足而舞的双头共命鸟，与扬目展巾的舞伎相映成趣。

榆林窟第19窟南壁有造型新颖的双人巾舞(图25)。这幅五代时期的经变画中的双人巾舞图虽然色彩比较单调，描绘人物及巾带的线条也不够生动，但是舞姿组合的造型

waving her sash.

A later style of ribbon dance for two people is displayed on the south wall of Cave 19 at the nearby Yulin Caves (Fig.25). Although the colors of this sutra painting from the Five Dynasties are a little monotonous, and the features as well as the line drawings are less lifelike, the combination of dance poses is fresh. The two dancers are short and sturdy, wearing the mountain style of coronet-like headdresses. The dancer on the right side twists her hips to the front, with the right hand

图25 造型新颖的双人巾舞(榆林窟第19窟南壁)
Fig.25 Ribbon Dance for Two Performers with Novel Poses (South Wall, Yulin Cave 19)

较为新颖。二舞伎身材矮壮，均头戴“山”字形花冠，身披绕肩长巾，右边舞者正面扭胯，右手向身左侧垂，左手执巾举至头侧；左边舞者侧面倾腰，双手合十高举头顶，似乎在强调舞蹈的礼佛功能。与唐代的同类壁画相比，五代、宋时期的舞蹈图像似乎缺少了流转飞动的态势，一般显得节奏比较缓慢，舞者的表情也略嫌呆滞。如莫高窟第 55 窟东壁宋代所绘巾舞场景，舞伎在八人乐队伴奏下执巾起舞，左手托掌，右手按掌，长巾垂绕，倾身向前，有缓舞慢转之势，舞者与伴奏者的神情都比较呆板。这很可能与当时的画匠缺乏实际的舞蹈生活感受有关。

pressing downward on the left side and the left hand holding her narrow scarf up to her head. The other dancer on the left side juts her hips forward while pressing her palms together above her head in a gesture resembling the *añjali* mudra, which seems to reinforce the devotional nature of the dance. Compared with the same murals in the Tang period, the dancing images in the Five Dynasties and Song Dynasty seem relatively static, with less bodily rhythm and less vitality in the facial expressions. For example, there is a ribbon dance scene on the east wall of Cave 55 at Mogao (not pictured), painted during the Song Dynasty. The performers extend their left arms and palms upward while pressing their left arms and palms downward, with their silk sashes coiling and bodies inclining forward. But the appearance of the dancers and accompanists seem rather dull and flat due to the lack of vitality in the poses. It may have something to do with the artists lacking a connection to any actual choreography of the time.

鼓舞

Drum Dance

在中国传统的打击乐器里，鼓类占有突出的地位。“城头叠鼓声，城下暮江清。”(李商隐《听鼓》)“鼗笙磬竽瑟，是必登清庙。”(陆龟蒙《杂讽》)除了打仗振奋士气的用途，鼓乐也是祭祀与宴乐歌舞不可缺少的，盘鼓、建鼓、铜鼓、腰鼓及鸡娄鼓、答腊鼓、羯鼓等都曾在各种图像中出现。唐人诗篇提到的鼓的种类亦多，大多作为伴奏乐器使用，相关史籍中明确记载用做舞具的却不多见。如腰鼓，是传自少数民族地区的乐器，《旧唐书·音乐志》记载“九部乐”“十部乐”里的《西凉乐》《高丽乐》《疏勒乐》《高昌乐》，均有腰鼓做伴奏乐器，而古文献及中原地区的出土舞俑与墓室壁画中却无“腰鼓舞”的遗存。唐代敦煌经变画中天宫乐舞的舞具，除了巾帛外，各式腰鼓、长

Throughout history, drums have played a prominent role in Chinese traditional percussion instruments. As the well-known lines from “Listening to the Drum” by Tang poet Li Shangyin (813–858) go: “I heard the drums from the top of the city walls / The river below was clear at sunset.” Drumming played an essential role not only in battle for the military, but also in sacrifices, ritual ceremonies, and feasts. Various types of drums, including the *pangu* drum, *jiangu* drum, bronze drum, waist drum, *jilou* drum, *dala* drum, and *jiegu* drum have been depicted in numerous types of visual arts and images. The categories of drums appearing in Tang Dynasty poetry were also numerous. Mostly they were used as accompanying percussion, with only a few for dance clearly documented in Chinese historical records. For instance, according to records in the *Old Book of Tang: Treaties on Music*, the waist drum was a kind of instrument originating from the Western Regions, a percussion instrument used in Xiliang (Western Liang) music, Gaoli music, Shule music and Gaochang music from the *Nine Books of Music* and later *Ten Books of Music*. On the other hand, other historical documents and certain unearthed dance figurines as well as mural paintings in chamber tombs from the Central Plains of China revealed no record of waist drums. In addition to

鼓则频繁出现,为我们鉴赏与研究当时的舞乐留下了珍贵的图像资料。

敦煌壁画中腰鼓舞伎乐天所用腰鼓大小不一,形制各异。有的挂在腰间或腹前,有的悬置胸前。舞伎姿态大多是立腿微屈,一腿屈抬,膝与腰齐做“端腿”姿;脚拇指用力翘起,双臂平展,奋张手指,做用力击鼓状。击鼓而舞的舞蹈形式至今流传在我国各地的民间民族舞之中,如山西的“花鼓”,藏族的“热巴鼓舞”,陕西安塞的“腰鼓”,朝鲜族的“长鼓”,等等。可见唐人经变画里的“腰鼓舞”,也是当时现实生活中普遍流行的一种舞蹈形式,而且一直演变、发展、流传至今,有着强大的生命力。

莫高窟第158窟佛坛下右侧有腰鼓舞画面(图26)。该窟正中主坛上是著名的中唐时期所塑释迦牟尼涅槃卧佛塑

images of sashes and ribbons in Tang period Dunhuang Buddhist art, people can find various waist drums and long drums, providing precious primary sources for their appreciation as well as research materials for dance and music of that time.

The waist drums that dancers use are not uniform in size or shape in Dunhuang wall paintings. Some hang on the side of the body, or in front of the waist, while others are suspended from the chest. The dance position is usually standing tiptoe on one leg, while lifting the other knee high toward the waist, with the foot flexed, the toes extended, and the big toe pointing upward. With arms outstretched, the performers spread their fingers to forcefully beat the drums. The technique of drumming while dancing has been handed down through the ages throughout the vast areas of the Chinese world, and includes the flower drum dance in Shanxi Province, the *reba* drum dance in Tibet, the waist drum dance in Shaanxi Province, and the long drum dance among the Korean people. As we can see, the waist drum dance of the Tang people as shown in sutra art was a popular dance form in daily life and since that time continued to evolve, develop, and spread.

In Cave 158 at Mogao, there is an image of a performing dancer with a waist drum hanging from the right side (Fig.26). In the center of this grotto is the famous reclining Buddha statue from the Middle Tang period. Behind this statue of the Buddha is a huge mural depicting bodhisattvas, arhats, and weeping royal princes from the Western Regions, all paying homage to the dying Buddha as he enters *parinirvāṇa*. To the right of this is a scene of “heretics slandering the Buddha,” which includes a

图 26　佛坛下右侧腰鼓舞(莫高窟第 158 窟)
Fig.26　Waist Drum Dance (Mogao Cave 158)

像,神态安详,造型生动。与塑像后所绘的巨幅各国王子举哀图相对,佛坛之下右侧绘有“外道谤佛”图,图中即有腰鼓舞场景:外道闻佛涅槃,欢呼跳跃,一人兴奋得手舞足蹈,那张臂抬腿、肌肉

scene of waist drum dancing. When these non-believers heard that the Buddha was entering *parinirvāṇa*, his final liberation from birth and death, they were overjoyed, exhibiting the common dance poses of the time with energetic choreography, lifted legs, taut muscles, and exuberant drumming. However, the dancers nowadays cannot bc seen very clearly, nor details of the drums they used, because these images were later intentionally defaced by

突显、奋击腰鼓的姿态，当是生活中常见的舞姿。因为是形容谤佛的场面，为历代礼佛的信众所厌恶，画面被严重刻画，以致我们今天已不能清晰地看到舞蹈者的神情和腰鼓形制等细节，这里展示了它们的临摹线描图（图 27）。

榆林窟第 25 窟南壁腰鼓舞（图 28），是中唐时期所绘的《无量寿经

pious devotees of Buddhism, who felt offended by this image. Figure 27 is a recreated line drawing of these figures (Fig.27).

Another example of the waist drum dance from the Middle Tang period can be found in Cave 25 in the southern section of the Yulin Caves (Fig.28). The scene, part of a painting illustrating scenes from the *Sukhāvatīvyūka Sutra*

图 27　佛坛下右侧腰鼓舞（莫高窟第 158 窟摹本）
Fig.27　Waist Drum Dance (Copy of Mogao Cave 158)

变画》中的单人鼓舞场面。舞者上身裸露，戴项圈、璎珞、臂钏、手镯，手挽长巾，向左侧身，吸提左腿做腾跳之势，双臂平展，十指大张，正欲拍击垂挂于胸下的腰鼓。其右脚五指用劲紧抓舞筵，左脚拇指用力翘起，似乎已经集中了全身的气力。长巾随节奏回转流动，形成优美的绸花。腰鼓型制较大，装饰美丽，与舞者腰间的佩饰相得益彰。两侧的八人伴奏乐伎使用了箫、横笛、排箫、方响、海螺、筚篥、笙、琵琶八种不同的乐器，神情各异；舞伎左侧还有一人首鸟身的伽陵频迦弹奏着琵琶，使整个画面更加生动和谐。

莫高窟第108窟南壁的胸鼓舞（图29）画面，为晚唐时期线描与敷彩双佳的杰作。舞伎头戴花饰，披巾，侧身、展臂、张手指、翘脚趾及一足屈膝高提等姿态，与其他腰鼓舞图无异，不同之处是舞者气质刚健，鼓形稍小，纹饰清晰，挂鼓位置提上至胸前，犹如今山西花鼓舞胸

(*Sutra of Infinite Life*), depicts a single waist drum dance. The dancer's torso is unclothed, except for such accessories as a jade and pearl necklace, armlets, bracelets, and a long silk ribbon. She inclines her body to the left, lifts her left leg in a jumping motion, and stretches her arms and fingers in order to beat the drum hung below the chest. The toes of the right foot grip the dance mat, and the left foot forcefully lifts upward; the dancer's body seems to be moving with full, concentrated strength. With a rotating rhythm, the sash turns into beautiful, rounded shapes. The large, gorgeously decorated drum coordinates well with the pendant hanging at the dancer's waist. Eight musicians, with varying facial expressions, play eight different musical instruments: the *xiao* (a vertical bamboo flute), transverse flute, *paixiao* (panpipes), *fangxiang* (mettalophone), conch, *bili* pipe (double-reed woodwind), *sheng* (a reed pipe wind instrument) and *pipa* (Chinese lute). Playing the *pipa* on the left side is a *kalaviṅka* with a man's head and bird's body, a complementary yet whimsical addition to the composition.

A mural with a chest drum dancer on the south wall of Cave 108 at Mogao is a masterpiece of line-drawing and surface pigments from the Late Tang (Fig.29). The performer wears flower ornaments in her hair and a narrow shawl around her body. Her sideways-leaning position, outstretched arms and fingers, tiptoe stance, and bent knees are essentially no different from other waist drum dance images. The differences lie in the clear decorative motifs, the bold, energetic

图 28　腰鼓舞(榆林窟第 25 窟南壁)

Fig.28　Waist Drum Dance (South Wall, Yulin Cave 25)

图 29　胸鼓舞(莫高窟第 108 窟南壁)

Fig.29　Chest Drum Dance (South Wall, Mogao Cave 108)

前挂鼓的样式。从舞巾形成的8字绸花,亦可看出舞蹈的动势与节奏。舞毯上的梅花图案被画工故意夸张地描画成繁星密布的模样,烘托出舞蹈的热烈气氛。

莫高窟第156窟南壁表现的是对舞中的击长鼓舞(图30)。莫高窟唐代经变画中有多幅舞伎分别击鼓与弹琵琶对舞的画面,这幅晚唐壁画是其中之一。位于舞筵左边的舞者肩披长巾,挂长鼓垂于腰间,双臂舒展,手指一张一收,正欲拍鼓;右腿微屈而立,左脚掩于长裙之中,可能正做“掖腿”或“踏步”动作;低头倾身,闭目凝神,表情温婉,姿态优美。画中鼓细腰宽面,长度似与今朝鲜族的《长鼓舞》相近。

莫高窟第5窟北壁鼓舞拉山膀舞姿(图31)。这幅五代时期的壁画上的鼓舞舞伎头梳双髻,身披长巾,左腿微屈而立,右腿屈膝高抬,一面大型腰鼓垂挂腹前。舞者右臂屈举,张掌

pose, the smaller drum shape, and the chest position of the drum on the body. The style is actually quite similar to the flower drum dance in present-day Shanxi Province. The figure-eight shapes, or “silk flowers” formed by the flowing, narrow shawl enable us to perceive the movement and rhythm of the dance. Closely-painted plum designs were intentionally added to the dance carpet to make it stand out in stunning contrast.

There are many sutra illustration paintings from the Late Tang Dynasty in which dancers beat drums or play the *pipa*, one of which can be seen on the south wall of Mogao Cave 156 (Fig.30). On the left side of the dance tapestry, the dancer wears a long, narrow scarf and has a long drum hanging on the waist. Her outstretched arms and fingers give the appearance of beating the drum. Her right leg bends slightly at the knee as she stands, while her left leg is tucked under her long skirt, giving the impression that she is taking steps with her head down and eyes closed. The facial expression is serene and the pose graceful. The choreography and percussion presented in this scene are similar to those of the long-drum dance of present-day Korean people of China.

Finally, on the north wall mural of Mogao Cave 5 we can see a *lashanbang* dance pose (of traditonal Chinese opera) from the Five Dynasties (Fig.31). The performer in this painting wears her hair in two buns, and a narrow shawl is draped around her shoulders. Her body inclines slightly to the left. She balances on her left leg and bends her right knee high in a high lifting position, with

图 30　对舞中的击长鼓舞(莫高窟第 156 窟南壁)
Fig.30　Long Drum Dance (Wouth Wall, Mogao Cave 156)

图 31　鼓舞拉山膀舞姿(莫高窟第 5 窟北壁摹本)

Fig.31　Drum Dance in *Lashanbang* Pose (Replica of North Wall, Mogao Cave 5)

欲单手击鼓；左臂提肘翻掌，其手姿与今天古典舞中的“拉山膀”十分相似。戏曲古典舞继承前代传统的线索，在本图呈现得相当清晰。

her foot flexed and turned out; a large waist drum covers her torso. She raises her right arm as if she is playing the drum with one hand. She holds her elbows up and turns her palms out, reminiscent of the classic *lashanbang* dance of today. The traces of this dance, passed from generation to generation down to the present day, are clearly evident.

琵琶舞及反弹琵琶舞姿

Pipa Dance and Dancing with the *Pipa* Behind the Back

“琵琶长笛曲相和,羌儿胡雏齐唱歌。”(岑参《酒泉太守席上醉后作》)“乐府只传横吹好,琵琶写出关山道。”(顾况《刘禅奴弹琵琶歌》)琵琶本是由西域传入中原的一种乐器，与秦汉时代中原的弹拨乐器弦鼗(后称阮、秦琵琶)一起不断被改造,演奏技法渐趋完善。到唐代,随着西域乐舞的繁盛，琵琶在众多乐器中占有独特地位，是既能独奏,又可合奏、伴奏的重要乐器。在敦煌壁画的天宫乐舞场景中，出现了许多执琵琶而舞的舞蹈形象。这些壁画中的舞伎，大多反弹琵琶而舞。其舞姿多为:上身微微前倾,琵琶反背于颈后,左臂伸直握弦,右臂屈于音箱,一足屈立,另一腿屈抬成“端腿”姿。这种造型独特的舞姿深受观者喜爱，但是我们在唐代的文献中并未见有正弹或反弹琵琶起舞的记载,琵

In his “Written After the Jiuquan Prefect Got Drunk at the Banquct”, the Tang poet Cen Shen (718? –769?) wrote, “The voice of *pipa* and flute are harmonious with each other/As the Qiang and Hu people sing together.”The *pipa*, a pear–shaped, plucked string instrument similar to the lute or oud, was probably originally introduced to the Central Plains via the Western Regions sometime during the late Qin or early Han dynasties. It underwent various changes and reached its height of popularity during the Tang Dynasty. The *pipa* has played a unique role among traditional Chinese instruments, and can be played solo, as an accompanying musical instrument, or as part of an orchestra or ensemble. Dunhuang wall paintings abound with scenes of dancers playing the *pipa* in celestial realms and heavenly palaces. In most of these dance scenes the performers hold the *pipa* behind the head with the right hand, with the back of the instrument facing the back of the head, as they reach around behind the instrument to strum the front side with the left hand. Their leg poses are the typical one–legged stance with lifted knee, prevalent in Dunhuang art. This kind of unique dance was supposedly popular among audiences of the time, however, there is no mention of this type of *pipa* dancing in any

琶一般均用作伴奏乐器。敦煌早期天宫伎乐壁画已多处出现一伎乐天弹奏琵琶，为身旁另一舞伎伴奏的图像，如莫高窟第272窟窟顶南披北凉时期的伎乐天(图32)、第248窟南壁北魏时期的伎乐天（图33)。在敦煌壁画表现民间赛神的民风习俗画面中，也多处出现女巫弹琵琶起舞的场景，可以确知当时现实生活中有边弹奏琵琶边舞的琵琶舞。至于反弹琵琶舞姿，在中唐以后的敦煌壁画里大量出现，舞蹈史研究者推测可能是吐蕃统治敦煌时期传入的。据舞蹈工作者考察，西藏定日地区至今还有反弹四弦琴起舞的形式。当然，也不能排除西域昭武九姓原有乐舞中就可能有反弹乐器而舞的动作，以显示舞蹈者的精湛技艺。有的研究者认为，琵琶作为乐器，反弹的姿态是不便于演奏的；但是既然作为舞具，其奏乐的功能削弱

extant Tang records or literature. As far as we know, the only actual use of the *pipa* was as an accompanying instrument at this time. However, there are many images from the early period of Dunhuang paintings of performing dancers that show one dancer playing the *pipa* while other musicians provide accompaniment. For example, celestial performers can be seen on the ceilings of both Cave 272 from the North Liang (Fig.32) and Cave 248 from the North Wei (Fig.33) in the southern part of the Mogao Caves. And in Dunhuang Grotto murals featuring folk customs and scenes of group worship, even sorceresses are shown playing the *pipa*. Hence, conclusions can be drawn that at that time it was common to play the *pipa* while dancing. In terms of performances of playing the *pipa* behind the back, these can often be found in the Mogao Caves after the Middle Tang period. Scholars and researchers believe that it was introduced during the time that the people of Tubo ruled Dunhuang. According to dance researchers, in Tibet a form of dancing with a four-stringed lute still exists today. Of course, it cannot be ruled out that the style of playing the *pipa* behind the back actually existed in the Western Regions, which would reflect the talented skill of these dancers. Some researchers contend that it would be extremely difficult to play the *pipa* backwards in this fashion, and would have served more as a dance prop than as an instrument. But through the Dunhuang artists' innovation and imagination, the elegant poses, incredible skills, and unique forms displayed by the performers present a charm all

图 32　北凉时期的伎乐天(莫高窟第 272 窟窟顶南披)
Fig.32　Celestial Musician, Northern Liang Period (South Slope of the Ceiling, Mogao Cave 272)

了，再经过画家的想象与艺术加工，突出了舞伎的优美姿态、高超技艺与独特造型，可谓别有一番风韵。

莫高窟第 112 窟南壁表现的是反弹琵琶舞姿(图 34)。这是敦煌壁画中最著名的一幅反弹琵琶舞蹈画面，

their own.

An example of playing the *pipa* behind the back can be seen in one of the most iconic *pipa* dancing images from the Middle Tang period, in Mogao Cave 112 (Fig.34). Two rows of three accompanying musicians each sit on both sides of the dance tapestry. Their facial features include slender "willow" eyebrows and pouting "cherry" lips, each

图 33　北魏时期的伎乐天(莫高窟第 248 窟南壁)

Fig.33　Celestial Musician, Northern Wei Period (South Wall, Mogao Cave 248)

绘于中唐时期。舞筵两侧各有三个伴奏乐伎，细眉秀目，樱桃小口，神态各异。舞伎上身向右前倾，左腿屈立，右腿屈膝，高提大腿，脚部上勾，拇指用力翘起；肩披长巾，反背琵琶于脑后，左手按弦，右手屈于音箱后拨弦。舞者高髻云鬓，面部丰腴圆润，表情温婉柔和，“朱唇一点桃花殷，宿妆娇羞偏髻鬟”(岑参《醉戏窦子美人》)，是典型的唐代宫娃特征。画匠将舞者矫捷的动势、

person with a different expression. The upper body of the dancer slants rightward; the left leg is pulled up as the right leg is firmly planted. She holds the *pipa* backwards against the back of her head, holding the fretboard with her left hand as she plucks the strings with the right. The dancer's hair is styled in an elaborate updo, highlighting her full, round face and soft expression. In the poem "The Drunken Beauty", the Tang poet Cen Shen gave us a typical depiction of aristocrats and court ladies during the Tang Dynasty, "Beautiful lips like peach blossoms/ The messy morning hair and makeup made the beauty blush." The painters of this mural

优雅的姿态、妩媚的神情汇聚凝固在侧身反弹的那一瞬间，给后世观赏者留下无穷的联想发挥和再创作的空间。

莫高窟第159窟西壁佛龛北侧有盛装反弹琵琶舞伎（图35）。这是乐舞场景里舞伎身姿的一个特写画面，亦绘于中唐时期。舞者宽胸细腰，面部丰满秀丽，盛装打扮，头饰、项圈、臂环、手镯、腰饰、脚环与舞裙上的珠串一应俱全，华丽夺目，不禁使人想起晚唐大诗人李贺《十二月乐辞》里的诗句："金翅峨髻愁暮云，沓飒起舞真珠裙。"舞者右腿屈膝高抬，脚趾张开，反背琵琶于脑后。长巾卷曲飞扬于全身上下，构成舞巾流动状的纹饰，成为一种表现飘逸意境的装饰性花饰。

莫高窟第108窟南壁与击腰鼓者对舞的反弹琵琶舞伎，是晚唐时代的壁画，构图朴素，似以线描取胜。击腰鼓与反弹琵琶舞伎身材较矮壮，近身相对而舞。头上的"山"字形花饰，颈下、腰间花饰均十分突出，更为夸张的是身上所

depicted all these idealized feminine traits, including the flexible movements, elegant gestures, and enchanting expressions, putting them into the flash of a moment when a performer dances with a *pipa* behind the head. It has captured the imagination of viewers ever since.

On the west wall of Mogao Cave 159 is another image of a dancer playing the *pipa* behind the back and wearing a splendid outfit (Fig.35). It is representative of the dance styles and ornamentation from the Middle Tang Dynasty. The dancer, who is plump and shapely with a beautiful face, wears a beaded skirt together with a headdress, necklace, armlets, bracelets, waist jewelry, and anklets. The performer bends her knees, lifts her right leg, stands on tiptoe as she spreads the toes of her right foot, and holds the *pipa* behind her head. The sash flying and swirling around the body further adds to the ornamental design.

A pair of dancers, one with a *pipa* behind the back and the other with a waist drum, comes from a Late Tang mural on the southern wall of Mogao Cave 108. Although its composition is simple, the lines are perfect. The performers themselves appear shorter and plumper than in many other mural depictions. The mountain style of coronet, the floral necklaces, and belts are all highlighted. The floor-length ribbon sashes are more exaggerated, seeming almost stationary in appearance. The *pipa* behind

图 34　反弹琵琶舞姿(莫高窟第 112 窟南壁)

Fig.34　Dancing with the *Pipa* Behind the Back (South Wall, Mogao Cave 112)

图 35　佛龛北侧盛装反弹琵琶舞伎(莫高窟第 159 窟西壁)

Fig.35　Heavenly Performer Dressed in Splendid Outfit Playing the *Pipa* Behind the Back (West Wall, Mogao Cave 159)

披垂地长巾，其卷曲的绸花并无动感可言，似乎仅是一种固定的造型。反弹琵琶舞伎背身反执的琵琶只用淡淡的线条勾勒而成，但画匠却突出了后伸的左臂与按弦的手指，使人仿佛感受到了舞者边舞边弹奏的高超技艺。此外，我们看到莫高窟第5窟中与舞长巾者对舞的反弹琵琶舞伎形象，举手投足的舞姿给人以对称的美感（图36）。我们这里展示的临摹图，采用了工笔重彩的手法，突出的是整个舞蹈的华美。

莫高窟第156窟南壁是与击长鼓者对舞的反弹琵琶舞伎（图37），此图在前面已经介绍了长鼓舞者的形象，而反弹琵琶的舞者做半蹲姿态，左腿屈立，臀部重心后移，画匠刻意描绘了反背的琵琶正面与伸臂按弦的左手、屈臂拨弦的右手，再加上掖腿左伸的右脚，更突出了这个动作的高难度。舞者倒执

the dancer's head is traced with only the faintest of lines, while the artist has chosen to emphasize the arms and hands of the player to make them more noticeable. The viewer has the impression that the performers are superbly skilled and talented. In addition, in Mogao Cave 5 we can see the symmetrical beauty of the dancers' gestures and expressions, one with a long, narrow shawl or sash and the other with a *pipa* behind the upper back. The reconstructed illustration we present here is an exact replica of the original, but with cleaner lines and deeper color saturation, so as to highlight the beauty of the entire dance (Fig.36).

We can get a better glimpse of a dancer playing the *pipa* behind the back—accompanied by a musician playing the long drum—from the southern wall of Mogao Cave 156 (Fig.37). From this angle, created intentionally by the artist, the viewer can see the front side of the *pipa* as it is played from its position behind the head. The true technical difficulty of playing the instrument behind the back is revealed in this image. The position of the *pipa* from behind partially covers the face of the performer, whose closed eyes, open mouth, and absorbed expression remind us of lines from "Song of the *Pipa*" by Tang poet Bai Juyi (772–846) : "The sad mood lingers in the sound of dense strings" and "sorrow and gloom rise quietly."

Finally, yet another *pipa* dancing scene can be found in a sutra illustration painting on the north wall of Cave 19, in the Yulin Caves (Fig.38). This sutra illustration from the Five

图 36　与舞长巾者对舞的反弹琵琶舞伎(莫高窟第 5 窟摹本)
Fig.36　Ribbon Dancer and the Dancer Playing the *Pipa* Behind the Back Arranged in a Set (Replica of Mogao Cave 5)

琵琶半遮面，垂目张嘴的依稀愁容，又使我们想起了白居易那首千古绝唱《琵琶行》中“弦弦掩抑声声思”“别有幽愁暗恨生”的诗句。

榆林窟第 19 窟北壁表现的是与长袖舞者对舞的琵琶舞（图 38）。这幅五代时期的经变画展示了宏大的乐舞场景，榜题说明为“十二药叉大将皆来集会”。乐舞画面分上下两层，上层舞伎在六人乐队伴奏下击胸鼓起舞，下层则为舞袖与正面执琵琶的双人舞，另有十人乐队伴奏，可惜本书无法展示。从临摹的线描图看，双人舞左边舞伎甩舞长袖，回

Dynasties shows a grand, epic dance scene of twelve *yaksas* gathering together, made up of two parts. In the upper part, dancers beat chest drums accompanied by a small ensemble of six people. In the lower part, there is a long sleeve dancer and a *pipa* dancer, accompanied by a band of 10 musicians. Unfortunately, this book cannot display these large images. From the copied line drawing, it can be seen that the dancer on the left shakes and waves her long sleeves, while looking at the *pipa* dancer. As the dancer shakes her sleeves to the left, the sash swings to the right,

图 37　与击长鼓者对舞的反弹琵琶舞伎(莫高窟第 156 窟南壁)
Fig.37　Dancer Playing the *Pipa* Behind the Back Accompanied by a Long Drum Performer (South Wall, Mogao Cave 156)

图 38　与长袖舞者对舞的琵琶舞(榆林窟第 19 窟北壁摹本)
Fig.38　Long Sleeve Dancer and *Pipa* Dancer (Line Drawing Copied from North Wall, Yulin Cave 19)

眸斜视舞琵琶者，舞袖向左，长巾右飘，给人以动势强烈的感觉。与我们多见的反弹琵琶舞姿不同，这里的舞者用了怀抱琵琶边弹奏边舞的姿势，左手按弦，右手则描绘了弹拨后放手的那一瞬间，也富有动感。舞者身材矮壮，面部丰满，显示出崇尚健美的风韵。

lending movement and a powerful dynamic to the image. Unlike the most common position of playing *pipa* behind the back, the dancer here embraces the instrument to her chest while dancing. She is buxom and shapely, with a broad, plump face, revealing a vigorous appeal and grace.

绳舞、盘舞等

Cord Dance, Plate Dance, and Other Dances

天宫伎乐乐舞舞具除最常见的巾帛、腰鼓、琵琶之外，还有花绳、铃铛、杯盘等。这虽是敬佛娱佛的贡品展示，也是现实生活的反映。有些舞具，本来是舞蹈者服饰的不可分割的组成部分，如杜甫所咏："百宝装腰带，真珠络臂鞲。笑时花近眼，舞罢锦缠头。"(《即事》）后来则渐渐独立成为一种新的舞蹈内容。有些则是西域少数民族习见生活与劳动场景经艺术加工而形成的舞蹈品种，如新疆民间的《献花串舞》《盘舞》《水罐舞》，内蒙古民间的《安代（舞巾）舞》《灯舞》等，也常常被画工吸收到宗教绘画中来，只是在敦煌壁画中表现得还不太充分。

敦煌莫高窟第435窟北壁（图39）有一幅舞花绳的伎乐菩萨形象，舞者袒右肩，身披类似印度纱丽的服装，屈臂，双手扭腕执下垂的长花绳而舞，可惜因为画面色彩氧化的

Besides the wide ribbon or sash, waist drum, and *pipa*, other props for dancers in the celestial realms include cords, flower garlands, bells, cups, and plates. These were articles used in Buddhist worship and as offerings to the Buddha; they were also a part of daily life at the time. Eventually, they worked their way into new choreographic styles. Some of these dance forms derived from the culture of the Western Regions, resulting in such forms as the garland offering dance, the plate dance, and the pitcher dance from Xinjiang, as well as the *andai* dance (scarf dance) and lantern dance from Inner Mongolia. These synthesized dances were eventually absorbed into religious paintings, although they do not appear in Dunhuang art that frequently.

The north wall of Mogao Cave 435 presents an image of a bodhisattva performing a dance with a flower garland. His right shoulder is bare, and the garment looks similar to an Indian sari. Unfortunately, the original color of the garland is unclear, due to oxidation over the years. On the east wall of Cave 20, at the Yulin Caves, there is a figure of a bodhisattva painted during the Five Dynasties (Fig.40). The bodhisattva kneels on a lotus throne wearing a coronet, earrings,

图 39　绳舞姿态(莫高窟第 435 窟北壁)
Fig.39　Cord Dance Pose (North Wall, Mogao Cave 435)

原因，今天已经看不清花绳原来的色彩。在榆林窟第20窟东壁(图40)有一幅五代时期所绘的供养菩萨像，菩萨右膝单跪于莲花宝座之上，头戴花冠，耳珰、项圈、臂钏、手镯俱全，双臂前举，两手略平伸执以小圆环连接的短花绳，绳上各色花串大而鲜明，形成铃铛效果。今天新疆南部麦盖提、库车等地的大

necklace, armlets, bracelets, with two arms outstretched in front of him holding a short garland of bright flowers which look almost like a string of bells. In present-day southern Xinjiang we can still see large-scale flower garland dances in this style. Moreover, we can find ancient cord dance images in the Kizil Caves, the Kumtura Thousand Buddha Caves, and many other places in

图 40　花串绳舞(榆林窟第 20 窟东壁)
Fig.40　Flower Garland Dance (East Wall, Yulin Cave 20)

型歌舞“麦西来甫”中均有《花绳舞》程式。我们还可以在新疆克孜尔、库木吐拉等处千佛洞壁画里看到更丰富的古代《绳舞》图像。

敦煌莫高窟第288窟南壁上部(图41)有一组西魏时期所绘的天宫伎乐形象,其中一身呈双腿跪坐的姿态,两臂屈肘上举,双手在头部前上方做捧抛花盘之状。画工将花盘刚脱手的一刹那情景定格了下来,舞者面部为典型的少数民族特征,表情专注而虔诚。同窟西壁还有一身手托果盘的伎乐形象,果盘上插满香花,可证亦为娱佛而绘,舞者头戴山字形冠,拧身回眸,似和西壁、东壁所绘伎乐相呼应。该窟东壁亦有一身手托花盘起舞的伎乐(图42),头戴花冠,转头回眸南壁。舞者双眉间额头上点有吉祥痣,神情虔诚安详,两肩披巾上扬有飞动之势。榆林窟第20窟东壁供养菩萨画像中亦有托花盘的舞蹈形象,菩萨双膝跪于莲花座上,左手略沉肘托花盘向前,右手摊掌垂于身体右侧,

Xinjiang.

On the upper south wall of Mogao Cave 288 (Fig.41), there is an image of a performer in a heavenly palace painted during the Western Wei period (535–556). One of them is kneeling in profile, with two hands overhead, appearing to lift a plate or tray of flowers. The dancer, who seems to have ethnic minority features, is attentive and devoted in this figure. On the west wall of the same cave, there is a dancer with a bowl full of flowers in both hands. This dance is part of the entertainments given as an offering for the Buddha. The dancer wears a mountain-style crown, and turns around to look back, echoing the performers painted on the east and west walls. On the east wall of the same cave, there is a performer dancing with a plate held in her hand and a coronet on her head; she is turning and looking back at the south wall. The devout and serene dancer, whose silk sash seems to lift up and fly on its own accord, has a *bindi* between the eyebrows (Fig.42). Similarly, in a painting of bodhisattvas making offerings, located on the east wall of Yulin Cave 20, there is an image of a dancer offering a bowl of flowers in both hands. The bodhisattva kneels on both knees on a lotus throne, the left arm lowered slightly and stretching forward a plate or bowl of flowers in her left hand, while she elegantly extends forth a six-petal flower in her right hand (Fig.43). Another dance, the plate dance, has a long history among ethnic minorities of the Western Regions. Originating

图 41　舞伎(莫高窟第 288 窟南壁上部)

Fig.41　Dancing Performers (Upper Part of South Wall, Mogao Cave 288)

掌心有一六瓣花朵，体态优雅(图 43)。《杯盘舞》是西域少数民族历史悠久的民间舞蹈,现今仍在新疆地区盛行不衰,而且无论托盘、顶盘、叠盘等动作,往往都盛上物品或装了水、乳,顶、接、抛、甩,乃至旋转和弯腰俯身,均准确自如,令观者惊叹。

还值得一提的是，在安西东千佛洞第 2 窟有一组西夏时期的双供养伎乐图(图 44),二舞者的左右两臂及双腿紧相勾连，缠绕的左右臂共同托举一巨大的花果盘于头顶,真是熔舞蹈与杂技于一炉,又隐现密宗色彩,堪称西夏时期宗教画里颇具特色的精品。通过这幅特殊风貌

in ancient Kucha, it still thrives in present-day Xinjiang. Their acrobatic dance movements include taking shallow bowls or plates, simultaneously filled with water or other items, and at the same time balancing, stacking, catching, tossing, throwing, and rotating them with a precision and agility that never fails to amaze audiences.

In addition, in Cave 2 at the Eastern Thousand Buddha Caves in Guazhou County, there is a painting of a pair of attendants, a fine example of art from the Western Xia period (Fig.44). The two dancers hook their two arms and legs together, their entwined arms lifting a large tray above their heads. It is an image mixing dance, acrobatics, and even Tantric elements. Through this, we can appreciate the outstanding folk dancing skills in ancient times, and at the same time we have to admire the ingenious design and exquisite artistry of this painting. Indeed,

图 42　托花盘舞伎(莫高窟第 288 窟东壁)
Fig.42　Dancer Holding a Plate of Flowers (East Wall, Mogao Cave 288)

的舞图，我们可以欣赏到我国古代民间舞蹈技巧的奇特与高超，同时也不由得不佩服当年画师构思的巧妙与技艺的精湛。当然,也有的研究者认为某些菩萨图像及姿态(还有佛的“手印”),具有特殊的宗教含义,不应解释为舞姿。我们则觉得这些图像姿态也来源于现实生活,还是与舞蹈有一定的关联。

although some scholars hold the view that Buddhist images and gestures with distinct religious connotations should not be interpreted as dance poses, we nevertheless maintain that these images derive from real life and have some connection with the choreography of the times.

图 43　托花盘的供养菩萨(榆林窟第 20 窟东壁)

Fig.43　Attendant Bodhisattva Holding a Plate of Flowers (East Wall, Yulin Cave 20)

图 44　双供养伎乐线描图(安西东千佛洞第 2 窟)
Fig.44　Two Performers Making Devotional Offerings
(Line Drawing Copied From Cave 2, Eastern Thousand Buddha Caves)

人间多曼舞
壁画里的民俗歌舞场面

Graceful Dance in the Mortal World: Folk Songs and Dance Scenes in Murals

敦煌隋、唐、五代时期的大铺经变画中，除了绘制体现佛国世界的天宫乐舞之外，还有一些绘有故事情节的零散的乐舞图像，形式多为两三人表演的小型民间歌舞，大致类似平民日常生活中的即兴舞蹈，舞者服饰多为窄长衣袖，圆领罗衫，紧束腰带，比较真实地反映出当时民间舞蹈表演的情况。此外，敦煌石窟中描绘的人间世俗乐舞形象也出现在供养人伎乐图里，或反映达官贵人宏大的出行场面，或表现下层民众供养人的乐舞活动，他们多以人间礼佛朝拜的舞乐人群像展现，更应该是现实生活的直接反映。

敦煌壁画中的民俗歌舞场面，从内容上大致可以分为民间宴饮、嫁娶、出行、观赏及宗教祭祀舞蹈等。例如嫁娶宴乐图，据统计在敦煌壁画中有46幅之多，主要绘于《弥勒经变》画中，其中绘于唐代的有35幅。十六国时期后秦高僧鸠摩罗什所译《佛说弥勒下生成佛经》里说，在弥勒的极乐

During the Sui, Tang, and Five Dynasties, in addition to paintings describing heavenly music and dance scenes in Buddhist realms, there were also music and dance images in Dunhuang which seem to relate more realistic stories. These are usually composed of two or three people performing folk songs or music, similar to the folk dances and entertainment of the common people of the times. The dancers usually wear clothes with long, narrow sleeves, rounded collars, and tight belts, reflecting authentic folk music and dance performances at that time. In addition, folk music and dance images from the Dunhuang caves also show up in paintings of performers making devotional offerings, depicting processional scenes of prominent officials and aristocrats as they travel, or the lower classes paying homage to the Buddha. All were a direct reflection of real life.

The folk songs and dances in Dunhuang's murals can be classified by their content into folk feasts, weddings, travel, sightseeing, and ceremonial worship. Taking paintings of wedding feasts as an example, there are 46 such paintings contained mostly within the *Maitreya Triple Sutra* illustrations, 35 of which were painted during the Tang Dynasty. *The Sutra that Expounds the Descent of the Maitreya Buddha and His Enlightenment*, translated by the prominent Buddhist monk Kumārajīva (343–413) of the Sixteen Kingdoms period, holds that in Maitreya's Tuṡita Heaven,

世界,"人寿八万四千岁""女人年五百岁,尔乃行嫁",于是画工描绘佛国世界女子出嫁的乐舞场景,就成为我们今天研究古代民间嫁娶舞蹈的珍贵资料。又如在唐代,宗教祭祀仪式中的舞蹈活动也十分兴盛,并逐渐向提高艺术水准以娱神兼娱人的方向发展。一方面,寺院成为兼有宗教活动与群众娱乐功能的重要场所,寺院歌舞既带有宣教性质,为了更贴近民众生活实际,也大量吸收世俗舞蹈,敦煌壁画中就有这样的舞蹈场面;另一方面,一般民间祭祀中的巫舞成为巫术活动的有机组成部分。唐五代时期,随着舞蹈艺术的高度发展,巫舞的神秘色彩渐趋淡薄,娱乐功能加强,更加讲究形式美与观赏性,敦煌壁画中出现了不少治病、驱鬼、赛神等巫术活动中的舞蹈场景。有的女巫,常常头戴簪花,身着唐服,手抱琵琶,随乐起舞。

"people can live up to 84,000 years old," and "women get married when they are 500 years old." As a result, these paintings of wedding music and dance scenes in Buddhist heavenly abodes have become invaluable primary sources for research on folk weddings in ancient times. Ceremonial and religious dance activities flourished during the Tang Dynasty, gradually raising artistic standards for the entertainment of both gods and humans. On the one hand, temples hosted religious events as well as recreational activities for the general public, so that temple music and dance was both missionary and at the same time incorporated elements of folk dance in order to get closer to the laity. On the other hand, dancing in folk ritual sacrifices became an organic part of exorcisms. During the Tang and Five Dynasties, the mystery of exorcism dance gradually diminished as highly developed dance artistry and its enhanced recreational purposes put emphasis on beauty of form and ornamental value. Dance scenes of therapy, exorcisms, and shamanistic activities show up in the Dunhuang murals. In these scenes, some sorcerers wear Tang clothing with flowers on their heads and dance to music with *pipas* in their hands.

供养人礼佛舞

Buddha Worshipping Dance

莫高窟现存早期的世俗舞蹈形象均为北周所绘，仅有两幅，因均位于洞窟显要位置而且都属西域舞蹈风格，颇引人注目。一幅是莫高窟第297窟的树下奏乐起舞供养人伎乐，绘于该窟西壁主佛佛龛下，正对窟门。图45画面上五个着突厥装的供养人，正奏乐起舞向佛朝拜。其中三人分别演奏笙、箜篌、琵琶，二舞者两手交叉举至头顶，大幅度摆胯，移颈动头，充满了西域风情。画面上还有一人因图像毁损，细部难以辨认，临摹图将其画成为肃立一旁的旁观者（图46)，似不确。从残存的形态看，应该也是一位舞者。天和三年(568年),北周武帝宇文邕迎娶突厥可汗俟斤之女阿史那氏为皇后。当时随同皇后到长安的还有来自康国、龟兹、高昌等地的庞大乐舞团，他们独具风格的表演轰动了京

There are only two primitive folk dance images found in the Mogao Caves. Both were painted in the Northern Zhou Dynasty. They are fascinating for their obvious position in the cave temples, as well as their depiction of choreography from the Western Regions. The first one is a painting of performers playing music under the trees, painted on the west wall under the Buddha niche facing the entrance in Cave 297. The five people are dancing to music for worshipping the Buddha (Fig.45). Three of them are playing the *sheng*, the *konghou*, and the *pipa*; the other two are dancing with their hands above their heads and their hips swinging in the exotic style of the Western Regions. Another image is barely discernable due to serious damage to the painting (Fig.46). In 568, Yuwen Yong, Emperor Wu of the Northern Zhou, married the daughter of Ashina Sijin, the Tujue's Mugan Khan. At that time, a massive musical dance entourage from Kang, Kucha (Qiuci), and Gaochang—ancient countries in the Western Regions—accompanied the queen, stirring the capital with their unique performance styles. The emperor ordered the entertainers to be organized into music and dance ensembles for the royal court, where they passed on their musical skills and songs, mixing the Western Regions music melodies with the

图 45　树下奏乐起舞供养人伎乐图(莫高窟第 297 窟)
Fig.45　Dancers and Musicians Performing Beneath Trees (Cave 297, Mogao Caves)

城。武帝特地下令将这些乐舞归入宫廷乐舞机构大司乐传习,采用西域音乐旋律,配置中原的传统乐器,融为北周的雅乐演奏。这幅敦煌供养人歌舞壁画,正是当时流行西域的乐舞在宗教艺术上的生动反映。

莫高窟第 299 窟西壁佛龛龛楣的莲花丛中乐舞(图 47)是另一幅北周时期所绘的礼佛舞蹈形象。画工在佛龛正中主佛头顶的莲花丛中绘了五身伎乐:一男性舞者赤裸上身,在花茎间交

traditional Chinese instruments of the Central Plains into the ceremonial music of the Northern Zhou Dynasty. This Dunhuang mural of performers is a vivid reflection of music and dance of the Western Regions.

The painting of people playing music and dancing in a cluster of lotuses on the lintel of the Buddha niche on the west wall of Cave 299 portrays another image of dancing figures who pay homage to the Buddha, painted in the Northern Zhou Dynasty (Fig.47). In the mid-right section of the niche are painted five musicians who sit in a patch of lotuses above the main Buddha. One dancer, who is topless, dances

图 46　树下奏乐起舞供养人伎乐图(莫高窟第 297 窟摹本)
Fig.46　Dancers and Musicians Performing Beneath Trees (Replica of Cave 297, Mogao Caves)

足而舞,他肩绕帛巾,腰系短裙,高举双臂,合掌头上,侧身扭胯,扬目移颈;他下边两侧的花蕾上各有两位伴奏者单腿屈膝盘坐,中间两位靠肩对视,分别弹奏着曲项琵琶与箜篌,旁边两位分别吹筚篥和笙。在主佛头顶出现俗舞场景,在敦煌壁画中实属罕见,也从一个侧面说明了西域民间乐舞在当时风行的程度。

莫高窟第 23 窟北壁拜

with a narrow silk shawl around his shoulders and a short *dhoti* tied at the waist. He holds his arms high, palms put together overhead, turns his body, twists his waist, and looks upward. There are two accompanists sitting on lotuses on either side of the dancer, legs dangling off the sides of the gigantic flower petals. They play the *bili* pipe (double reed woodwind) and the *sheng*. Two performers in the middle look at each other, and respectively play the *pipa* and the *konghou*. It is rare to see a scene of folk dancing above the main Buddha, which reflects the popularity of the Western Region folk musical dance at that time.

Stupa-worship dancing on the north wall of Mogao Cave 23 shows that there were various

塔舞蹈(图 48)。民间礼拜佛祖菩萨的形式多种多样,因为佛塔亦是佛法与人间功德的象征,所以拜塔也是礼佛的形式之一。这幅盛唐时期的世俗画表现的就是民间拜塔起舞的场面。一位舞者着短袖上衣与短裙，两臂上举，抬头仰视面前的佛塔,右腿屈膝立地,左腿

forms of Buddhist worship (Fig.48). Because stupas contain relics of the Buddha and other Buddhist saints, stupa worship also became one of the forms of sacred Buddhist devotional activity. This secular painting from the Tang Dynasty reveals a scene of stupa worship dance. The dancer in a short-sleeved tunic raises his arms and looks up at the stupa in front of him. He stands with his right knee bended, and lifts his left heel up behind him, close to the buttocks. He appears to be dancing with vigorous movements. A six-man musical ensemble sitting on the carpet behind the dancer accompanies him with flutes, drums, and string instruments. Four children,

图 47　佛龛龛楣的莲花丛中乐舞(莫高窟第 299 窟西壁)
Fig.47　Group of Performers Among Lotus Flowers on Niche Lintel (West Wall, Mogao Cave 299)

图 48　拜塔舞蹈(莫高窟第 23 窟北壁)
Fig.48　Stupa-worship Dance (North Wall, Mogao Cave 23)

提收使脚后跟贴近臀部，正以大幅度的跳踏动作礼拜起舞。舞者身旁有一人正匍匐在地做跪拜姿势。舞者身后的地毯上坐着六人乐队,吹击弹拨,为舞蹈伴奏。画面右侧榜题下有四个正聚沙筑塔的儿童,穿着肚兜,稚朴可爱,充满了生活情趣。榜题上的文字依稀可辨,说明香花、称名、乐舞礼拜等均是供养佛祖的形式。

each wearing a *dudou*—a traditional bib-like Chinese garment worn as a shirt or undergarment—can be seen in the lower right corner of the painting, building a sand castle, enjoying life to the fullest. There is an inscription in Chinese characters to the side, explaining that fragrant flowers, incantations, music, dance, and prayer are all forms of worshipping the Buddha.

宴饮舞与敦煌舞谱

Dancing for Feasts and Choreography Notations

中国的宴饮乐舞是饮食文化的重要组成部分，一般可区分为宫廷宴乐、官僚贵族宴乐与民间宴乐。它们之间除了规模、服饰、乐队、场景、气氛的差别外，主要表现为娱乐对象的不同。在敦煌壁画里的宴乐图，最具观赏与研究价值的是描绘民间嫁娶宴饮活动的乐舞场面，充满了浓厚的生活情趣。例如绘于莫高窟第445窟北壁的婚宴舞图（图49），非常真实地反映了盛唐时期西北地区的民间习俗：屋外的庭院中搭起了帐篷，婚礼则在帐内举行，左上侧宴席桌旁端坐宾主，右侧为拜堂行礼的新郎新娘，中央是翩翩起舞的舞伎，右上方有五人的伴奏乐队，右后方有作为洞房的圆顶青庐。舞伎扬袖抬足、扭腰回眸，使我们想起

China's musical dance for feasting was an important part of food culture, which generally can be categorized into music for palace banquets, music for banquets of officials and aristocrats, and music for folk feasts. In addition to differences in scale, costume, musical instruments, occasion, and atmosphere, they were mainly different in terms of the entertainment's purpose. In paintings of banquet entertainment, those scenes which portray musical dance for wedding feasts offer the most in aesthetic enjoyment and research value. These scenes also reflect happy and joyous moments in life. For example, the painting of a dance at a wedding on the north wall of Mogao Cave 445 accurately reflects the folk customs in the northwest during the High Tang period (Fig.49). A tent is erected in the courtyard and the wedding is held inside. The host and guests sit on the upper left side of the banquet table, while the bride and groom perform formal bows on the right side. Dancers perform in the center with a five-person ensemble on the upper right. There is also a blue-green cottage with dome serving as the bridal chamber in the background on the right. Dancers wave sleeves, raise feet, gyrate their torsos, and glance back. Some researchers believe the rhythm and clothing style of "slow dance with elegance" on the painting is similar to the *wangwushan* dance, or *ruanwu* ("soft dance")

图 49　婚宴舞图(莫高窟第 445 窟北壁)
Fig.49　Marriage Feast Dance (North Wall, Mogao Cave 445)

白居易“妆成剪烛后，醉起拂衫时”的诗句。有的研究者认为图中“慢态不能穷”的韵律风格及服饰与著名的《韩熙载夜宴图》里王屋山舞软舞《六幺》(又名“绿腰”“乐世”)十分相似，但舞图上的青庐氛围却和大官僚豪宅的穷奢极侈迥然不同。另外，青庐之俗源于

depicted in the Chinese painting *Evening Banquet at Han Xizai's Residence*. The blue-green tent in this painting, however, is different from the luxurious mansions of Chinese nobles. In addition, the custom of blue-green tents originated from the northwest nomadic people, and then spread to India. Its reappearance in the Dunhuang murals reflects the charm of cultural integration. The musical accompaniment in *Evening Banquet at Han Xizai's Residence* includes a bass drum, clappers, and hand-clapping by two people. But in this scene of musical dance, one accompanist is

西北游牧民族，后又传入印度一带，在敦煌的壁画里再现，正体现了民族文化交融的魅力。《韩熙载夜宴图》里的伴奏是一架大鼓、一个拍板，还有二人击掌；这个乐舞场面中伴奏者除一人吹箫外，其余的人分别在拍板、击钹、按掌，均起着掌控舞蹈节拍的作用，显示这类舞蹈是比较讲究节奏的。

又如榆林窟第 38 窟西壁五代时期所绘的婚宴场面也特别引人注目（图 50），因为从画面看是回鹘与汉族通婚的典礼：帷帐里的新娘头戴桃形凤冠，这正是回鹘贵妇的标志，新郎则是汉族官人打扮。左边帐篷里坐着男女宾客、亲友，桌上摆着大盘菜肴。帐前空地上有一位男性舞者，正面对一位手执团扇的年轻女子扬袖起舞；另一男性侍者托盘站在舞者身后，盘中放着酒碗，显然和这个舞蹈密切相关。

莫高窟第 98 窟北壁绘有五代时期的一幅《贤愚经变》，其中也有民间宴饮舞蹈

playing the *xiao* while others use clappers, beat cymbals and clap hands. They all play the role of controlling the dance beats, indicating that this kind of dance is more particular about rhythm.

Another mural which fascinates people is the wedding scene painted during the Five Dynasties, located on the west wall of Yulin Cave 38 (Fig.50). The scene depicts a marriage ceremony of Uyghurs intermarrying with Han Chinese. The bride in the tent wears a peach-shaped phoenix coronet, a symbol of wealthy Uyghur women, and the groom is dressed in the Han style. Guests, friends, and relatives sit on the left side in the tent and dishes from different cuisines are laid on the table. In the open space in front of the tent, a male dancer dances as he waves his sleeves, facing a young woman who holds a paper fan. Another male attendant who is carrying a tray with bowls on it stands behind the dancer; apparently, he is closely related to the dance.

The illustration painting of *Sutra of the Wise and the Foolish* on the north wall of Mogao Cave 98 from the Five Dynasties also portrays a scene of dance for folk feasting (Fig. 51). Five men in informal dress sit at the table on which there are some dishes of food. A man at the table in similar dress rolls up his sleeves and tightens his waistband. He opens his arms with fists clenched and lifts up his right leg, which makes it seem that he is twirling. A man on the left side of the dancer accompanies the performance with clappers, and the man on the

图 50　婚宴舞场面(榆林窟第 38 窟西壁)

Fig.50　Marriage Feast Dance (West Wall, Yulin Cave 38)

的场面(图 51):五位着常服的男子，围坐在放了菜肴的酒桌前；一位同样着常服的男子，则在桌前临时卷袖束衣，平展两臂，双手握拳，吸提右腿，似在做旋转而舞的动作；舞者左侧一人执拍板为舞蹈击节，右侧一人则端盘而立，准备进酒。

舞蹈史研究者推测以上壁画的宴饮舞蹈，很可能即是唐五代时期广泛流行的

right side is standing with a tray in his hands, about to propose a toast.

Researchers of dance history speculate that it is likely that dances for feasting in the above-mentioned murals are the popular *daling* dance from the Tang and Five Dynasties—a kind of entertainment dance of etiquette and custom which stressed rhythm. It was inseparable from the words and music of various *qupai* (names of melodies) and had prescriptive rituals and dance patterns. "A Hundred-Verse Poem for Yuan Zhen" written by Tang poet Bai Juyi (772-846) reads, "We sat close and laughed together, while the

图 51　宴席前舞蹈场面(莫高窟第 98 窟北壁)
Fig.51　Part of Marriage Feast Dance (North Wall, Mogao Cave 98)

"打令舞"——这是酒宴上带娱乐性的礼俗舞蹈，讲究节拍，与各种曲牌的"打令词、曲"密不可分，有规定的仪礼与舞蹈程式。白居易《代书诗一百韵寄微之》诗云："密坐随欢促，华尊逐胜移。香飘歌袂动，翠落舞钗遗。筹插红螺碗，觥飞白玉卮。打嫌调笑易，饮讶卷波迟。"（注：抛打曲有《调笑令》，饮酒曲有《卷白波》）而敦煌的这些舞蹈壁画，正好启示我们去认识藏经洞文献里发现的唐代舞谱。

敦煌舞谱残卷自 1925 年经我国学者刘复（字半农）首先从法国巴黎藏敦煌写卷中发现定名并编入《敦煌掇琐》，至今已经陆续发现并刊布多个写本。20 世纪六七十年代以来，中外多位学者对它们进行了整理、释读与研究，20 世纪 80 年代末，由柴剑虹整理出 S. 5643、P. 3501 两卷的 8 名 24 谱（如《浣溪沙》《双燕子》《南乡子》等）（图

gorgeous goblet was passed to winners of the drinking game / Waving sleeves and spreading perfume everywhere, the Dancers were performing so fast that their hairpins fell on the ground / We put chip counters in the red whorled bowl, and toasted each other with cups and jade wine vessels / We performed the clapping music but thought it too easy; We sang the drinking song but were surprised by its slow pace." The murals portraying dancing in Dunhuang shed light on choreography notations from the Tang Dynasty that were found in the documents from the Library Cave (Cave 17) at Mogao.

Beginning in 1925, scroll fragments of Dunhuang choreography notations were first found by Chinese scholar Liu Fu in the Dunhuang manuscripts in Paris. He named these scroll fragments and compiled them in *A Collection of Dunhuang Manuscripts*. Since then many manuscripts have been gradually located and published. Since the 1960s and 1970s, a number of Chinese and Western scholars have collected, interpreted, and studied these manuscripts. At the end of the 1980s, Chai Jianhong collected eight melody names and 24 choreography notations from two scrolls, No. S. 5643 and P. 3501. Some examples include "Silk-Washing Stream," "A Pair of Sparrows," and "Song of a Southern Country." (Fig.52) Five other choreography notations have been discovered in the Dunhuang manuscripts since 1984. These include "A Southern Song for Offering Wine" discovered by researcher Li Zhengyu as well as scroll fragment No.820, with notations for "Two-Clap Leads for

52)；由于 1984 年后又陆续发现了敦煌写本中 5 个不同内容的舞谱残卷，尤其是李正宇研究员发现的 S. 5613 号题署为《上酒曲子南歌子》及方广锠研究员在国家图书馆藏品里发现的北图残 820 号《两打引令》谱（图 53），更进一步证实了罗庸、叶玉华等前辈学者的科学判定。经过两位笔者多年的合作研究，结合古代文献记载与民间舞蹈遗存，可基本上确定现存敦煌舞谱为排演与记录唐人酒宴上自娱与礼仪性的“打令”舞字谱，大致由曲名、词序、字组三部分组成，其中最关键的就是舞蹈节拍的规定（如 “慢二急三”“慢四急七”）与舞蹈动作（如打、令、皇、送、摇、据、挼等）的提示。笔者与其他一些研究者对这些舞蹈动作进行的释读，将古代舞谱的研究推进了一大步。另外，S. 7111 号《曲子别仙子》四首词前亦有“慢三急三、慢二急三”的节拍规定，为我们研究唐人酒宴上的打令舞蹈曲、词、舞三者的密切关系提供了弥足珍贵的资料。

Drinking Games” (Fig.53) discovered by the researcher Fang Guangchang in the National Library, further confirming the scientific judgments of senior scholars such as Luo Yong and Ye Yuhua. After years of collaborative research by two authors of this book, combined with records of ancient documents and remnants of folk dances, what can be confirmed is that Dunhuang choreography notations are manuscripts that choreograph and record entertainment and ceremonial *daling* dance during the Tang Dynasty. The notations are mainly divided into three parts: melody names, order of songs, and lyrics, in which the most critical parts are provisions of dance beats (e. g. , “two slow beats and three quick beats,” and “four slow beats and seven quick beats”) and the suggestion of dance movements (e. g. , “throw, beat, send, shake, cross, ”etc.). Along with several other researchers, we have studied and analyzed these dance movements, facilitating the study of ancient choreography notations. In addition, manuscript No. S. 7111, “Poem for Songs: Farewell to Fairies” also has the notation of “three slow beats and three quick beats” and “two slow beats and three quick beats” which has provided invaluable information for us to study the close relationships of tunes, lyrics, and choreography for banquets held during the Tang Dynasty.

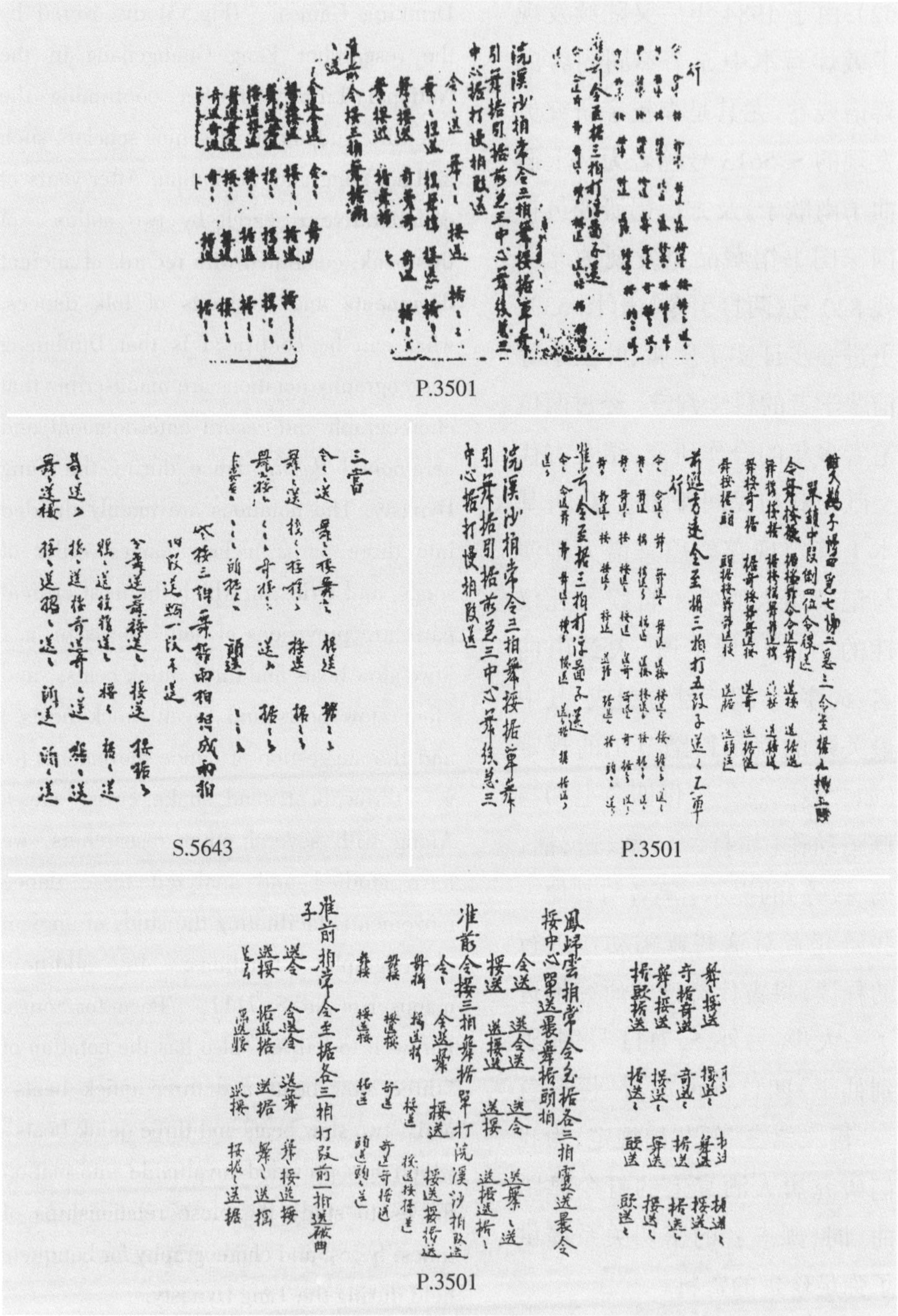

图 52　敦煌舞谱残卷

Fig.52　Scroll Fragments of Dunhuang Choreography Notations

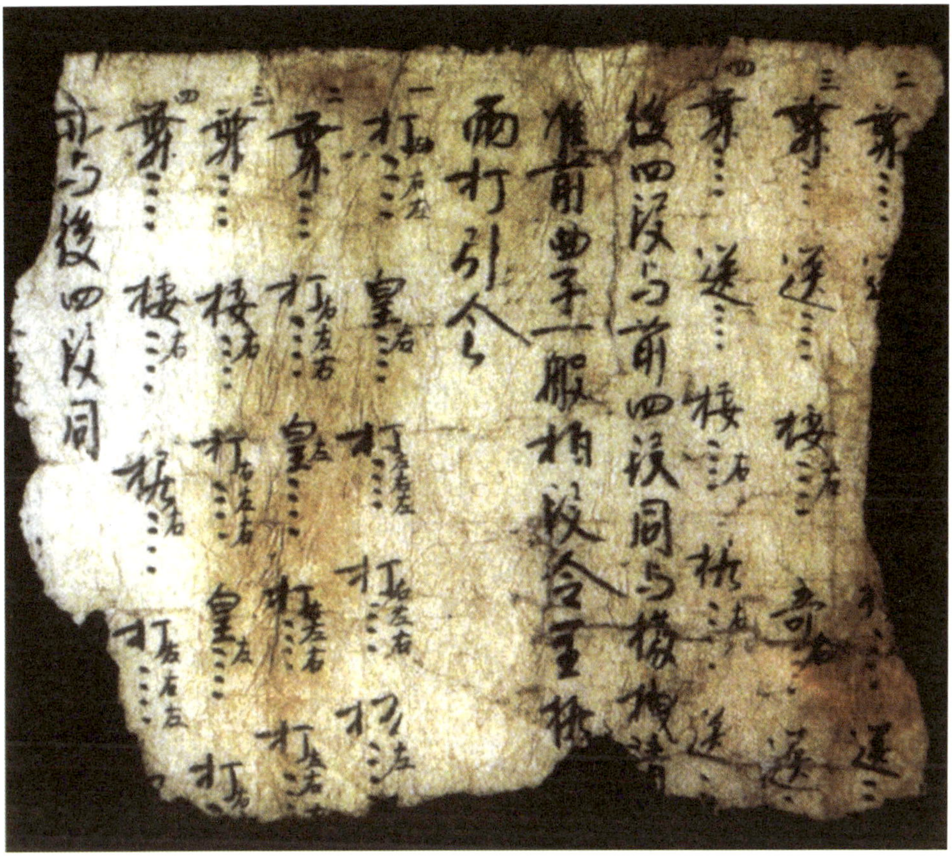

图 53　敦煌舞谱残卷(BD. 10691)

Fig.53　Scroll Fragment of Dunhuang Choreography Notations (BD. 10691)

出行舞

Dancing in Processional Scenes

敦煌壁画里的出行舞以莫高窟晚唐归义军时期第156窟的《张议潮出行图》与《宋国夫人出行图》中的舞乐场面为代表。这两幅特殊的供养人壁画由于主题系颂扬敦煌归义军政权的创始人，其描绘的出行场景自然非同一般，真实地再现了当时河西地区权贵豪门出行巡游时载歌载舞的盛况。这两幅壁画的共同特点是表现出中心人物的张议潮及其夫人宋氏形象高大，出行队伍庞大而气派：前者马队迤逦，旌旗猎猎，气宇轩昂；后者车轿整齐，服饰鲜丽，雍容华贵。两支队伍里均有乐舞伎人，前者以吹铜鼓大角的骑兵为先导，乐队演奏大鼓、腰鼓、鸡娄鼓和箜篌、笙、琵琶、筚篥、横笛；后者以百戏戴

Examples of dancing in processional scenes in Dunhuang murals include the painting of *The Procession of Zhang Yichao* as well as the painting of *The Procession of Lady Song*, a noblewoman from the Kingdom of Song in Mogao Cave 156, created during the Guiyijun period in the Late Tang (Figs.54, 55). Since the theme of these two special patron paintings is to extol the founder of the Guiyijun military regime in Dunhuang, the paintings portray unusual scenes of excursions, recreating grand occasions of singing and dancing while the nobles travelled in the Hexi area. Common characteristics of these two paintings are that they both depict the main character, Zhang Yichao, and his wife, whose surname was Song, accompanied by an impressive entourage. In the first painting (Fig.54), a meandering cavalcade makes an imposing appearance with flags fluttering, while in the latter painting (Fig.55), carriages and sedan-chairs form an orderly procession with bright clothing that seems elegant and stylish. Both entourages include musicians and dancers. There is a cavalry officer acting as a leader or conductor in Zhang Yichao's entourage, blowing a trumpet. The orchestra plays the bass drum, waist drum, *jilou* drum, *konghou*, *sheng*, *pipa*, *bili* pipe, and transverse flute. The other ensemble, led by performing acrobats, plays instruments including waist drum, transverse flute, *pipa*, *xiao*, and *sheng*.

竿为先导,乐队演奏腰鼓、横笛、琵琶、箫、笙等。二者各有风采,既宣扬文治武功,又渲染歌舞升平。

《张议潮出行图》中的八人舞蹈(图 54)为四男四女,成双行队舞,男子穿汉装,戴幞头,女子着吐蕃装,束双髻,裹彩巾,均斜张双臂,甩长袖相向而舞。舞者顿足挥臂而舞的矫健姿态,与今天藏族舞蹈的行进舞姿很像,有的研究者则

Each has its own style. They not only commemorate political and military achievements, but also celebrate peace through song and dance, as well.

Eight people dance in the painting of *The Procession of Zhang Yichao*, four men and four women in two rows (Fig.54). Thc men wear Han-style clothing and black gauze caps. Women are dressed in ancient Tubo-style clothing, wearing their hair in double topknots, with colored scarves wrapped around their heads. The rows

图 54 《张议潮出行图》中乐舞形象(莫高窟第 156 窟)
Fig.54 Dance Scenes Painted in *The Procession of Zhang Yichao* (Mogao Cave 156)

认为颇接近藏族传统的“跳锅庄”，舞者边唱边舞，甩袖踏足，动作奔放有力。

《宋国夫人出行图》（图 55、图 56）中的四位舞伎分站四方，相对而舞，均高髻云鬓，穿裙襦，肩披长巾，脚着云头鞋，挥动长袖，翩翩起舞，既有中原长袖舞风格，又透出藏族“弦子舞”的风韵。相传“弦子”是唐代文成公主入藏时带到藏区的，后融会了藏族民间舞蹈顿足张臂的特点，成为典雅、舒缓、优美的风格鲜明的民族舞蹈，正是民族文化交流的结晶。为了更好地品鉴人物的姿态与神情，我们将这幅壁画的原照片及线描图同时展示给读者。

face each other, and dancers stand with arms outstretched to the side, waving long sleeves. The vigorous, stomping feet and waving arms are similar to the choreography of the modern-day Tibetans. Some researchers think that they are quite close to the *guozhuang* dance in Tibet, in which people stand in a circle, hand in hand, singing and dancing, spinning and jumping, stomping their feet and waving their arms.

Four dancers in the painting of *The Procession of Lady Song* stand in a square formation, facing each other as they dance (Figs. 55, 56). They wear their hair in topknots covered with caps or small turbans, and dress in robes with jackets over them. Long, narrow scarves are draped over their shoulders. They dance nimbly and gracefully, moving their long sleeves in a style which reveals a cross between that of the Central Plains and the *xianzi* dance of the Tibetans. According to legend, the *xianzi* (a three-stringed plucked instrument) was brought to the Tibetan area by Princess Wencheng of the Tang Dynasty. It was later combined with the stamping feet and outstretched arms of Tibetan folk dance. *Xianzi* dance then evolved into an elegant, soothing, beautiful folk dance with a distinctive style. We can say it is a crystallization of cultural exchange and integration. Both the original image and a line drawing of the painting are shown here to readers, in order to better appreciate the poses and expressions of the characters.

图 55 《宋国夫人出行图》中乐舞形象(莫高窟第 156 窟)
Fig.55 Dance Scenes Painted in *The Procession of Lady Song* (Mogao Cave 156)

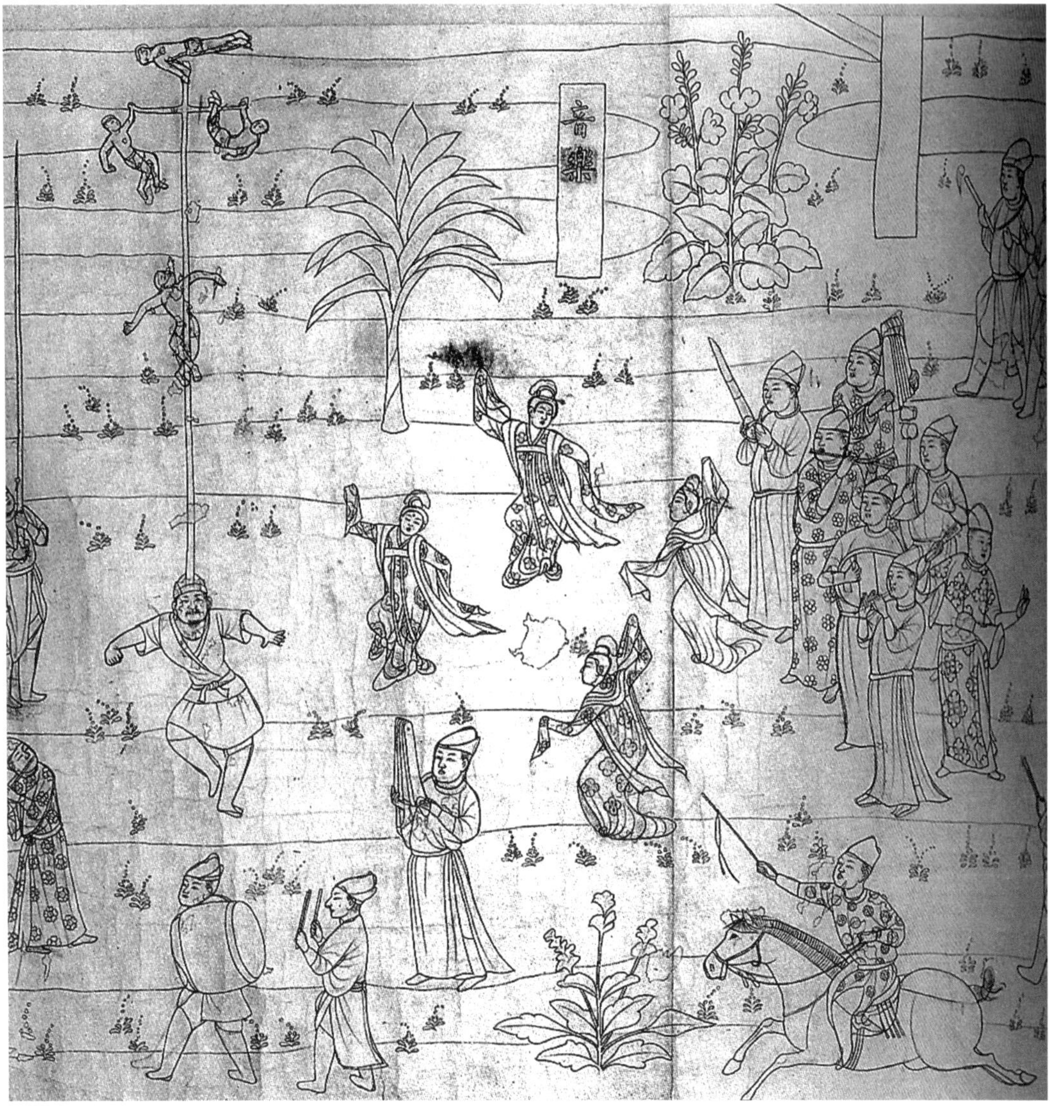

图 56 《宋国夫人出行图》中乐舞形象(莫高窟第 156 窟摹本)

Fig.56 Dance Images Painted in *The Procession of Lady Song* (Replica of Mogao Cave 156)

祭祀舞与拟兽舞

Sacrificial Dance and Masquerade Ceremonies

“歌舞散灵衣，荒哉旧风俗。”(杜甫《南池》)在我国民间的祭祀活动中，迎神、送神仪式中的乐舞是必不可少的。祭祀乐舞是中国古代各民族共有的普遍的乐舞形式，既因地域、民族、宗教、时代的不同而各呈风貌，又在长期的文化交汇里形成了一些共同的特征，并渗透到其他的民族民间舞蹈种类中去。例如佩带假面的傩舞，扮演动物形态的兽舞，手持法器、祭物(金刚杵、花、绳、杯盘等)的菩萨乐舞形象等。因此，我们在敦煌壁画里虽然一般不易指出特征明显的祭祀舞蹈，却仍然可以找到它们异彩纷呈的各类形象。距敦煌地区很近的古凉州(今甘肃武威)，巫舞赛神颇为流行，敦煌地区岁时节日的赛神活动更为活跃，而舞蹈往往是这些活动不可或缺的内容。

As the Tang poet Du Fu in his poem “South Lake” wrote, “People are dancing and singing in spirit clothes to practice sorcery/How absurd these old customs are! ”In Chinese folk sacrifice, music and dance played an essential role in both receiving (“welcoming”) and expelling (“sending off”) spirits. Ritual sacrifice with music and dance was ubiquitous in ancient China. Their forms varied owing to differences in geography, ethnicity, culture, religion, and historical period. However, they also share some common features due to long term transcultural diffusion. These ritualistic dances eventually permeated other kinds of ethnic folk dances as well. Types of ritual dances include exorcism dances in which shamans wear masks, masquerade ceremonies in which people imitate animals as totems, and music and dance images in which bodhisattvas make devotional offerings holding various sacred implements in their hands, including Dharma-vessels (i. e., musical instruments used in Buddhist or Daoist rites), flowers, garlands, cords, trays, and bowls. Although the distinguishing characteristics of sacrificial dance are not easily defined, we can still find various extant images today. For example, in ancient Liangzhou (present-day Wuwei in Gansu Province), not far from Dunhuang, the practice of dancing to appease

图 57　巫舞形象(莫高窟第 12 窟北壁)

Fig.57　Exorcism Dance (North Wall, Mogao Cave 12)

诚如王维的诗所云："女巫进，纷屡舞。"（《迎神》）"纷进舞兮堂前""神之驾兮俨欲旋"（《送神》）。

莫高窟第12窟北壁晚唐时期的壁画里，有一位头戴簪花，身着唐服，手抱琵琶，随乐起舞的女巫形象（图57）。她怀抱曲项琵琶，歌舞娱神，为人治病消灾。女巫面对神坛，面部丰腴，虽然因色彩的褪落看不清她的表情，那张开的樱桃小口却告诉我们她正唱着动听的歌曲；她上身斜倾，长裙曳地，右脚在裙内微微后抬，体态婀娜，舞姿优美。画的右下部有病人及侍者。巫人弹奏琵琶，有一种特殊的风格和韵味。据《乐府杂录》记载，唐代琵琶名手段善本，在听了另一名家康昆仑的演奏后论："本领何杂，兼带邪声？"昆仑惊曰："段师神人也！臣少年初学艺时，偶于邻舍女巫授一品弦调，后乃易数师。"所谓

and worship spirits was prevalent. The sacrificial activities for these spirits were conducted during festivals and other designated special days in Dunhuang. Dance always formed an indispensable part of these ceremonies.

In Mogao Cave 12 in Dunhuang, there is an image of a sorceress on the north wall from the Late Tang period (Fig.57). She wears flower ornaments on her head according to Tang costume, holding a *pipa* close to her chest as she sings and dances for the entertainment of the spirits. Facing the spirit altar, her songs form a sort of incantation, beseeching the spirits to cure people and remove ill fortune. Her face is plump, although her features are indistinguishable due to color fading and paint deterioration. Her small "cherry" lips indicate that she is singing a beautiful song. She leans her upper body forward and her right foot lifts backward slightly under her floor-length skirt. Her body is shapely and her movements graceful. There are supplicants with illnesses and servants at the bottom right of the picture. The sorceress plays the *pipa* with a special style and zest. This style of exorcising dancing while playing a *pipa* was known as *xiesheng* ("evil voice"). In certain bodhisattva images in Dunhuang, we can also see musical instruments and sacrifice merged into a unified whole. For example, on the east wall of Cave 20 in the Yulin Caves, there is an image of a bodhisattva holding a conch shell in his hand (Fig.58). He wears a crown on his head and kneels with his left leg on a lotus seat. The bodhisattva extends his arms with bended elbows. The conch lies flat on his left palm. He holds his right hand up in a *mudra*

“邪声”，当是巫人弹奏琵琶所具有的风格。当然在有的菩萨供养图里，我们也可寻见供品与法器、祭物合而为一的图像。如榆林窟第20窟东壁就有一幅手捧海螺被称作南无甘露供养菩萨的画面：头戴花冠的菩萨左腿单跪于莲花座上，双臂前伸，肘略下沉，左手平摊捧海螺，右手伸食指与中指，手姿优美，似另有寓意（图58）。也有的研究者认为这些手势的佛教意义更为突出，与舞蹈关系不大。

拟兽舞形象源远流长，大概最初和远古时期及游牧民族的狩猎活动有关，后来发展为祭祀活动的内容，再逐渐演变为独立的舞蹈门类。到隋唐时期，在元宵灯节，不仅有热闹非凡的观赏各色花灯活动，也伴随演出各类百戏杂技与乐舞，其中戴兽面、仿百兽形态的拟兽舞也很得群众喜爱。薛道衡在《和许给事善心戏场转韵诗》里曾形象地描写了这种拟兽舞表演：“抑扬百兽舞，盘跚五禽戏。狻猊弄斑足，巨象垂长鼻。青羊跪复跳，白马

(symbolic hand gesture in Buddhist and Hindu iconography), his forefinger and middle finger extended upward, with the other fingers and thumb downward. Some researchers believe these poses have more to do with Buddhist significance and little to do with dancing.

Animal imitation dance, a type of masquerade ceremomy, has a long history in ancient China. Initially related to nomadic people’s hunting activities, it later developed into ritual masquerade ceremonies and then gradually evolved into dance forms of its own. By the time of the Sui and Tang dynasties, people enjoyed acrobatic and dance spectacles during the lunar Lantern Festival. Animal imitation dances in which performers wore masks and imitated beasts were a very popular part of these entertainments. In “Verses Composed with Xu Shanxin at the Theater”, Sui Dynasty poet Xue Daoheng (535–609) described these animal dances vividly: “The Beasts dance rise and fall, but five mimicked animals hobble and limp / The lion plays with its spotted foot, while the giant elephant hangs down its long trunk / The goat kneels and leaps, but the white horse revolves and runs / ... / The deer climbs down, and the monkey crouches and stands on its toes.”In some of the sutra illustration paintings in the Mogao Caves, we can see images of human–headed *kalaviṅkas* with bird bodies, and we can also find images of masquerade ceremonies or animal imitation dance. For example, on the north wall of Mogao Cave 465, there is a

图 58　手捧海螺的菩萨(榆林窟第 20 窟东壁)
Fig.58　Bodhisattva Holding a Conch Shell (East Wall, Yulin Cave 20)

图 59　猴面人身舞形象(莫高窟第 465 窟北壁)
Fig.59　Image of Figure with Monkey Head and Human Body (North Wall, Mogao Cave 465)

回旋骑。... 麋鹿下腾倚，猴猿或蹲跂。”我们除了在莫高窟的一些经变画场面中，可以看到许多人首鸟身的迦陵频伽乐舞形象外，也可找到民间拟兽舞的图像。例如莫高窟第465窟北壁有一幅舞图（图59），舞者猴面人身，全身赤裸，左腿屈蹲以左脚全掌着地，右腿侧抬并翻脚掌，左臂屈肘抬至胸前，手中似抓取一物，右臂屈举做虚拳之状。该窟壁画为元代所绘，保留着许多精彩的舞姿图，有的舞者手中持有铃、杵之类法器，研究者认为这些风格特异的舞图属于金刚乘藏密画派，舞蹈形象则使人联想起元代著名的《十六天魔舞》。虽然也是宗教宣传画，同样洋溢着浓厚的生活气息，是民族民间舞蹈的奇葩。论者常津津乐道的莫高窟第148窟的“六臂飞天”，一飞天乐伎分别持琵琶、金铃、横笛、铜钹演奏飞舞，虽为画匠的想象夸张，同样也应是实际乐舞场景的浓缩与提炼（图60）。

painting of a nearly naked dancer with a monkey face and man's body (Fig.59). The creature's left leg bends slightly as he stands on his left foot in a kind of single-legged plie. His right knee is bent and lifted high at a 45-degree angle, with the sole of the foot flat and the toes pointing downward. The left arm is also bended at a 45-degree angle, with the hand in front of the chest;he appears to be holding something in his left hand. The right arm is lifted up and bended at a 90-degree angle and the right hand is held up in a *mudra* gesture. The wall paintings in this cave temple were painted in the Yuan Dynasty and many images of marvellous dance poses have been preserved in them even until the present day. Some dancers also hold musical instruments in their hands such as bells. Some researchers believe that these specific dance images belong to Esoteric Buddhism. Many of the dancing images remind people of the famous Dance of the Sixteen Demons in the Yuan Dynasty. Although they are paintings for disseminating religion, they are also brimming with vitality and are exquisite examples of ethnic folk dances. A painting which experts never tire of discussing, the six-armed flying *Apsara* located in Mogao Cave 148, depicts a flying celestial musician with six arms simultaneously playing the *pipa*, transverse flute, brass cymbals, and a bell as she dances and flies around. Although the image comes from the painter's imagination, it is also a reflection of real-world musical dance (Fig.60).

图 60　六臂飞天(莫高窟第 148 窟摹本)

Fig.60　Six-armed Flying *Apsara* (Replica of Mogao Cave 148)

剑器舞

Sword Dance

剑既是我国古代运用历史悠久的传统兵器，也是中国武术与舞蹈的最习见的用具。先秦典籍中记载了子路戎装见孔子、拔剑起舞的故事。著名的纪传体史书《史记》中“项庄舞剑，意在沛公”的故事成为后世家喻户晓的典故。如果说子路和项庄的舞剑还是中原地区一种半武术、半舞蹈的即兴发挥的话，至迟到了隋唐之际，剑舞已经汲取了西北游牧民族的文化营养，成为“健舞”系统中不可或缺的、有特定程式的表演性舞蹈。唐代大诗人杜甫曾在晚年写下《观公孙大娘弟子舞剑器行》一诗，回忆起他少年时代在郾城观看公孙氏舞《剑器浑脱》的情景：“昔有佳人公孙氏，一舞剑器动四方。观者如山色沮丧，天地为之久低昂。”诗中称

The sword was a traditional weapon used in ancient times, and it remains the most common weapon or prop used in Chinese martial arts and dance today. The pre-Qin classics record the story of Zi Lu, one of the main disciples of Confucius, meeting the master in martial attire and performing a sword dance. The famous book by Sima Qian, *Records of the Grand Historian*, records the story that “Xiang Zhuang performed a sword dance as a cover for his attempt on Liu Bang’s life, ”a story of a political assassination attempt in the guise of a sword dance, a legend which is well-known to most Chinese people. If we believe that Zi Lu and Xiang Zhuang’s sword dances were a combination of martial arts and ethnic Han dance choreography, then by the Sui and Tang dynasties the sword dance had already absorbed elements of the northwestern nomadic tribes. The great Tang poet Du Fu wrote a poem describing a similar scene in “On Watching the Sword Dance of Aunt Gongsun’s Disciple.” The poet recalled his childhood memories when he watched a woman called Aunt Gongsun performing the sword dance: “There was a beautiful woman named Gongsun who would astonish the watchers whenever she performed the sword dance / The crowds were huge and so amazed were they at her dancing skills, and even heaven and earth shook from her dancing.” Aunt Gongsun was indeed a real person, and it was

赞“妙舞此曲神扬扬”“先帝侍女八千人,公孙剑器初第一”,也感慨安史之乱后“梨园子弟散如烟”“玳筵急管曲复终,乐极哀来月东出”。据《明皇杂录》记载:公孙大娘善舞各种套路的剑器,如《西河剑器》《剑器浑脱》《裴将军满堂势》等。裴将军即当时的舞剑高手裴旻,因特善舞剑,与“书圣”张旭、“画圣”吴道子一起被誉为“唐人三绝”。公孙大娘所舞,亦当得到裴将军剑舞之精粹。另一位大诗人李白也留下了不少描述剑舞的动人诗句,如“三杯拂剑舞秋月,忽然高咏涕泗涟”(《玉壶吟》)。“起舞莲花剑,行歌明月弓”(《送梁公昌从信安北征》)。对剑舞与乐曲及酒的关系,著名的边塞诗人岑参的名作《酒泉太守席上醉后作》有更集中的描述:“酒泉太守能剑舞,高堂置酒夜击鼓。胡笳一曲断人肠,座上相看泪如雨。”敦煌藏经洞所出写本里就发现了岑参此诗的唐代写卷。舞蹈史研究者曾经就古代的“剑器”是舞双剑还是雄装空手或持彩球而舞,进行过讨论。上述诗歌可以作为文献的证据,而我们从莫高窟的壁画里似乎可以找到一点剑舞图

recorded that she was skilled in performing all the sword dances of the day, including the "Western River Sword Dance", the "*Huntuo* Sword Dance" (one that integrates the sword dance with the *huntuo* dance), "General Pei's Sword Dance" and so on. Another great Tang poet, Li Bai, also wrote many lines about sword dances, such as, "After three cups of wine, I started the sword dance in the autumn moonlight / Chanting aloud while dancing, mixed feelings came over me and I could not keep myself from crying," in "Song of the Jade Wine Vessel". The frontier poet Cen Shen in his poem "Written After the Jiuquan Prefect Got Drunk at the Banquet," described the relationship between sword dancing, song, and wine in detail: "The Jiuquan Prefect was skillful at performing the sword dance, and bottles of wines were placed in the hall and the drums were beaten at night / The moment a piece of heartbreaking Hu music was played, all the audience burst into tears." This ancient poem written by Cen Shen was among the cache of manuscripts discovered in Mogao's Library Cave. Researchers of dance history have debated whether "sword" indicates dancers holding two swords to dance, or holding colored balls, or holding nothing. The poems above can provide evidence for the use of swords in dancing, but we can also find examples of sword dance from the murals in the Mogao

像上的例证。

莫高窟第 154 窟东壁有一幅盛唐时期所绘《金刚经·忍辱波罗密品》,其中有生活气息浓郁的画面：画中三人均着当时的文人服装，一人盘腿端坐于床榻之上，手捧经卷念诵；床榻右后方一人做骑马蹲裆的弓箭步，右手执竹剑而舞；床前另一人亦做弓箭步,做挥拳击掌状。床上的诵经者却毫不理会,依然诵经不止。研究者认为这个场景真实反映了当时流行的剑舞和武术相映成趣的豪健姿态,栩栩如生,有很强的视觉效果。此外,前几年王克芬研究员又在榆林窟第 3 窟南壁西夏时期的菩萨伎乐图里发现了剑舞的新图像(图 61)。图中三身伎乐菩萨均单足脚尖着地持舞具而舞,自东向西依次为腰鼓舞、剑舞和拍板舞。跳剑舞者右手持剑,侧身回眸,做腾越之状,姿态夸张、豪放,具有鲜明的西域风格。无独有偶,榆林窟第 25 窟的《未生怨》图中有“追杀”画面,持剑相追者的

Caves.

On the east wall of Mogao Cave 154, there is an illustration painting (not pictured) of *The Diamond Sutra: Chapter 14, Lead All Beings to Nirvana*. It was painted during the High Tang. The scene is incredibly lifelike. There are three men in the painting: all wear the scholarly clothing of the literati. One of them sits cross-legged on a bed, studying Buddhist scrolls; on the right, behind the bed, a man is practicing martial arts movements with a bamboo sword in his right hand. In front of the bed, the third man is also practicing martial arts movements, striking his palm with his fist. The man on the bed pays no attention and keeps on reading. Researchers believe that this scene reflects the synthesized form of popular sword dancing and martial arts prevalent at that time. This image is so vivid it is somewhat arresting to the viewer. In addition to this, several years ago scholar Wang Kefen discovered a new image of sword dance created during the Western Xia period. The image is found among figures of Buddhist musical dance on the south wall of Cave 3 at Yulin (Fig.61). The three Buddhists in the picture all stand on one leg and dance with various props. From east to west, the dancers perform the waist drum dance, sword dance and clapper dance. The sword dancer holds a sword in the right hand and leans to the side as he turns his head. The distinctive leaping pose is dramatic and bold, characteristic of the Western Regions style. This painting has

图 61　剑舞画面(榆林窟第 3 窟南壁)

Fig.61　Sword Dance (South Wall, Yulin Cave 3)

出剑动作亦和剑舞的姿态有异曲同工之妙，可证此舞也是从实际生活中提炼而成。

莫高窟藏经洞所出文学写卷中还有题名为《剑器词》的作品(编号S.6537)，其中一首写道:“排备白旗舞,先自有来由。合如花焰秀,散若电光开。喊声天地裂,腾踏山岳摧。剑器呈多少,浑脱向前来。”既可证明剑器舞有气势恢弘的群舞场面,在表演时有曲词的配合,也说明它和印度及西域传来的“浑脱”(苏幕遮)常常是穿插或融合在一起演出的。

its counterpart in Cave 25 at Yulin, which contains a mural scene of a deadly pursuit with a sword. The chaser holds a sword in hand with a pose similar if not identical to that of the sword dance, which lends credence to the claim that these sword dance images had their basis in real life.

Among the manuscripts found in the Library Cave (Mogao Cave 17), there is a volume named *Poems of Swords* (S.6537). One of the manuscripts records: [The performers were] “dancing with the white flags held in their hands, and the dance got its name with reasons /When gathered, they looked like fireworks; When dispersed, they looked like lightning/ Their shout could split heaven and earth, and their steps and kicks could destroy the mountains / They began to perform *huntuo* Dance while the audience were still immersed.” It can not only prove the magnificent scene of sword dance along with music, but it also proves that sword dance was usually performed with or within *huntuo* dance originated from India and the Western Regions.

胡舞动心弦
特色鲜明的民族舞蹈

Hu Dance: Distinctive Ethnic Choreography

西部少数民族乐舞传入中原地区，早在汉武帝凿空西域时就开始了。到东汉灵帝时代(168—189年)，西域乐舞等曾在内地盛行一时。据《后汉书·五行志》载："灵帝好胡服、胡帐、胡床、胡坐、胡饭、胡箜篌、胡笛、胡舞，京都贵戚皆竟为之。"丝绸之路上的中外各民族之间的文化交流，在唐朝达到极盛的状态。京畿地区的长安、洛阳，丝路重镇的敦煌，不仅人员交往十分频繁、经济贸易空前繁荣，而且成为文化交融特征明显的国际都会城市。在文化交融上，最为当时人及后人津津乐道的便是体现在时尚、乐舞上的浓郁"胡气"。开元、天宝时期，体现大唐景象的"胡风唐韵"，更是充斥着宫廷民间，弥漫在都市边陲。著名文人元稹有几句诗形象地写出了当时这种风气之盛："女为胡妇学胡妆，伎进胡音务胡乐。""胡音胡骑与胡妆，五十年来竞纷泊。"(《和李校书新题乐府十二首·法曲》)在唐代敦煌这个各民族聚居的移民社会大舞台上，活跃着各色民族乐舞，而它们精彩纷呈的画面也必然反映到石窟壁画中来。

Ethnic minority dances from the Western Regions began to make their way into China's Central Plains during the reign of Emperor Wu (157 BC–87 BC) of the Han Dynasty. Under the reign of Emperor Ling (168–189) of the Eastern Han Dynasty, music and dance from the pastoral nomads of the Western Regions were flourishing. It was recorded in the *Book of Later Han: Records of Five Elements* that "Emperor Ling likes Hu clothing, Hu tents, Hu beds, Hu seats, Hu dinners, Hu *konghou,* Hu flute and Hu dance; all the nobles in the capital like them, too." The cultural exchange between the Chinese and these Western nomads on the Silk Road reached its peak in the Tang Dynasty. Personal communication became frequent, and commercial trade was thriving as never before in Chang'an, Luoyang, and Dunhuang. Cities emerged as international metropolises of distinctive cultural integration. People of that period and later took delight in talking about "Hu Style" reflected in fashion, music, and dance. During the Kaiyuan and Tianbao periods, the "Style of Hu and Charm of Tang reflected the prosperity of the period. It permeated the palaces and imperial court and spread to the urban areas. Various forms of performing arts were active in Dunhuang during the Tang Dynasty, and these were reflected in the mural images in the grottoes.

胡旋舞

Huxuan Dance

"胡旋"是唐代最为盛行的一种民族舞蹈,据史籍记载,因西域康国献胡旋女而传入中原。《旧唐书·音乐志》记载:宫廷燕乐九部、十部乐中的"康国乐,工人皂丝布头巾,绯丝布袍,锦领。舞二人,绯袄,锦领袖,绿绫浑裆袴,赤皮靴,白袴帑。舞急转如风,俗谓之胡旋。乐用笛二,正鼓一,和鼓一,铜钹一"。其实,康国属于"昭武九姓",原居地在河西走廊南侧的祁连山,后迁徙中亚,所以"胡旋"很可能是河西地区少数民族民间舞蹈融会了中亚乐舞而形成的。该舞最显著的特点是左旋右转,急速如风。因为唐玄宗时期的宠臣安禄山与爱妃杨玉环均擅长跳"胡旋",《旧唐书·安禄山传》说安"晚年益肥壮,腹垂过膝,重三百三十斤,每行以肩膊左右抬挽其身,方能移步。至

Huxuan dance (meaning"the Sogdian whirl") was one of the most popular ethnic dances in the Tang Dynasty. According to historical records, *Huxuan* dance came to the Central Plains of China when the Kang state, an ancient kingdam in the Western Regions, offered *Huxuan* dancing girls as a gift to the people of the Central Plains. According to *The Old Book of Tang: Treatises on Music*, "Musicians play Kangguo music in black silk headscarves and dark red silk gowns with brocaded collars. Two dancers wear dark red jackets with brocaded sleeves and collars, green damask silk trousers, red leather boots, and white knee-high hose. *Huxuan* dance demands dancers to whirl as quickly as the wind and hence the name. Two flutes, one main drum, a pair of brass cymbals, and one echo drum are used to play the music."The Kangju, called the Kang state by the Chinese, was one of the names of the Nine Zhaowu Clans, the prominent ethnic Sogdian families in China. They originally lived in the Qilian Mountains, south of the Hexi Corridor; they later relocated to Central Asia. As a result, it is highly possible that *Huxuan* dance originated from the combination of ethnic minority folk dances in the Hexi area and Central Asian musical dance. *Huxuan* dance's most obvious feature was that dancers whirled and spun quickly. During the reign of Emperor Xuanzong in

玄宗前，作胡旋舞，疾如风焉”。所以胡旋舞在当时最为畅行。白居易、元稹等都有题为《胡旋女》的诗篇传诵于世，尽管他们写此诗的本意是讽喻明皇喜好声色误国，导致了安史之乱，而诗中对“胡旋”的描述则为我们今天研究这种舞蹈提供了珍贵的资料。如白诗云：“胡旋女，胡旋女，心应弦，手应鼓。弦鼓一声双袖举，回雪飘飖转蓬舞。左旋右旋不知疲，千匝万周无已时。人间物类无可比，奔车轮缓旋风迟。”元诗云：“胡旋之义世莫知，胡旋之容我能传。蓬断霜根羊角疾，竿戴朱盘火轮炫。骊珠迸珥逐飞星，虹晕轻巾掣流电。潜鲸暗嗡笪波海，回风乱舞当空霰。万过其谁辨终始，四座安能分背面？”令今人欣喜的是，我们在敦煌莫高窟的

the Tang Dynasty, An Lushan, the leader of the later An Lushan Rebellion, and Yang Yuhuan, an imperial concubine, were both good at *Huxuan* dance. *The Old Book of Tang: Biography of An Lushan* said that An "was obese in his later years. He weighed over 165 kg and the flesh around his belly almost swung below his knees. He could not walk without two people's help. But when he was performing the *Huxuan* dance before Emperor Xuanzong, he flew like the wind." As a result of being in vogue among the nobles, *Huxuan* dance gained popularity. Both Bai Juyi (772–846) and Yuan Zhen (779–831) wrote poems titled "*Huxuan* Dancers". The original intention of these poems was to satirize the libertine Emperor Xuanzong, blaming him for the An Lushan Rebellion because he neglected government affairs. A serendipitous consequence is that their description of *Huxuan* dancing provides valuable reference sources for us. As Bai Juyi's poem stated, "*Huxuan* dancers, *Huxuan* dancers, they danced with music / Once musicians played their stringed instruments and the drum, *Huxuan* dancers raised their hands and whirled with their dresses puffed / They whirled and whirled tirelessly, as they would never stop / Nothing in the world could whirl as quickly, neither running wheels nor the whirlwind." Yuan Zhen likewise described in his poem, "Common people did not know much about *Huxuan* dancers, and let me tell you what they were like / They danced like the whirlwind, and they whirled like the fiery wheels / They danced as fastly as the shooting star, and they danced as lightly as the rainbow / Their dance was as powerful as a whale, which generated giant waves / They whirled ten thousand times and who knew when they would end / They whirled so quickly, but who

经变画中又看到了较诗句更为生动形象的胡旋舞图像。

在莫高窟第220窟盛唐时期所绘的大幅经变画中，既有动作相对缓慢的双人舞（可看作是胡旋的起始形象），又有特征明显的急速胡旋图（图62）。其南壁经变图

could see their faces clearly?" It is fortunate that we have discovered images of *Huxuan* dance, more vivid than these poems, in the sutra illustration paintings in Dunhuang.

In Mogao Cave 220, the sutra illustration painted during the High Tang Dynasty shows both a relatively slow dance for two people (which can be seen as an early prototype of *Huxuan* dance), and a fast *Huxuan* dance with

图62　双舞图（莫高窟第220窟）
Fig.62　*Huxuan* Dance for Two People (Mogao Cave 220)

下端中间,有两位身着裙衫的舞伎正侧向对舞,二人均做"吸腿"之姿单足站立于小圆毯上,双臂一上一下,挥动彩巾,十分对称。从飘带飞扬的动势及腿部姿势,可以想见正在做急速旋转前的准备动作。其北壁药师经变图下端,则绘有场面辉煌的胡旋舞图(图 63~ 图 65)——四位舞伎,分成文、武两组,都足踏小圆花毯翩翩起舞。左(西)边一对舞伎头梳武髻(或戴头盔,因画面有损难以确认),上身穿紧身戎服短装,下身着波浪形下摆的长裙,肩披绕背长巾,背向而舞;一腿后勾,脚掌翻上,踏毯一足的脚跟着力;一手抓巾用力上伸,一手握巾侧垂做"提襟"之姿。仿佛是古典戏剧里武将在急速舞动之后猛地立停准备做"亮相"的动作,透出一股英武之气。右(东)边一对舞伎梳多根发辫(似今日维吾尔

its typical characteristics (Fig.62). In the lower central area of the sutra painting on the south wall, two dancers in skirts dance together side by side. They dance in unison symmetrically. Both of them are standing on one leg on a small round rug, waving colorful silk sashes with one arm up and the other pressing down. The flying ribbons and their leg positions indicate that they are performing a series of quick dance turns. There is a splendid *Huxuan* dance picture on the bottom of the sutra illustration painting on the north wall of the same cave (Figs.63–65). There are four dancers in the painting. All of them are dancing gracefully on a small round rug. The pair of dancers on the left side have topknots similar to soldiers in ancient China, but it is also possible that they are wearing helmets. It is difficult to see clearly, because the painting is damaged. They wear vests or sleeveless jackets that appear similar to military armor of the period; their long skirts have wave-like fringe at the hems. With long ribbons on their shoulders and across their backs, they dance turned away from the viewer. They raise one leg behind the body with the sole upward, leaving the center of gravity on the heel of the other foot planted on the rug. They hold the ribbon with one hand high and another hand low beside the body. They look heroic, like generals in Chinese operas who suddenly stop to strike a dramatic pose after quick movements. Another pair of dancers on the right side of the painting are also dancing with backs partially turned. Just like modern Uyghur girls, they wear their hair in several braids. They each wear a mountain-style crown on the head, wearing only a white floor-length skirt for

图 63　胡旋舞图之一(莫高窟第 220 窟)

Fig.63　Image of *Huxuan* Dance, 1 (Mogao Cave 220)

族姑娘),戴山形冠,上身半裸,着白色曳地长裙,亦背向而舞;两臂平举,双足着毯,从舞巾的抛撒飞动之势,可以想见她们正在做急速的旋转,不禁让我们想起了元、白等诗人对胡旋女舞姿的描写,也印证了《新唐书·音乐志》中说"胡旋舞,舞者立球(毯)上,旋转如风"的记载。无论是武扮还是红妆,都说明这个舞蹈属

clothing. They hold their hands out flat and stand on the dance carpet. The undulating ribbons suggest quick whirling movements. Their attire, a mix of military and feminine, indicates that this is a kind of "vigorous dance."Two more points about this picture of *Huxuan* dance are noteworthy. One of them is the large scale of the orchestra. The ensemble includes 13 players with almost every kind of string and percussion instrument on either side. *The New Book of Tang: Treatises on Rites and Music* said that "Musicians from the state of Kang have one leading drum and one accompanying drum; two flutes and two brass cymbals. There are two

图 64　胡旋舞图之二(莫高窟第 220 窟摹本)

Fig.64　Image of *Huxuan* Dance, 2 (Replica of Mogao Cave 220)

于“健舞”一类。另外，这幅胡旋舞图还有两处值得关注：其一，伴奏乐队规模较大，两侧各有十三人的庞大乐队，管弦、鼓乐几乎一应俱全。《新唐书·音乐志》上讲“康国伎，有正鼓、和鼓，皆一；笛、铜钹，皆二。舞者二人”，而“龟兹伎，有弹筝、竖箜篌、琵琶、五弦、横笛、笙、箫、觱篥、答腊鼓、毛员鼓、都昙鼓、侯提鼓、鸡娄鼓、腰鼓、齐鼓、檐鼓、贝，皆一；铜钹二。舞者四人”。而壁画中的伴奏乐器更接近于后者。可见胡旋自康国传入中原后，又折回河西地区，自然又融合了“特善诸国”的龟兹乐舞。其二，舞场中央摆有五层灯台，舞者两侧又各置三层灯树，既造成了光芒耀眼的热烈气氛，又有照明的实际功用，两侧还各有两位添灯火的菩萨，也类似人间舞台上的负责灯光、场地的服务人员。如此盛大的乐舞场面，恐怕正是唐朝宫廷胡旋舞的特色。因为胡旋的主要特色——旋转如风——常常用飞动的巾帛表示，所以在前述敦煌壁画中的巾舞形象中，

performers dancing with music, ”while “Musicians from Kucha (Qiuci) have a Chinese zither, a *konghou*, a *pipa*, a banjo, a transverse flute, a *sheng*, a *xiao*, a *bili*, a *dala* drum, a *maoyuan* drum, a *doutan* drum, a *houti* drum, a *jilou* drum, a waist drum, a *qigu* drum, a *yangu* drum, a conch, and two brass cymbals (19 people in total). There are four performers dancing with music.” The accompanying instruments in this mural painting are more like the latter description. It can be observed that after being disseminated to the Chinese interior, *Huxuan* dance returned to the Hexi Corridor, where it naturally absorbed Qiuci dance, considered the best among all the ethnic dances. Another noteworthy observation is the lighting. There is a five-tiered candelabrum in the center of the stage and a three-tiered candelabrum on each side of the dancers. It helps to create an atmosphere for the dance, while at the same time providing the practical function of lighting. There are also two attendant bodhisattvas in charge of the candles on both sides of the stage, similar to stagehands responsible for lighting on a set. Such a spectacle of musical dance was supposedly a feature of *Huxuan* dance in the Tang imperial court. Since whirling, the main feature of this dance style, is mainly presented through long flying ribbons or sashes, people can also find *Huxuan* dancers among images of ribbon dancing in the murals discussed previously. In the Song Dynasty, *Huxuan* dance was still popular both at court and as a folk dance, with

图 65 胡旋舞图之三(莫高窟第 220 窟摹本)
Fig.65 Image of *Huxuan* Dance, 3 (Replica of Mogao Cave 220)

应该还能找到胡旋女的身影。胡旋舞到了宋代，应该仍然活跃在宫廷、民间，而且有了新的发展变化，如宋代词人贺铸的《换追风》词里就有这样的句子："掌上香罗六寸弓，雍容胡旋一盘中。"只是这种"掌上""盘中"的"追风胡旋"究竟是什么样子的，舞者又是何方人氏，今天已经难知其详了。

new developments and changes. For example, He Zhu (1052–1125), a Northern Song poet, wrote in the poem "On Exchanging Steeds", "... [a dancer] like a six-inch bow which can stand in the palm of the hand / She spins her *Huxuan* dance, as on a plate." However, it is difficult for us today to know exactly what "in the palm" or "on a plate" was supposed to look like, or who the dancer was.

胡腾舞

Huteng Dance

"胡腾"亦是唐代时自中亚昭武九姓的石国传入内地的民族舞蹈。此舞以左右跳跃腾踏为特征,故名,舞者多为男子。《全唐诗》中现存明确描述"胡腾舞"的诗歌有四首,其中两首对该舞舞者服饰、动作、气氛等的描写最为详细生动,不妨照录全诗如下:

石国胡儿人见少,蹲舞尊前急如鸟。织成蕃帽虚顶尖,细氎胡衫双袖小。手中抛下葡萄盏,西顾忽思乡路远。跳身转毂宝带鸣,弄脚缤纷锦靴软。四座无言皆瞪目,横笛琵琶遍头促。乱腾新毯雪朱毛,傍拂轻花下红烛。酒阑舞罢丝管绝,木槿花西见残月。(刘言史《王中丞宅夜观舞胡腾》)

胡腾身是凉州儿,肌肤如玉鼻如锥。桐布轻衫

Huteng dance ("leaping Hu dance") was another ethnic dance from Central Asia introduced to inland China during the Tang Dynasty. It was named after its feature of leaping and jumping movements. As it was an athletic dance, most *Huteng* dancers were male. There are four existing poems in *Complete Tang Poems* that clearly describe *Huteng* dance. Two of them in particular provide detailed and picturesque descriptions of *Huteng* dancers' attire, movements, and bearing. Tang poet Liu Yanshi (742–813), in his poem "Enjoying *Huteng* Dancing at Night in Official Wang's House" wrote,

"It was rare to see Hu people from the country of Shi, who danced as quickly as birds / The tops of their knitted hats were slightly pointed, and their shirts made of fine wool cloth had tight cuffs / Putting down the wine cups and looking to the west, how faraway their hometown was! / They jumped and twirled with jeweled belts rattling, they danced so quickly their brocaded boots wore out / Audiences were all watching silently, mesmerized by the rapid tunes of the flute and *pipa* / Their jumps shredded the carpet into pieces which flew like snow, and the red candles were snuffed as day broke / The wine was finished and the music and dancing had stopped, when the waning moon set in the west above the hibiscus."

Another poet Li Duan (743–782) in his poem "*Huteng* Dancers" wrote, "The *Huteng* dancer came

图 66　背身而舞的伎人(莫高窟第 98 窟北壁)

Fig.66　Image of a *Huteng* Dancer with His Back to the Viewer (North Wall, Mogao Cave 98)

前后卷，葡萄长带一边垂。帐前跪作本音语，拾襟搅袖为君舞。安西旧牧收泪看，洛下词人抄曲与。扬眉动目踏花毡，红汗交流珠帽偏。醉却东倾又西倒，双靴柔弱满灯前。环行急蹴皆应节，反手叉腰如却月。丝桐忽奏一曲终，呜呜画角城头发。胡腾儿，胡腾儿，故乡路断知不知？（李端《胡腾儿》）

可见该舞蹈程式中有急速蹲跳、环行腾踏、扬眉动目、反手叉腰等主要特征。根据这些特征，虽然我们在敦煌壁画中还没有寻见胡腾特征特别明显的舞伎图像，却也可以找到他们在佛教经变画中的踪影。例如莫高窟第 98 窟北壁、第 61 窟北壁有两位背身而舞的伎人（图 66、图 67），从面部特征与身材比例来看，似带有明显的阳刚之气，身体居于舞毯边缘，似正持巾带做腾踏环行的动作，这是五代时期所绘。再早一点，如莫高窟

from the Western Regions, who had fine, fair skin and a high-bridged nose / He wore a light shirt made of fine wool of sycamore flowers, with the grape-pattened belt hanging on the side/ He kneeled before the curtain and spoke his mother tongue before he lifted his coat and rolled up his sleeves and began to dance / The former governor of the Anxi Grand Protectorate tried to hold back his tears, and poets from Luoyang offered lyrics for him to play / He leaped and jumped on the tapestry with raising eyebrows and rolling eyes, while the sweat fell down from his forehead but his beaded hat hung askew / He swayed eastward and westward as if drunk, with his feet in soft boots moving lightly / Whether jumping or twirling, all his movements were made to the rhythm, and he rested the hands on the hips akimbo like a half moon / The dance suddenly stopped when a tune was played, and the horns were blown on the top of the city wall / *Huteng* dancer, *Huteng* dancer, didn't you know the way back home has been cut off ?"

It can be seen from the poems that *Huteng* dancers often leaped and jumped quickly while moving in circles, raised their eyebrows and rolled their eyes, put their hands akimbo, and so on. Those appear to be the main features of *Huteng* dance. We have not yet found images of *Huteng* dancers in the Dunhuang murals, but traces of them can still be observed in sutra illustration paintings. For example, two different dancers with their backs to the viewer on the north wall of Mogao Cave 98 and Cave 61 appear to have masculine facial features and figures (Figs. 66, 67). They hold ribbons as they bounce and jump at the edge of a dance tapestry. Both paintings

图 67　背身而舞的伎人(莫高窟第 61 窟北壁)

Fig.67　Image of a *Huteng* Dancer with His Back to the Viewer (North Wall, Mogao Cave 61)

图 68　舞伎(莫高窟第 286 窟南壁)
Fig.68　Dancer (South Wall, Mogao Cave 286)

第 286 窟南壁中唐时所绘舞伎(图 68),正在花毯边做腾踏动作,呈宝带飞卷、落英缤纷之势,虽然因是佛画未着蕃帽锦靴,上身所穿的束袖布衫也和其他舞伎不同。时代晚些的,如莫高窟第 308 窟前室西壁和榆林窟第 3 窟南壁西夏时期所绘的两位舞者,都体形健壮,在花毯上做东倾西侧的腾踏动作(图 69、图 70)。这表明当年画工在绘制佛教图像时,既揉进了现实生活中胡腾舞的姿态,也根据需要做了适当的改变。

were created during the Five Dynasties. Another painting created earlier during the Middle Tang on the south wall of Cave 286 shows a dancer bouncing at the edge of a dance mat with ribbons flying and petals falling (Fig.68). Since this is a Buddhist painting, the dancer wears neither Hu cap nor brocade boots. His shirt with tight cuffs is also different from other dancers. Murals created in later periods, like the one on the west wall of the front room of Mogao Cave 308, and another on the south wall of Yulin Cave 3, show two fit and strong dancers performing leaping movements as they lean to the left or right (Figs. 69, 70). This indicates that painters at that time made necessary and appropriate changes on the basis of original *Huteng* dance positions while painting Buddhist images.

图 69　舞者(榆林窟第 3 窟南壁摹本)
Fig.69　Dancer (Replica of South Wall, Yulin Cave 3)

图 70　舞者(莫高窟第 308 窟前室西壁摹本)
Fig.70　Dancer (Replica of West Wall, Mogao Cave 308)

柘枝舞

Zhezhi Dance(Mulberry Branch Dance)

“柘枝”也是从中亚石国(今塔什干一带)传来的民族舞蹈。据《全唐诗》中的佚名《柘枝词》的序语讲，柘枝可分为健舞(羽调柘枝)和软舞(商调柘枝)两类,一般是“用二女童，帽施金铃,抃转有声”,系双人对舞，到宋代发展成多人的队舞，居中间者称“花心”。服饰上也有变化，从头戴卷檐尖帽或绣花镶珠帽改为凤冠。唐人描写柘枝舞的诗歌甚多（仅大诗人白居易就有五首),从中亦可见其舞容、舞姿及舞服。写得最具体的是章孝标的《柘枝》:

柘枝初出鼓声招,花钿罗衫耸细腰。移步锦靴空绰约，迎风绣帽动飘飖。亚身踏节鸾形转，背面羞人凤影娇。只恐

Zhezhi dance (mulberry branch dance) also comes from the country of Shi in Central Asia (present-day Tashkent area, Uzbekistan). According to the preface to “Poem of *Zhezhi*” in *Complete Tang Poems*, *zhezhi* can be divided into “energetic dance” and “soft dance.”Generally, it consisted of “two girls wearing hats with golden bells, and clapping their hands while whirling.”At first it was a dance for two people, but it developed over time into group dances by the Song Dynasty. There were also changes in attire. Peaked hats with turned-up brims, or embroidered and beaded hats were replaced by crowns and coronets. Many Tang poets wrote about *zhezhi* dance—the great poet Bai Juyi wrote no less than five poems on the subject. People can also use these poems to study the make-up, attire, poses, positions, and movements of *zhezhi* dancers. Tang poet Zhang Xiaobiao (791-873), in his poem “On *Zhezhi*”, gave the most details about this dance:

“The *Zhezhi* dancer came onstage with drumbeats. She gyrated her slim waist wearing silk clothes and flower-shaped headwear / Her feet in brocaded boots, she gracefully took quick short steps while her embroidered hat wobbled in the wind / Lowering her body, she moved in a circle tapping the ground to the rhythm of the drums, while her slender back, when she turned around, looked so flirtatious / She was dancing so quickly as if she could fly into the sky, while the audience were still intoxicated by

相公看未足，便随风雨上青霄。

我们从唐诗中可知柘枝舞最重要的伴奏乐器是鼓，无论是大鼓、羯鼓，还是画鼓、蛮鼓，可统称“柘枝鼓”，其服饰最显眼的则是带金铃的绣帽、罗衫。我们在敦煌壁画里似乎还没有寻到特征明显的柘枝舞蹈图像，却同样可以在前面所介绍的双人巾舞、鼓舞及后面要介绍的莲花童子舞等形象中依稀看见它的影子。如敦煌西千佛洞第 15 窟北壁中央的乐舞画面（图 71），舞者击鼓腾踏的动作十分明显，似兼有胡腾、柘枝二舞的特征。又如前面所引的“用二女童，帽施金铃，抃转有声”，成为晚唐至宋初流行的“屈柘枝”舞的主要特征，而这个舞蹈的主要场景、道具为莲池、荷花，在敦煌经变画中也多有出现。如莫高窟第 320 窟南壁经变图中在莲花上的舞者，就有研究者认为也应该是柘枝舞的形象（图 72）。

her beauty! ”

From reading Tang poetry, we can see the most important musical instrument in *zhezhi* dance was the drum. These included the bass drum, *jiegu* drum (a drum used in ancient China), *huagu drum*, and the *mangu* drum (a large drum used in southern China). All these drums were collectively called *zhezhi* drums. The embroidered cap with a golden bell and the cambric shirt are the most noticeable clothing in *zhezhi* dance. Although we have not obtained any evidence of *zhezhi* dance in the Dunhuang murals, images of this dance can actually be found in the ribbon dance for two people and drum dance introduced in the previous section, and also the lotus boy dance introduced later. For example, in the central image on the north wall of Cave 15 in the Western Thousand-Buddha Caves, the dancer is clearly beating a drum and walking with legs held high, combining the features of *Huteng* dance and *zhezhi* dance together (Fig.71). Lily ponds and lotuses are the major stage settings and props for this dance. People can find many examples of it in Dunhuang sutra illustration paintings. For example, some scholars believe that in the sutra illustration painting on the south wall of Cave 320, the dancer is performing a *zhezhi* dance (Fig 72).

图 71　乐舞画面(敦煌西千佛洞第 15 窟北壁中央)

Fig.71　Musical Dance Scene (Center of North Wall, Cave 15, Western Thousand-Buddha Caves)

图 72　莲花上的柘枝舞(莫高窟第 320 窟南壁)

Fig.72　*Zhezhi* Dance on Lotus (South Wall, Mogao Cave 320)

“惊破霓裳羽衣曲”

“Raiment of Rainbows and Feathers”

《霓裳羽衣》是盛唐开元天宝年间最著名的乐舞。此舞来源，有不少传说，都与那位精于音律的风流天子唐玄宗李隆基有关，后来人们将传说与史实结合起来加以落实，如王建《霓裳辞》的诗注中说：“罗公远多秘术，尝与明皇至月宫，仙女数百，皆素练霓衣，舞于广庭，问其曲，曰‘霓裳羽衣’。帝晓音律，因默记其音调。及归，但记其半。会西凉府节度杨敬述进婆罗门曲，声调相符，遂以月中所闻为散序，敬述所进为曲，而名‘霓裳羽衣’。”史载此曲有十二遍之多。可见《霓裳羽衣》是融合了中原与西域舞乐，经唐玄宗亲自改制的大型法曲乐舞，用白居易《法曲歌》中的诗句来概括，就是“法曲舞霓裳”“法曲合夷歌”。它的舞蹈特

“Raiment of Rainbows and Feathers” was the most famous musical dance during the Kaiyuan and Tianbao periods of the Tang Dynasty. There are many legends about the origin of this dance, many of which are associated with the Emperor Xuanzong (personal name Li Longji), who was musically talented. The legends later merged with historical records. For example, Tang poet Wang Jian (768–830) wrote in the notes to his poem “Raiment of Rainbows”: “Luo Gongyuan was a mystic. He has been to the Moon Palace with Emperor Li Longji. There were hundreds of celestial fairies dancing there. Luo asked them the name of the music they danced to, and the fairies told him it was called ‘Raiment of Rainbows and Feathers’. The emperor was good at music, and memorized the melody of it. When he returned, the Emperor could only remember half of the notes. At this moment, Yang Jingshu, the military governor of Xiliang Prefecture offered him a Brahmin tune, which was similar to the one the Emperor has memorized. Then Li Longji ordered the music they heard in the Moon Palace as the prelude, and the one Yang offered as the main stanza, and the two were put together and named ‘Raiment of Rainbows and Feathers.’” According to historical records, this music consisted of 12 repeated parts. “Raiment of Rainbows and Feathers” combined the musical dance of both the

点，应该是在融会华夷之曲的大型乐队的伴奏下，人数众多的舞伎身着鲜丽缤纷的霓裳(“羽衣”则是强调其仙人身份，可有象征性的“翅膀”，但并非一定是插上羽毛)，翩翩起舞。据说杨贵妃及其侍儿张云容等表演过独舞、双人舞的《霓裳羽衣》，恐怕只是特例而已。另外，据《新唐书·礼乐志》说：“凡曲终必遽，唯《霓裳羽衣》将毕，引声益缓。”这种尾声缓长的大型舞曲，正好符合了颂扬歌舞升平盛世的需要。

既然如此，那么为什么舞蹈史研究专家至今未在敦煌壁画中找出明确为《霓裳羽衣》舞的图像来呢？对此，有两种并不成熟的推测。其一，天宝后期爆发安史之乱，唐王朝自此走向衰落，许多人归咎于唐明皇的喜好声色，归咎于杨玉环的“红颜祸水”，乃至归咎于“胡夷之声乱华”，所谓“渔阳鼙鼓动地来，惊破霓裳羽衣曲”(白居易《长恨歌》)，于是胡旋、霓裳等舞蹈也受到牵连而逐渐

Central Plains and the Western Regions. Its significant feature was that a large number of dancers wore colorful rainbow-colored costumes. The phrase “raiment of rainbows and feathers” is a reference to the immortals in Chinese mythology and the clothes they wore. It does not mean that the dance costumes were actually made of feathers. It is said that Yang Guifei, a famous imperial concubine in the Tang Dynasty, and her servants performed “Raiment of Rainbows and Feathers” both as a solo dance and a two-person dance, but it was most likely just a special performance. In addition, according to the *New Book of Tang: Treatises on Rites and Music*, “All the songs speed up at the end, but ‘Raiment of Rainbows and Feathers’ ends slowly.” This sort of slow ending for a full-length dance conformed to the demands of extolling life in peacetime.

However, why have dance history researchers not yet found any clear images of “Raiment of Rainbows and Feathers” in Dunhuang art? There are two theories regarding this, neither of which can be verified. The first one is that after the An Lushan Rebellion, the Tang Dynasty was on the verge of collapse. Many people blamed Emperor Xuanzong (Li Longji) for his love of music and aesthetics instead of politics; many also regarded Yang Guifei as a femme fatale. Many people even blamed foreign songs for bringing chaos to China. Tang poet Bai Juyi in his poem “Song of Everlasting Regret” wrote, “As the Hu army invaded us, we heard the enemy’s drum, which suddenly interrupting

衰微。这样,它们便不易在壁画中得到表现。其二,霓裳羽衣与别的舞蹈不同,场面宏伟辉煌,文宗时期的霓裳羽衣舞更是舞者成群,乐队庞大,很难在壁画中描绘出来;而传说中又与道士、仙乐有关,也难以在佛画中表现。其实,我们认为第一种推测虽有一定道理,却不尽然,因为一直到唐文宗、宣宗时期,该舞蹈还是因皇帝的青睐而不断在宫廷宴乐中表演,所以白居易的《霓裳羽衣歌》云:"我昔元和侍宪皇,曾陪内宴宴昭阳。千歌百舞不可数,就中最爱霓裳舞。"第二种推测应该比较符合实际。即便如此,在数以百计的唐代舞蹈图像中,尤其是在敦煌舞伎色彩斑斓的服饰上,还是处处可以看到宫廷霓裳的吉光片羽。例如莫高窟第12窟南壁所绘晚唐时期的独舞舞伎,不仅服饰华丽,而且衣裙间露出翼状装饰(图73);又如第205窟所绘两位正侧相对、缓步慢舞的舞

the tune of 'Raiment of Rainbows and Feathers'." As a result, the dances such as the *Huxuan* dance and "Raiment of Rainbows and Feathers" began to fade out gradually. Thus, it is not easy to find an image of it in any Dunhuang murals. The second theory is that "Raiment of Rainbows and Feathers" is simply too large-scale with too many dancers and orchestra members, making it difficult to fit onto a mural. It is also associated with Taoist priest and its related music, so it can hardly be shown in Buddhist paintings because of religious grounds. Actually, although there is some truth to the first theory, the argument is not completely valid, because "Raiment of Rainbows and Feathers" was popular and performed continuously in court up until the reigns of the emperors Wenzong and Xuanzong of Tang Dynasty due to royal patronage. As Bai Juyi wrote in the poem "Song of Raiment of Rainbows and Feathers," "I have accompanied the Emperor enjoying so many feasts / Among thousands of dances and concerts have I seen, the best of which was 'Raiment of Rainbows and Feathers'." The second theory seems more plausible. Even so, people can find highly treasured remnants of "Raiment of Rainbows and Feathers" in dance garments of the Tang Dynasty, especially in the images at Dunhuang. For example, we can see the image of a solo dancer from the Late Tang period on the south wall of Mogao Cave 12. The dancer not only has magnificent garments, but also wing-like decorations on her dress (Fig.73). Then there is the image of two dancers on the wall of Cave 205.

图 73　晚唐时期的独舞舞伎(莫高窟第 12 窟南壁)
Fig.73　Solo Dancer from Late Tang Dynasty (South Wall, Mogao Cave 12)

图 74　胡旋舞图(莫高窟第 220 窟摹本)

Fig.74　*Huxuan* Dance (Replica of Mogao Cave 220)

伎(见前图 16),画面经临摹者细心描绘复原,色彩十分鲜丽夺目。这些都使我们想到了霓裳羽衣的丰采。由于许多壁画图像色彩经千年的剥蚀氧化变得较难确认,以往的舞蹈研究者对敦煌壁画舞伎形象服饰缺乏细致入微的分析,漏失了一些珍贵的信息。现在,有的研究者已经开始弥补这方面的缺失,从纺织技术及服装设计等角度致力于敦煌舞伎服饰的复原研究。

One dancer faces another dancer's side with slow dance steps (Fig.16). The details are clear after careful work by the line artist. All these things remind us of the dazzling style of "Raiment of Rainbows and Feathers". Many wall paintings have become difficult to identify because of long years of deterioration and oxidation. Much valuable information has been lost, but some researchers are now trying to fill this gap. They are committed to the study of recovering and reconstructing Dunhuang dance garments from the perspective of textile technology and costume design.

稚气伴欢颜
生动活泼的童子舞姿

Cherubic Smiling Faces: Dance Poses of Children

“化生”为佛教中“四生”(胎生、卵生、湿生、化生)之一,即“莲花(华)生”,因化生者均做童稚形象,故称“化生童子”。佛教经变画中的化生童子往往做嬉戏舞蹈的姿态或手持各种乐器,研究者即取名为“化生乐伎”并列入舞蹈形象的研究范围之内。当然,敦煌壁画里的童子舞蹈并不只限于莲花童子,在百戏杂技与嬉戏图中也不乏他们天真可爱的身影,成为我们今天研究佛教图像和古代实际生活的生动资料。

In traditional Buddhist thought there are four forms of birth for all living beings: birth from wombs (*taisheng*), birth from eggs (*luansheng*), birth from moisture (*shisheng*), and birth by miraculous spontaneous materialization (*huasheng*; Sanskrit: upapkrit:). In Chinese, *huasheng* is sometimes also called "birth from lotuses," and includes various divine beings. The lotus has long been a sacred symbol in Buddhism. In Chinese Mahayana Buddhist iconography, images of those born from materialization usually appear as young children, referred to as "*huasheng* children," or "lotus children." In sutra illustration paintings, these cherubic children also appear playing or dancing, with musical instruments in hand. Because of this, there is the additional category of "*huasheng* performers," or "*huasheng* dancers." Their images are now being researched as sources of dance and choreography. Without doubt, images of *huasheng* dancers in Dunhuang murals outnumber those of lotus boys. People can also find images of lotus boys doing acrobatics. All of these images provide essential material for research into Buddhism as well as the daily lives of ancient people.

莲花童子舞
Lotus Child Dance

莲花童子在壁画里主要描绘在经变画的莲花上或莲池中，也有画在装饰佛龛两侧的莲纹图案上的。这些童子或赤裸全身，或只戴肚兜，或兼有肚兜、短裤，一个个憨态可掬，动作稚朴，不禁让人们联想起唐代花蕊夫人《宫词》中的诗句："旋折荷花伴歌舞，夕阳斜照满衣红。"

莫高窟第 329 窟（图 75）佛龛左右侧各饰有竖形莲花纹图案，图中童子均单腿立足踏于莲花之上，另一腿做或踢、或抬、或踏、或扬的各种动作。他们圆胖敦实，有的系围嘴，有的戴肚兜，双手举莲花、托莲苞、抚莲蕾，既活泼可爱，又具舞蹈之美。莫高窟第 14 窟南北二壁晚唐时代的如意轮观音图中均有莲池舞童画面，南壁左右二童子分立池中，臂挽巾带，戴项

In the Dunhuang murals, lotus children can appear standing on individual lotus flowers, or among a lotus patch or lotus pool; they also appear on lotus designs in Buddha niches. These children usually appear naked or wearing minimal clothing, such as the *dudou* —a Chinese garment similar in appearance to a bib—or shorts resembling a *dhoti*. They are charming and adorable. It brings to mind the lines of "Palace Lyrics" by concubine and notable Tang poet Madame Huarui (883 - 926): "[The maids are] singing and dancing with lotuses in their hand, with their clothes turning red in the setting sunlight."

In the painting decorating both sides of the Buddha niche in Mogao Cave 329, lotus boys stand single-legged on top of giant lotus flowers, with the other foot kicking, lifting, raising, or treading (Fig.75). They are chubby and stocky. They each wear a sleeveless *dudou* (bib-like garments), as they hold or touch the lotus flowers and stalks. People can see another image of lotus childen performers in a mural from the Late Tang depicting the Avalokitesvara Bodhisattva in Cave 14 (not pictured). On the south wall, two children stand on both sides of the pool, with broad silk sashes around their arms, wearing necklaces, armlet, bracelets, *dudou* and dhotis, as they lift their palms and lunge slightly. Their dance poses form a delightful contrast with the lotuses. On the north

图 75　佛龛左右侧竖形莲花纹图案上的童子舞(莫高窟第 329 窟)
Fig.75　Lotus Children Dancing in a Lotus Patch (Both Sides of Niche, Mogao Cave 329)

圈、臂环、腕镯，着肚兜、短裤，扬首蹬弓步，一手托掌，一手叉腰，摆出造型舞姿，与碧池中的荷花相映成趣。北壁左右二童子则做双臂上扬的对称动作，与池中腾涌而起的水花合拍而舞(图 76)。莫高窟第 285 窟西壁龛楣上有绘于西魏时期的一组化生童子伎乐(图 77)，均总角裸体，出于莲花之中，或吹奏乐器，或合掌拜舞，姿态优雅，使我们看到了早期的童子舞蹈形态。

榆林窟第 15 窟南北两壁所绘的莲花童子则是宋代的作品(图 78、图

wall of the same cave, two boys hold their arms up, dancing amongst lotus flowers and fountains of water (Fig.76). In Cave 285, there are more images of lotus boys on the lintel of the niche, located on the west wall (Fig.77). Some play musical instruments such as the *pipa*, while others dance with clasped hands, displaying elegant poses.

There are painted images of lotus children on both the north and south walls in Yulin Cave 15, constructed during the Song Dynasty (Figs.78, 79). Naked, the children dance on one leg on top of lotuses, displaying various poses

图 76 莲池舞童画面(莫高窟第 14 窟北壁)
Fig.76 Lotus Children Dancing in a Pool of Lotuses (North Wall, Mogao Cave 14)

图 77　龛楣上化生童子伎乐(莫高窟第 285 窟西壁)

Fig.77　Lotus Dancers on Niche Lintel (West Wall, Mogao Cave 285)

79),这些童子均赤裸全身,单足立莲花上做各种舞蹈动作,或手持莲花、花蕾,或握拳扬手,虽童趣天真,姿态不免呆板,也说明了宋代敦煌壁画在技法上的呆滞。当然,莫高窟第 400 窟的壁画中也有莲花童子伎乐,形象就略为生动一

and movements. Some hold lotuses or flower buds while others clench their fists or raise their hands. Though childlike and innocent, they seem a bit dull, which reveals the deterioration in artistic quality during the Song period. The image of the lotus children dancing in the mural from Mogao Cave 400 is much more dynamic. By contrast, on the proper left side of the south wall in Yulin Cave 25, there

些。可以与此做对比的是榆林窟第25窟南壁西侧经变画里有几对赤身裸体的莲花童子嬉水画面，其中有一对童子，一人跪坐于荷叶之上，右手下指；另一人在水中站立，双手摆弄荷叶。另一对童子则在池中嬉戏，一人正倒栽在水中做翻滚动作，臀部朝上；另一人左足站水中，右腿抬起，双臂上举合掌，使人们联想起花毯之上舞伎的优美姿态。25窟的经变画绘于唐代，在人物的描绘上显然要比15窟的宋代画作生动活泼得多。又，莫高窟第

are images of several naked lotus boys playing in the water. Among them, one of a pair kneels on a lotus leaf with right hand pointing to his companion who is standing in the water, moving the lotus leaf back and forth with two hands. In another pair, one boy dives headfirst into the water, making a rolling motion, while his playmate stands in the water at his left foot, with his right leg lifted, raising hands up and putting palms together in *añjali*, reminding us of the elegant dancers on the dance mat. The above images of lotus children in Mogao Cave 25 were painted during the Tang Dynasty, and are more vivid and dynamic than those in Mogao Cave 15 from the Song Dynasty. In addition,

图78　莲花童子形象之一(榆林窟第15窟)
Fig.78　Lotus Dancer, 1 (Yulin Cave 15)

图79　莲花童子形象之二(榆林窟第15窟)
Fig.79　Lotus Dancer, 2 (Yulin Cave 15)

172窟有一身从莲池中跃出冲天起舞的童子，也给观者留下了深刻的印象(图80)。

榆林窟第12窟前室西壁“梵天帝释赴会图”中的“云端莲花童子乐舞”画面(图81)颇为特别：在一朵飘飞天际的祥云上，有几位天真可爱的童子乐伎。两个仅着肚兜、腰裙，跪坐于莲花之中，左侧一位吹筚篥，右侧者打拍板；另一位着长袖大翻领衫、短

in Mogao Cave 172, there is an image of a lotus child leaping out of a lotus pool as he dances, making a stronger impression on the viewer (Fig.80).

The mural *Brahma and Indra Attending the Buddha's Sermon* in Yulin Cave 12 is a rather special painting with images of lotus boy musicians and dancers (Fig.81). There are several lovely child performers on a flying cloud; two of them wear short tunics and kneel on lotuses. The boy on the left side of the painting plays a *bili* pipe and the one on the right wooden clappers. Another

图80　经变画中莲花童子飞天(莫高窟第172窟)

Fig.80　Flying Lotus Child *Apsara* in Sutra Illustration Painting (Mogao Cave 172)

裙，单足站立于莲花之上扬袖而舞，其舞姿使我们想起了汉代风行的“袖舞”。最有意思的是童子的额头上均贴有翼状饰物,不知其有何用途或含意。这幅展示佛天情景的图画却充满了世俗的生活情趣。可惜我们这里只能展示它的临摹图,服饰等都经过了临摹者的加工与再创造,与原图已不尽相同。

boy wears a long-sleeved costume with turned -down collar and a short *dhoti*. He stands on a lotus flower on one leg and dances, waving his sleeves. The wing-like designs on the children's foreheads present an intriguing motif. Their purpose and meaning are unclear. This section of the mural reflects the delights of the secular, mortal world. Unfortunately, we can only present a line drawing facsimile here, due to deterioration of the original work.

图 81　云端莲花童子乐舞画面(榆林窟第 12 窟前室西壁摹本)
Fig.81　Lotus Child Dancing on Flying Clouds (Replica of West Wall, Yulin Cave 12)

百戏童子舞

Child Acrobat Dance

自汉代以来"童子杂耍"就是"角抵百戏"里的重要内容,是融会乐舞杂技的综合性表演项目。敦煌壁画中的百戏童子舞蹈,虽然出现在经变画中,也显然是民间或宫廷歌舞百戏的反映。莫高窟第361窟南壁的乐舞场面中即在中央舞毯边缘描绘了六个生动活泼的百戏舞童(图82):中间两

Since the Han Dynasty, child acrobats were an important part of acrobatic performances, usually combining musical dance, tumbling, and juggling. Although these child acrobats were shown in Buddhist sutra paintings, they actually reflect folk street acrobatics and court performances. In the mural located on the south wall of Mogao Cave 361, six naked child acrobats can be seen on the margins

图82 乐舞场面的百戏舞童(莫高窟第361窟南壁摹本)

Fig.82 Acrobatic Dance in Sutra Illustration Painting (Replica of South Wall, Mogao Cave 361)

童子，一人反身下腰，另一人单足站立于反身者腹上，另一足及双手耍盘；两侧各有两人做倒立、扬手等舞蹈动作。虽然细节因画面的褪色已经辨认不清，经画家临摹后，人物的轮廓姿态仍旧栩栩如生，留给我们充分的想象空间。

of the central dance carpet (Fig.82). Two of the children, on each end, perform handstands. The boy in the center balances and juggles three plates with his hands and feet while standing on the stomach of a child doing a backbend. The two others perform dance movements, swinging their arms in rhythm. The composition forms a triangular or pyramid shape overall. Though the details are blurred due to fading and wear, the line drawing facsimile still presents an outline of these lively figures and their movements, while leaving some blank space for the imagination.

火宅童子舞

Children Dancing in the Burning House

敦煌经变画中根据《法华经》的“火宅喻”品宣扬佛教的出世思想，描绘某富人住宅着大火，而“诸子等于火宅内乐著嬉戏，不觉不知，不惊不怖”，身陷大火，仍作乐不止的场景，因而有儿童歌舞的画面。这些舞蹈形象，取材于现实生活，儿童们身着民间服装，跳的也应该是日常生活里的即兴舞蹈。

莫高窟第 449 窟南壁《法华经变》中有一中唐时期的“火宅童子舞”画面，在用夸张而简洁的手法表现的火宅内，有一群着各色世俗装的小儿正在挥舞长袖，做腾跳、蹲、跪等各种舞姿。限于水平，笔者仅临摹出其中一位舞童的形象供读者观看（图 83）。研究者认为这些颇似胡腾舞的动作，与中亚石国少儿善此舞有关。莫高窟第 154 窟南壁也有一幅火宅舞图（图 84），只是舞者系一

The parable of the burning house comes from the *Lotus Sutra* (*Saddharma Puṇḍarīka Sutra*), a key religious text in Mahayana Buddhism. In the parable, children play and dance heedlessly inside the house of a rich man, unaware that the house is on fire. The images of the dancing figures in Dunhuang murals are based on the real life of the times. The children are all dressed in folk costumes, showing the style of dance in daily life.

On the south wall of Mogao Cave 449, there are paintings illustrating the *Lotus Sutra* that were created during the Middle Tang. One of these depicts the parable of the burning house in a bold and concise style. The children in the burning house wear different colorful long-sleeved costumes, performing various dance movements such as leaping and springing up, crouching down, and kneeling. A line drawing reproduces the image of one of the children (Fig.83). Researchers believe these movements are similar to those used in *Huteng* dance from Central Asia, discussed in the previous chapter. On the south wall of Cave 154 in Dunhuang, there is also a painting representing the burning house parable (Fig. 84). There is a single figure of a dancing youth dressed in Hu tribal clothing. He waves his long sleeves and stomps his feet, accompanied

胡装的青年，正在两乐工的伴奏下踏靴挥长袖而舞，这恐怕是画工自己离开佛经原典的即兴创作。

by two musicians. It is an unconventional creation by the artist, inspired by the parable from the *Lotus Sutra*.

图 83 《法华经变》中的火宅童子舞画面（莫高窟第 449 窟南壁摹本）
Fig.83 Scene of Boy Dancing in the Burning House in *Lotus Sutra* Illustration
（Replica of South Wall, Mogao Cave 449）

图 84　火宅舞图(莫高窟第 154 窟南壁)

Fig.84　Children Dancing in the Burning House (South Wall, Mogao Cave 154)

萧管霓裳：敦煌乐舞

Raiment of Rainbows and Feathers: Music and Dance from the Dunhuang Murals

多元荟萃，植根中华
敦煌乐舞的文化特征

Culturally Diverse Yet Rooted in Chinese History: Features of Dunhuang Dance

我们从前面各章的简略介绍和分析可以得知，敦煌石窟佛教内容壁画中所表现的各地区、各民族、各时期的舞乐，都带有本地区、本民族以及某个特定历史时期的文化特征。因为任何宗教，都要努力采用当时、当地人民喜闻乐见的方式来传播，争取信徒，所以，也必然采取各地人民的传统艺术为其服务。这就形成了世界各地的佛教艺术，创造了包括佛教舞蹈在内的各自不同风格的佛教文化。

因此，敦煌佛窟中的舞蹈壁画，也是随着时代的变迁，地域及民族传统文化的不同而显示出各自不同的风格与审美特征。早期敦煌舞蹈壁画，无论舞姿或服饰都带有不少印度、尼泊尔风韵，

Based on the introduction and analysis in previous chapters, readers could know that the Buddhist murals at Dunhuang have their own cultural features reflecting different peoples, regions, and times. This is largely because any religion that attempts to recruit more followers has to tailor its teachings to popular tastes of the times, giving rise to various regional art traditions serving that purpose. This has resulted in tremendous differences in Buddhist art styles around the world, including Buddhist dance.

The same can be said with the artistic styles at Dunhuang. As time passed, there emerged huge differences among regional cultural traditions, hence these diversified aesthetic tastes and artistic styles are reflected in Dunhuang paintings and sculptures. In the earliest murals, there existed a strong Indian and Nepali influence on dance positions and costumes, as well as traces of the tough, wild spirit of the pastoral nomads from the north. Later there was considerable cultural influence

同时又显示出北方游牧民族的强悍精神。随着时间的推移，中原“汉风”慢慢浸润其中。到了中期的隋唐时代，在显示多元舞蹈因素的同时，新的隋唐舞风逐渐形成并占据重要地位。如隋唐敦煌壁画中的飞天、伎乐天，都身披肩绕长长的巾带，长巾成了飞天翱翔云间的翅膀，形成了变化万千的美妙舞姿，千百年来，令世人赞叹不已。中原传统的继承和发展，北方和西域、南亚乐舞内容与风格的传入和影响，不断孕育出创新的因素，逐渐形成了多元荟萃兼容的文化特征。

from the Han people who came from the Central Plains surrounding the Yellow River. During the Sui and Tang dynasties, the already multi-ethnic dance murals took on new characteristics of the time, which had a significant impact on Dunhuang art. One of these new elements was the flying *apsara* holding music instruments, with narrow shawls or broad silk sashes on their shoulders and arms. The long silk sashes are like wings for these celestial maidens so that they can fly in the sky. In addition, the sashes enhance the aesthetics of the various dance movements, making this style of art appreciated around the world. The inheritance and development of traditions from the Han Chinese, as well as the influence and integration of styles from the north, the Western Regions, as well as South Asia contributed to the formation of a diverse cultural phenomenon.

汉风胡韵，源远流长

History of Han and Hu Cultural Integration

我国中原地区的乐舞，本来就有其悠久的历史文化渊源。例如前面介绍的唐代丰富多彩的巾舞，就可以追溯到三千多年前。早在公元前11世纪立国的周代，在其创立的“雅乐(舞)”体系中，就有教育国子(贵族子弟)的《六小舞》,《六小舞》中的《帗舞》执五彩缯而舞，这大概是古巾舞、今长绸舞的源头。据《隋书·音乐志》记载：“始开皇初定令，置‘七部乐’……其后牛弘请存鞞、铎、巾、拂四舞……因称：‘四舞’按汉魏以来，并施于宴飨。”(中华书局1973年版，第二册，377页）可见在公元前3世纪初至公元3世纪的汉魏时代，巾舞已正式用于宴飨。留存至今的汉代画像石中，更有大量巾舞的生动画面。如四川杨子山汉墓出土的一块百戏画像砖(图85)，一女舞者头梳双髻，身穿短衣及镶边

Music and dance in China enjoy a long history. The ribbon dance, so popular in the Tang Dynasty, can be traced back to over 3,000 years ago. In as early as the Zhou Dynasty, established in the 11th century BC, a ceremonial musical dance system called *yayue* came into existence. It consisted of the six minor dances for teaching nobles in small-scale rituals, which included the embroidered cape dance. This ritual dance most likely is the origin of the Tang ribbon dance. According to *The Book of Sui: Treaties on Music:* "In the beginning, the Emperor approved the *Seven Books of Music*... Then Niu Hong proposed the four types of dance performed respectively with a drum, large bell, broad silk ribbon and whisk... Ever since the Han and Wei dynasties the four types of dances were popular at banquets."So people can deduce that roughly between the 3rd century BC and the 3rd century AD, dances with broad silk sashes or ribbons were part of official banquet entertainment at court. On stone relief portraits excavated from Han Dynasty tombs and other architecture, there are figures reflecting this kind of dance. For example, on the stone relief portrait of acrobats discovered in a tomb from the Han Dynasty from Yangzi Mountain, Sichuan Province, a female dancer with hair in two topknots is waving long

长裤，双手舞长巾，横飘空中。手握的一端，明显包有短棍，这样舞起来既省力，又便于舞出一些难度较大的绸花。女舞者身后，有一蹲步而行，形象滑稽的男舞者，似在追逐舞巾女子。另一幅山东安丘汉墓出土

ribbons with both hands (Fig.85). Following her movements, the ribbons are flying in the air. It is clear that there is a stick attached to each of the ribbons. This design makes it easier for the dancer to maintain better control of the ribbon to present complex undulating movements. Next to the female dancer, to the viewer's left, a male performer is crouching behind her in an amusing way, as if he is pursuing her. On another stone relief image of

图 85 四川杨子山汉墓出土的汉百戏画像砖拓本

Fig.85 Han Dynasty Stone Relief Portrait of Ribbon Dance Excavated from a Tomb at Yangzi Mountain, Sichuan Province

的男子舞巾画像砖（图86），画像舞姿豪健洒脱，舞者脚踏一鼓，双臂飞舞菱纹长巾，甩展两侧。从巾与人身高的比例看，约有两丈长，长绸舞起来在空际萦绕卷扬，变幻莫

acrobatics discovered in a tomb from the Han Dynasty in Anqiu, Shandong Province, the male dancer to the viewer's right center performs in a bold and masculine way (Fig.86). With one foot on a drum, he waves a long silk ribbon, holding it by the middle section. Based on the proportion of the dancer and the ribbons, the probable length of the ribbon is two *zhang* (about 6.6 meters). The ribbon

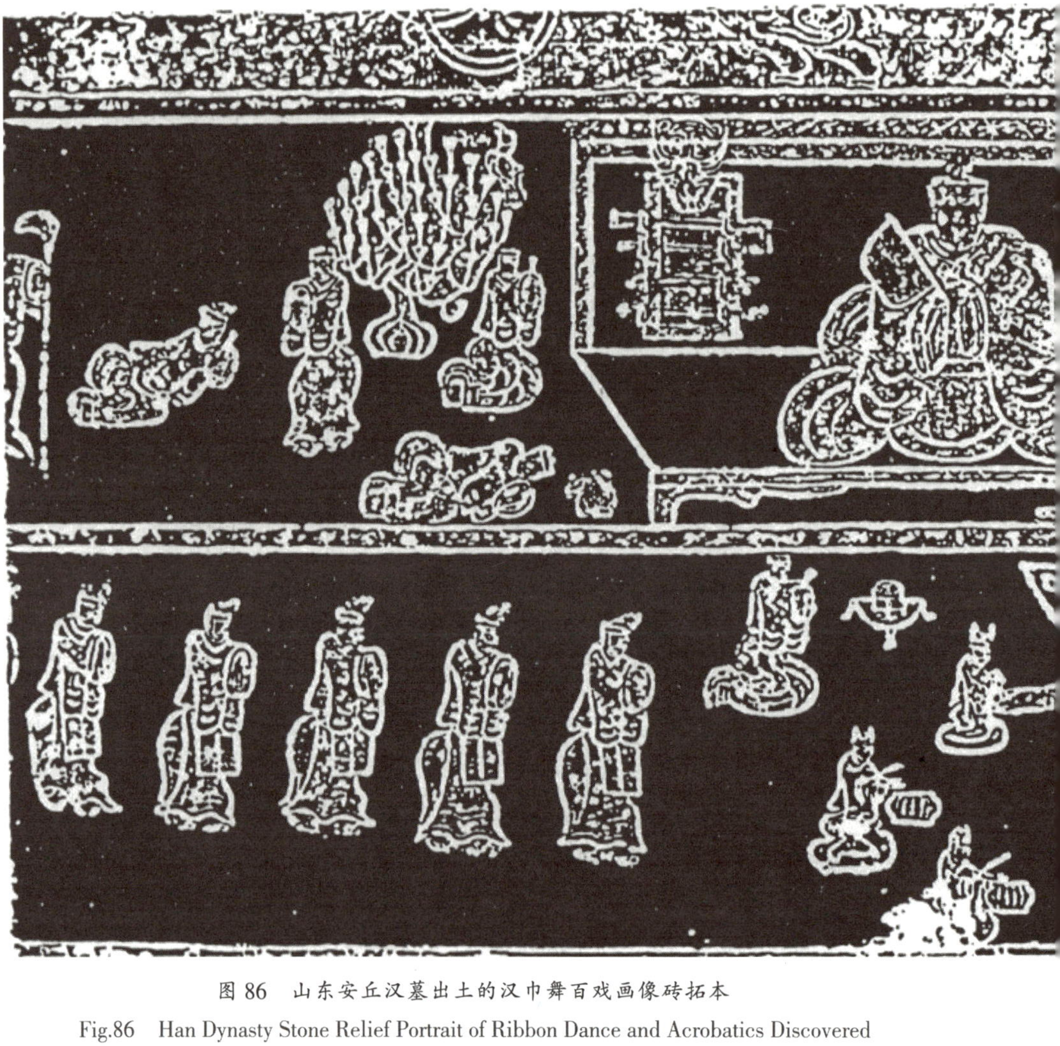

图 86　山东安丘汉墓出土的汉巾舞百戏画像砖拓本

Fig.86　Han Dynasty Stone Relief Portrait of Ribbon Dance and Acrobatics Discovered at a Tomb in Anqiu, Shandong Province

测，如风卷流云，似炊烟袅袅。也许正是由于这种视觉效果，启示莫高窟的画工们也给神佛世界的舞蹈之神披上了长长的绸带，轻盈飘逸，美丽多姿。这是佛教艺术在中国

flutters, curls, and spirals in the air, moving like clouds flowing with the wind or smoke curling up to the sky. Inspired by these types of visual images, the painters of Dunhuang brought these long ribbons into the world of gods and Buddhas, creating a sense of sprightly elegance and breathtaking beauty. This creation of Buddhist art is unique to China, rooted deeply in the ribbon dance of its ancient history.

传播过程中，中国艺术家的独特创造。而这一创造的灵感，很可能来自生活中源远流长的巾舞。时至今日，中国舞蹈家们已运用这种独特的舞蹈形式，创作出了《飞天》《红绸舞》等舞蹈，戏曲《天女散花》等，并在国际比赛中获奖。

又如敦煌舞蹈壁画中，常常出现类似“顺风旗”“提襟”“端腿”“托掌”“按掌”等舞姿，这些舞蹈造型，也应该是在中原地区漫长的舞蹈实践的过程中创作并固定成型的。它们既在汉代画像砖上频繁出现，又仍然是今日古典戏曲舞中的常用动作，均具有浓郁的中华舞风。

另外，壁画里的一些伎乐天舞者，巾带低垂，柔曼温婉，低眉蹲身，亦饱含中原含蓄典雅的汉风。榆林窟19窟出现了甩舞长袖的伎乐天，与一执琵琶舞蹈的舞者对舞。其甩袖而舞的舞姿及头妆的样式均与戏曲舞者相似。它的出现距戏曲兴起的宋代不远，当不是偶然的巧

Even today, Chinese dancers and choreographers still find inspiration in this traditional art, which can be seen in several recent dance works that have won international dancing competitions, including “Flying *Apsaras*”, “The Red Silk Dance”, and “Heavenly Beauties Scattering Flowers.”

Also, among Dunhuang murals people can see the presence of numerous choreographic movements, such as “*shunfengqi*” (fluttering the flag), “pulling the lapels,” “straightening the leg,” “lifting the palm upward,” and “pressing the palm downward,” all of which originated in dance performances in the Central Plains. Such distinctively Chinese dance moves are often observed on tomb art from the Han Dynasty, and can even be seen in traditional dance performances performed today.

In addition, the celestial musicians and dancers on the mural walls always present soft and gentle gestures, lowering their gaze, wearing loose silk sashes and flowing clothes, which reflects the elegance of the Han civilization. The heavenly performer painted in Cave 19, at the nearby Yulin Caves, wears long sleeves, and next to her is another dancer holding a *pipa*. Her dance movements and the way she wears her hair is identical to those often seen in traditional dance. This painting dates back to the Song Dynasty, which is not a coincidence in that it mirrors the dramas and operas popular at that time. Dance using long sleeves has a long history in China. Of the six minor dances developed in the Zhou Dynasty, dancing without

合，应是时代风尚使然。“长袖善舞”历史久远。西周《六小舞》之一的《人舞》，其特点是不执舞具，“以舞袖为容”（见《十三经注疏·周礼注疏》，中华书局 1979 年版）。春秋战国时代，诸侯贵族，醉心于歌舞作乐，表演性舞蹈有很大的发展。出土文物中，玉器、漆器出现了许多十分优美生动的舞蹈形象，如河南金村出土的战国玉雕舞女佩饰（图 87、图 88，今藏美国弗利尔博物馆），二舞者着长袖舞衣，细腰长裙，一手做“托掌”姿，飞舞长袖于头上，另一手做“按掌”姿，拂垂长袖于腰侧，相对而舞。另有传世的挽臂玉雕舞人、断一臂玉雕舞人，姿态各异，娟秀华美（图 89）。四川成都百花潭出土的战国“宴乐渔猎攻战纹壶”（图 90），表现了战国时期多方面的生活场景。

musical accompaniment was one type of dance performed using a long-sleeved costume. During both the Spring and Autumn and Warring States periods (altogether 770 BC–221 BC), the nobility were drawn to singing and dancing entertainments, which resulted in the rapid development of the performing arts. Among excavated relics from this period, there are jade and lacquer objects showing beautiful figures of dancers. One example is a jade pendant carved in the form of a pair of female dancers discovered in Henan Province, now displayed in the Freer Gallery of Art at the Smithsonian Museum (Figs.87, 88). The two dancers wear costumes of long-sleeved, tightly belted dresses, performing the same dance movements side-by-side. With one palm lifted and the other pressed downward, the dancers throw one sleeve overhead and leave the other hanging down by the waist. The line drawing in Figure 88 provides a clearer view of the details of this gorgeous ornament. Other similar jade objects have come to us through the ages, such as a dancer with a broken-off arm with beautifully wrought sleeve details and an elegant pose (Fig.89). The bronze wine vessel discovered in Baihua Tan, Chengdu, gives us a glimpse into various daily activities during the Warring States Period (475 BC–221 BC) (Fig.90). On the vessel's neck, there is a scene of people harvesting mulberry leaves; one of them is performing a long sleeve dance. A close-up of the dancer can be seen in Figure 91. The appreciation of long sleeves and slender waists on dancers was passed on from the Kingdom of Chu to the Han Dynasty. It was documented in *Miscellaneous Records of the Western Capital* that the first emperor of the Han Dynasty,

图 87　河南金村出土的战国玉雕舞女佩饰(今藏美国弗利尔博物馆)
Fig.87　Jade Jewelry in the Form of Female Dancers Unearthed at Jincun Village, Luoyang, Henan Province (Warring States period)

图 88　玉雕舞女线描图
Fig.88　Line Drawing of a Jade Pendant in the Form of Female Dancers

图 89　战国玉雕断臂舞女
Fig.89　Jade Female Dancer with a Broken-off Arm (Warring States Period)

图 90 四川成都百花潭出土的战国"宴乐渔猎攻战纹壶"线描图
Fig.90 Line Drawing of a Bronze Wine Vessel Discovered in Baihua Tan, Chengdu (Warring States period)

壶颈部分还有一幅采桑图：人们正在采摘桑叶，其中一个正飞卷长袖作舞，体态婀娜秀美(图 91)。这正是“桑间濮上”民间歌舞场面的生动写照。汉代继承了战国楚舞袅袅长袖、细腰欲折的传统，如《西京杂记》载：汉高祖宠姬戚夫人，多才多艺，“善为翘袖折腰之舞”。上有所

Emperor Gaozu, favored the imperial concubine Qi because she was very talented at the long sleeve dance. Since the emperor enjoyed it so much and approved greatly of this dance, it spread to all social classes and flourished.

The nobility and upper classes from the Han Dynasty left a fair amount of choreographic description. For example, in “Ode to Watching Dances”, the Han Dynasty poet Zhang Heng (78–139) wrote, “The dress flies like lissome swallows and sleeves flutter like spiraling snowflakes, ” and in his poem “On Dancing”

图 91 “宴乐渔猎攻战纹壶”上的采桑舞女图
Fig.91 Female Dancer Picking Mulberry Leaves on Bronze Wine Vessel

好，又大加提倡，遂风行于社会。

汉代文人对舞袖美姿的描写也不少，如张衡《观舞赋》有“裙似飞燕，袖如回雪”之叹，傅毅《舞赋》有“罗衣从风，长袖交横”等描画，都是对袖舞的生动描写。从战国经汉唐以至明清两千多年间，描述舞袖的文字，史不绝书。各代出土文物中的舞袖形象，更是层出不穷，从未间断。笔者最近在法国巴黎塞尔努斯基博物馆的陈列品中，看到前几年出土的一对东汉时期的舞蹈彩陶俑（图 92），女俑穿紧身衣，男俑舞长袖，神态生动逼真。戏曲兴起后，吸收融合了历史悠久的舞袖技法，借以表现各种人物的不同思想感情。时至今日，戏曲舞与民间舞中，保存了十分丰富且富于表情的舞袖古法，加强了袖舞的表现力，也提高了袖舞的观赏价值及震撼力。中华民族的舞蹈传统之深厚，历经数千余年，其不绝不灭的顽强生命力，不能不令人惊叹。

敦煌壁画中的各色胡舞，也有其鲜明的文化特征与各自的源流可寻。我国是一个由 56 个民族组成的多元一体的中华民族大家庭，舞蹈传统极为悠久丰厚。例如

the poet Fu Yi (?–90) wrote, “Silk clothes flutter in the wind and long sleeves sway side to side.” Throughout the two thousand years beginning with the Warring States Period, continuing through the Han and Tang dynasties, and culminating in the Ming and Qing dynasties, there emerged countless writings about sleeve dance that have been matched by various excavated relics. Recently, we came across a pair of painted ceramic sculptures of dancers from the Eastern Han Dynasty discovered not long ago, and displayed in the Musée Cernuschi in Paris (Fig.92). The female dancer wears a tight, figure-hugging costume, and the male shakes his long sleeves, both looking lively and realistic. Chinese opera which was developed much later also adopted the techniques of sleeve dance as a way of express the emotions of different characters. Even today’s folk drama and dance exhibit obvious influences of the ancient sleeve dance, which audiences find impressive. These traditions are truly remarkable in that they run so deep, standing the test of thousands of years.

The Hu dances depicted in the Dunhuang caves also have distinctive cultural features and origins. As China is made up of 56 ethnic groups, their dancing traditions are long-established and thus vary one from another. For

图 92　东汉舞蹈彩陶俑(今藏巴黎塞尔努斯基博物馆)
Fig.92　Painted Ceramic Sulptures of Dancers Displayed in the Musée Cernuschi, Paris (Eastern Han Dynasty)

敦煌舞蹈壁画中多处出现的单手弹指,或双手捧掌弹指,以及移颈动头等舞姿,早在唐人杜佑编著的《通典·乐二》第 142 卷中,就已经生动地描绘了此类胡舞的乐情舞态:“胡舞铿锵镗错,洪心骇耳……举止轻飚,或踊或跃,乍动乍息,跷脚弹指,撼头弄目,情发于中,不能自止。”可知远在千余年前传入中原的西域(包括今我国新疆等西部地区)舞,已有“跷脚弹指,撼头弄

example, the dance poses, such as the flicking of the fingers or the movement of the dancers' necks and heads, have already been depicted vividly in *Tongdian*, a Tang period encyclopedia: “The Hu dance is sonorous and powerful. The dancers dance with swift steps. They jump and leap, raise their feet and flick their fingers.” People have learned that the Hu dances were brought into the Central Plains nearly a thousand years ago from the nomadic Western Regions (Fig.93). Typical dance movements such

目”富于表情的俏丽舞蹈动作(参见图93 唐代胡人戏狮俑)。至今,中亚及我国西北少数民族如维吾尔、哈萨克等民间舞中,仍保存了弹指、撼头(移颈动头)等特色舞蹈动作。其他如西夏党项羌人的舞蹈壁画风格独具(图94),元代蒙古族人的舞蹈壁画矫健奔放,也都是中华民族百花园中不同形态、不同色调的舞蹈之花。在我国许多传世的典籍中,可以找到十分丰富的有关西域和北方各

as flicking the fingers, and moving the neck side-to-side can still be seen in today's folk dances of the Uyghur and Kazakh people. Other murals depict the dances of the Qiang people from the Western Xia (Fig.94), as well as the dances of the Mongols during the Yuan Dynasty, with their bold, passionate styles. Dances of the Western Regions along the Silk Road from

图 93　唐代胡人戏狮俑(仿制品)

Fig.93　Replica of a Painted Pottery Figurine of a Hu Dancer Performing Lion Dance (Tang Dynasty)

图 94　西夏时期壁画中持凤首箜篌伎乐天(莫高窟第 327 窟)
Fig.94　Mural of a Heavenly Musician Holding a Phoenix-Headed *Konghou* (Mogao Cave 327, Western Xia)

民族乐舞音乐特色、舞蹈程式和乐器及服饰的记载;而留存至今的敦煌壁画中的乐舞形象,更使我们有可能追寻一千多年前西域与印度乐舞在丝绸之路演变的脉络。

over a thousand years ago are readily found in the Dunhuang caves. These dances have also been documented in abundant Dunhuang murals, which give us a detailed account of their characteristics, musical types, dance patterns, instruments, and costumes used in them.

佛教舞蹈，风格各异

Various Styles of Buddhist Ceremonial Dance

敦煌壁画所集中展示的佛教舞蹈，是影响深远的宗教文化的重要组成部分。佛教在世界各地传播的同时，各国各族人民创造了各具特色的佛教艺术，其中也包括舞蹈艺术。佛教自从至迟在东汉明帝永平十年(67年)传入我国后，我国各族人民在各自传统舞蹈文化的基础上，创造了不同风格、不同形式的佛教舞蹈(图95)。它们深深地扎根在人民群众之中，有的出现在敬佛的祭礼仪式中，有的出现在宗教节日或其他节日的群众游乐场合，娱神、娱人兼而有之。中原汉族地区，佛事活动以舞祭祀的风俗，至南北朝及唐代还很盛行，到宋以后舞祭之风渐衰，这与舞蹈发展的总趋势有关，也与科学技术的发展和对神的崇信程度减弱有关。

在我国，地处边疆的少数民族地区，佛教舞蹈一直相当兴盛，传承至今。例如藏族的

The murals of Buddhist dance in the Dunhuang caves constitute a great monument to the far-reaching influence of religious culture. Through their conversion to Buddhism, people around the world created various religious arts unique to their own regions, dance included. Buddhism was probably first introduced into China around AD 67 during the Eastern Han Dynasty. From that time, Buddhist followers developed religious dances of various features and types (Fig.95). Rooted deeply in daily life, they were used in ritual ceremonies for venerating the Buddha. During religious festivals and holidays, they also served as entertainment to both divine beings and secular people. In Chinese civilization, ritual dance for worshiping the Buddha remained popular until the Northern and Southern Dynasties. After the Song Dynasty, this custom declined due to the development of science and technology which caused people to gradually reduce their superstitious beliefs.

However, in remote areas dominated by ethnic minorities, Buddhist dance flourishes even to today. For example, *cham* (Chinese: *qiangmu*) dance as practiced by the Tibetans is a distinctive dance that has been passed on for nearly a thousand years. It originated

图 95　安阳修定寺砖雕中胡人舞蹈形象
（今藏巴黎吉美博物馆）
Fig.95　Image of Hu Dancers in Brick *Bas-Relief* at Xiuding Temple, Anyang, Henan Province (Currently Displayed in the Musée Guimet in Paris)

“羌姆”，是一种风格独特、传承千年的佛教舞蹈，大约在公元 7 世纪，由印度尼泊尔传入西藏。大乘佛教与藏族本土宗教——苯教在长期的相互斗争、相互融合中形成了藏传佛教。在西藏第一座佛寺——桑耶寺建成的开光典礼上，天竺高僧莲花生，将藏族土风舞与

in the Nepal region near India and was brought to Tibet around the 7th century. Mahayana integrated with Bön, a native religion, which gave birth to Vajrayana or Tibetan Buddhism. At the consecration ceremony of Bsam yas Temple (Samye Temple), the first temple established in Tibet, the eminent monk Padmasambhava combined regional Tibetan dance and the ideology of Buddhism, creating a new type of performance

佛教哲理内容相结合，编成“羌姆”表演。举行了“戴上面具，击鼓跳舞”的仪式，这便是最早的藏族佛教舞蹈《羌姆》。每逢宗教节日，佛寺都要跳《羌姆》。“羌姆”藏语为驱鬼跳神的动作，借以酬神驱邪，守护佛法，祈丰年，求神佑。跳《羌姆》的僧人，都要经过严格的训练。撒拉族舞蹈学硕士古兰丹姆深入考察了青海塔尔寺《羌姆》，并查阅了相关文献，了解到清康熙五十七年（1718年），七世达赖喇嘛格桑加措曾下令，在塔尔寺建立了“乾巴扎仓”（法舞学院），该学院设在塔尔寺较偏僻的东北角，俗人、女子都不准进入，完全是封闭式的教学。这里训练从事乐舞活动的僧人，也成为排练《羌姆》的场所。在寺院专门设立“法舞学院”来传授《羌姆》，对这种宗教舞蹈的传承与发展起到了非常积极的推动作用（参见图96今天的藏族《羌姆》舞形象）。

藏传佛教传到蒙古族地区，《羌姆》也随之传入，但蒙古族不称“羌姆”，转用“羌姆”

called *cham* in Tibetan (Chinese: *qiangmu*) in which performers wearing masks dance to drumming. *Cham* in Tibetan language means a spiritual dance that can invoke good spirits and ward off evil ones. This early version of *cham* has now become routine in all Tibetan temples during religious festivals, where it is performed to defend Buddhist doctrines, pray for good harvests, and seek blessings from deities. The monks who were chosen to perform *cham* had to undergo strict training. In 1718, the 7th Dalai Lama, Kelzang Gyatso, approved the establishment of a *cham* teaching institute in Kumbum Monastery, which was off limits to lay people and females. The training, practice, and rehearsal of *cham* is closed to outsiders. The establishment of the *cham* training academy contributed much to the transmission and development of this religious dance (for contemporary *cham* figures, see Fig.96).

With the conversion of the Mongols to Tibetan Buddhism, *cham* was adopted and went by its Mongolian name *chama*. The Mongols believed in shamanism. However, after Kublai Khan established the Yuan Dynasty in 1271, he unwaveringly promoted Lamaism and as a result it flourished across the country. Combining the rituals used to invoke deities in shamanism and other elements of tribal dance, this distinctive Buddhist *chama* dance gradually took on a Mongolian flavor.

Today, some temples in Inner Mongolia

的蒙古语音译为“查玛”。蒙古族传统信奉“萨满教”(原始多神教)。元世祖忽必烈于公元1271年建立元朝，大力扶持喇嘛教，封藏僧八思巴为国师，于是，喇嘛教大兴。随着喇嘛教在蒙古草原的传播，《查玛》不断吸收蒙古族原始宗教萨满教“跳神”和其他蒙古族舞蹈，形成了具有蒙古族特色的佛教舞蹈——《查玛》。

内蒙古一些寺院也有专门训练跳《查玛》的僧人。这些跳《查玛》的僧人，都是经过挑选，近似舞蹈学校选拔学生一样，看其身体条件以及对舞蹈动作的领悟能力如何等等，特别是鹿神的扮演者，要求更高。因为鹿在蒙古族人民心目中是吉祥自由的象征，鹿神的扮演者要表现鹿的敏捷与灵活，跳得高，奔跑快，这就需要有一定的功力，所以要选年轻的僧人加以训练。

《羌姆》与《查玛》的共同特点是：戴面具，装扮各种神像而舞。它们的根源是

give *lamas* special training to perform *chama*. These *lamas* are handpicked through rigid selection. Basic requirements include optimal physical condition and a profound understanding of the dance movements, of which the most demanding are the ones for performing God of Deer. For Mongolians, deer are a symbol of auspiciousness and freedom, so these performers are expected to make swift and nimble movements, jump high and run fast, a skill that could take years of training to master. Needless to say, they all start very young.

What *cham* (*qiangmu*) and *chama* have in common is that performers dance in various masks to represent spirits and deities, which stem from ancient and widespread masked exorcism dances.

The Yugurs, or Yellow Uyghurs as they have been traditionally known, are one of China's 56 officially recognized ethnic groups. They inhabit the Sunan Yugur Autonomous County and the Jiuquan area, where they co-exist with other ethnic minorities of China, including Mongolians and Tibetans. Beginning in the 14th century, the majority of the Yugur people were converted to Tibetan Buddhism. The Dharmapala dance, the most representative Buddhist dance of the Yugurs, is performed every January 16th and June 6th according to the Chinese lunar calendar. It is considered a way of expounding the Dharma, or Buddhist doctrine. The performers are *lamas* who have been trained for many years, and the characters portrayed in this

图 96　今天的藏族《羌姆》舞形象

Fig.96　Contemporary Image of a Modern *Cham* Performer

历史久远,流布极广的面具舞。

裕固族大都居住在甘肃肃南裕固族自治县和酒泉一带，长期与蒙、藏等族和睦相处。14世纪以后,裕固族主要信仰喇嘛教。《护法神舞》就是裕固族最有代表性的佛教舞蹈,其主要内容是张扬佛法的威力,每年农历正月十五和六月六日在寺院表演。舞者都是经过训练的喇嘛,所扮演的角色多是偶像化的神灵,头上戴着狰狞神怪的面具,手执金刚杵等法器而舞,借以驱鬼、消灾、求佛保佑。舞队中有牛、马、鹿、鹰、骷髅、乌鸦、喜鹊等各种护法神出场。其中，鹰、乌鸦、喜鹊等护法神是裕固族独有的。这与该民族常年生活在深山密林中的自然环境及游牧生活有密切的联系。

地处中原的山西五台山诸寺院流行一种佛教舞蹈《金刚舞》,俗称"跳

dance are mostly deities. Performers wear boldly exaggerated masks of deities, spirits, and demons; they dance with instruments such as the *vajra* (thunderbolt) club in their hands, in a ritual designed to ward off ghosts and misfortune and to ask blessings from Buddhas and bodhisattvas. The masks and deities include oxen, horses, deer, skeletons, eagles, crows and magpies. Among them, the deities of eagles, crows, and magpies were based on animals that lived in closed proximity to the Yugurs in the deep mountain forests.

Another Buddhist dance can be found at Mount Wutai in Shanxi Province, a well-known Buddhist site. This mountain is said to be the dwelling place of *Mañjuśrī*, the bodhisattva of wisdom and insight. The *vajra* dance is faithfully practiced in the temples there. Every year on June 10th according to the Chinese lunar calendar, religious activities and grand ceremonies are held to celebrate *Mañjuśrī*'s birthday. Yellow Temple, a *lama* temple, is especially famed for the *vajra* dance performed there by professionally-trained *lamas*. With the exception of the one who plays *Mañjuśrī*, the other characters such as Dharma protectors, warriors, and demons all wear masks and colorful brocade costumes and use armor-like props. The highlight of the whole dance is the ritual of warding off evil spirits and giving prayers for the blessing of all sentient beings.

As Buddhist ceremonial dancing goes, *vajra* dance from Mount Wutai shares many similarities with *cham* from Tibet and *chama* from Mongolia. As Buddhist ceremonial dancing goes, *vajra* dance from Mount Wutai shares many similarities with

神”“跳鬼”或“跳布扎”。相传五台山是文殊菩萨的居住地。文殊菩萨是释迦牟尼的左胁侍，每年农历六月十日文殊生日都要举行盛大的佛事活动。在黄庙（喇嘛寺院）表演的《金刚舞》颇负盛名，舞者由经过专门训练的喇嘛担任，除扮演菩萨者外都戴面具，身穿各色锦袍、软靠，装扮成各种护法神、金刚力士、鬼怪等，其内容是表现大威德金刚降妖伏魔的故事。其中“斩鬼”一节，是整个舞蹈的核心内容，意为驱除妖魔，为人类祈福。

五台山的《金刚舞》与藏、蒙佛寺舞蹈《羌姆》《查玛》有传承关系，相同之处颇多。同时，由于五台山位于汉族聚居区的中原之地，故《金刚舞》又明显地具有一些汉族舞蹈的特点。

北京地区的《跳布扎》，又称“跳鬼”或“跳神”，是流行于北京各喇嘛寺院驱鬼祈福的佛教舞蹈。北京《跳布扎》起源于何时，已难考

Tibetan *cham* and Mongolian *chama*. However, the *vajra* dance exhibits highly distinctive features of the ethnic Han, as Mount Wutai is located in Shanxi Province in China's Central Plains.

Popular among *lama* temples around Beijing, *tiaobuzha* (*buzha* dance) is a Buddhist dance with the intention of warding off evil spirits and praying for blessing. Although it is difficult to determine exactly when it originated, there is literature documenting this kind of dance. For example, *tiaobuzha* was described by the eunuch Liu Ruoyu in *Records of the Imperial Palace* during the Ming Dynasty (1368–1644). It was apparently the ancient version of the modern *buzha* dance. Dancers wore high bamboo hats and five-colored robes, while in today's *buzha* dance, dancers also wear various masks, probably influenced by the *chama* dance of Mongolians. In the Qing Dynasty (1616–1911), the Lama Temple (also called the Yonghe Palace) sent *lamas* to temples in Inner Mongolia to learn *buzha* dance; eminent *lamas* from Inner Mongolia also came to Beijing to teach these skills. Every year on January 30th in the Chinese lunar calendar, the Lama Temple is flooded with excitement over the *buzha* dance. This ceremony consists of 13 parts, including invoking spirits, invoking the deity of butterflies, invoking *vajras*, invoking heavenly kings, invoking dharma protectors, and invoking Maitreya, the future Buddha. The last part exorcises demons. With all evil spirits eradicated, *buzha* dance ends on a high note.

证。明人所著《酌中志》已有记载，书中所载“跳步叱”即今天的《跳布扎》。当时的服饰是头戴高顶笠，身穿五色大袖袍，而后世的《跳布扎》主要是头戴各式面具而舞，这很可能是受到蒙古族本土佛教舞《查玛》的影响所致。清代雍和宫曾派僧人到内蒙古佛寺学习《跳布扎》，内蒙古也曾派高僧到北京传授技艺。每当农历正月三十日，雍和宫《跳布扎》时，热闹非凡。跳舞分 13 个段落，其中有“跳白鬼”“跳黑鬼”“跳蝶神”“跳金刚”“跳天王”“跳护法神”“跳弥勒”等佛教之神，最后是“跳斩鬼”。魔鬼已除，皆大欢喜，《跳布扎》结束。

南传佛教大约在公元 1 世纪后，从天竺传到东南亚缅甸、泰国后，再传入我国西南傣族等地区，属小乘教派。

傣族的佛教舞蹈有《孔雀舞》《大鹏鸟舞》《鱼舞》《蝴蝶舞》《象脚鼓舞》等。这些舞蹈的形成与傣族地区林木密布、动物繁多的生存环境有密切的关系。这些舞蹈本身

After the 1st century, Theravada Buddhism spread from India to Burma and Thailand in Southeast Asia, then to Southwest China where the Dai people lived. Theravada became the accepted doctrine of that region.

Buddhist dances developed by the Dai people include the peacock dance, thc dancc of *peng* (a gigantic mythical bird in ancient China), the fish dance, the butterfly dance, the elephant foot drum dance, and so forth. The dense forests and numerous animals in the Dai region gave birth to these picturesque dances. Actually, these dances themselves have very little to do with religions, having been passed on among the people long before their conversion to Buddhism. Nonetheless, the peaceful and beautiful nature of the animals shown in these dances could be incorporated into Buddhist practice as a way to attract converts; as a result, the dances became a common sight at Buddhist festivals. In light of this, it is safe to say that animal imitation dances in the Dunhuang murals have a sound basis in daily life.

Buddhists in Yunnan also perform dances as part of their worship, including the De'ang ethnic group's elephant foot drum dance, and the Bai people's lotus lantern dance and eight-treasure flower dance. The eight-treasure flower dance, also known as the scattering flowers dance, has six parts, each one respectively using flowers, incense, seven-star lamps, holy water, fruit, and music as devotional offerings to the Buddha.

并没有多么浓重的宗教色彩，且早已在民间传承。佛教传入后，以这些模拟善良、优美动物的舞蹈供养佛、娱佛，并在佛教节日向群众展示演出，又成了欢度节日的娱人舞蹈。我们不难从这些舞蹈中找到敦煌壁画中拟兽舞的生活基础。

云南其他信仰佛教的兄弟民族，也都用自己的民间舞供养佛、娱佛。例如德昂族的《象脚鼓舞》、白族的“绕坛”《莲花灯舞》《八宝花舞》（即《散花舞》），以花、香、灯、涂、果、乐 6 个舞段，形象地演示了佛经中规定的对佛多种方式的供养。

大理白族，佛教盛行，民族歌舞活动“绕山林”，既与宗教活动有关，又是群众的游乐歌舞集会。其中包含许多舞具丰富的歌舞表演，如《霸王鞭》《八角鼓》（“金钱鼓”）等。其他如维吾尔族著名的《灯舞》（顶灯起舞），朝鲜族的《僧舞》（击鼓飞舞长袖）、《波罗舞》（击钹而舞），浙江的《跳净童》等，都是我国各民族人民创造的各具特色的佛教舞蹈。

以上这些，都是敦煌佛教壁画创作的文化基础与生活源泉，都会在林林总总的壁画乐舞形象中反映出来。应该承认，我们的舞蹈史研究者对此的探究还是很粗浅的，有待在更全面的资料收集与分析的基础上进一步深入。

Most of the Bai ethnic group believes in Buddhism, and their folk ceremony known as “Through the Mountains” is a song and dance rally for both mass amusement and religious purposes. There are a variety of song and dance performances in this activity, such as rattle stick dance (also called gold coin drum), the octagonal drum dance, etc. Other dances, including the oil lamp dance of the Uyghurs (dancing while balancing an oil lamp on the head), the monk dance (dancing with drums and waving long sleeves), the pungmul dance (also called farmers music dance) of the Korean ethnic group in China, and the *tiaojingtong* dance (a kind of comic folk dance) from Zhejiang Province, are all unique Buddhist dances created by various ethnic groups in China.

The dances from daily life mentioned above serve as cultural background for the Dunhuang Buddhist murals. The truth is, researchers of dance history know very little in this area. More work needs to be done to acquire further information for comprehensive analysis and understanding.

多元荟萃，植根中华

Culturally Diverse Yet Rooted in Chinese History

人们不禁要问，为什么两千年前，由印度、尼泊尔传入中国的佛教艺术，能在敦煌这片神奇的戈壁绿洲里，经过各民族文化艺术长期的碰撞、交融、浸润、发展，既能保持和发展异彩纷呈的各自传统，又能和谐地统一在中华民族的大家庭里，具有深深的中国情，浓浓的中国韵呢？

这个问题的核心，涉及文化交融的目标与规律，也涉及包括乐舞、美术在内的敦煌文化艺术的品格、特性问题，限于学识水平，我们只能尝试将自己初步思索的答案简略地写出来供读者参考并求指正。

首先，敦煌文化虽然表现为一种特色鲜明的地域文化，但构成这一文化的核心是以儒家为基础，儒、释、道及其他宗教文化

People cannot help but ask: spreading from India and Nepal into China nearly two thousand years ago, how did Buddhist art manage to flourish in Dunhuang, this miraculous oasis on the edge of the Gobi Desert? After thousands of years of cultural contact, diffusion, and integration among various ethnic groups and nationalities, how did Buddhist artistic traditions stay regionally distinctive while thriving harmoniously side by side? And how did this art gradually take on strong sinicized characteristics over time?

These questions relate not only to the processes which govern cultural diffusion, but also to the characteristics and features of Dunhuang art itself in the areas of music, dance, and paintings. On the basis of our limited understanding, we can only attempt to present brief answers for readers' reference and hope that they will use these for further investigation.

First, though showing a distinctive mix of different regions and ethnic groups, Dunhuang culture shared mainstream cultural values which were a combination of Confucianism, Daoism, and Buddhism—with Confucianism at its core of social norms. What these intrinsic sociopolitical and philosophical elements from China and Buddhism from South Asia had in common was that they all advocated tolerance, harmony, and

融会贯通的主流文化。中华民族固有的儒家文化和道家思想，与自印度、尼泊尔传入的佛教宗旨，均带有宽容、兼容、包容的精神，这就决定了它们之间有互相交流、吸收和融合的基础，也有吸取其他民族、地域、宗教文化营养的可能性。

其次，敦煌文化是在中华大地上开放的一朵奇葩，它表现出对华夏主流文化的认同，却又不固步自守、停滞不前，而是在新的人文环境与时代条件下不断创新；它体现出对来自其他民族与异域文明的尊重与吸纳，同时也并不生搬硬套、囫囵吞枣，而总是注意消化吸收和适应本土需要，使外来文化能够植根于中华文明的沃土之中。在长期汇流交融中吸取的各民族文化，今天已经成为中华主流文化不可分割的组成部分。

再次，敦煌文化特性的形成，得益于多元文化的荟萃，而这种交融又因其处于丝绸之路咽喉的特殊环境，而兼有华夏主流文化、敦煌本土文化与外来各族文化三者的直接影响与多渠道回流的特色。以壁画来说，今天，我们的研究者与观赏者虽然可以辨认一些具体图像、作品的内容和风格，却难以回答究竟是谁

inclusion. This laid a firm foundation for their mutual exchange, acceptance, and integration, opening up the possibility of borrowing cultural and religious elements from other civilizations.

Next, as a unique phenomenon, Dunhuang culture was based on Chinese mainstream culture in many aspects, yet it did not stop there. It developed its own innovations under fresh circumstances in every new era. It respected and accepted various civilizations in a selective way. It did not just gulp down everything that was put on the table, but chose, digested, and adapted to what was needed according to the situation, which allowed these overseas cultures to thrive on Chinese soil. Over a long period of diffusion, integration, and assimilation, cultures from different nationalities are now an indispensable part of the Chinese mainstream cultural system.

Finally, the distinctive features of Dunhuang culture are the result of contact by a variety of civilizations. With Dunhuang's status as the major crossroads on the Silk Road, it had both direct and indirect access to Chinese mainstream culture, local culture, and foreign cultures through multiple channels. Take cave murals

影响谁(主动被动)的问题,也难以一一确定这些影响孰前孰后,某些成分哪主哪次。这种扑朔迷离的特色,恰好证明了文化的汇流是一种十分复杂的现象(图97)。

总之,灿烂辉煌、多姿多彩的敦煌舞蹈壁画,既具有多民族文化交融的鲜明特征,又形成为一个完整的体系,它们不仅记录了中华民族广取博采、兼收并蓄、吸纳百川的兼容精神,展示了中华民族根深叶茂的舞蹈艺术,而且也在异域文化雨露的长期滋润下,对中华文明的进步产生了重要的影响,做出了不可磨灭的贡献。

as an example: while researchers and audiences can make out some content and style from a few paintings, nobody can say for sure which culture is the creator, which one came first, or which one enjoyed dominant status. This obscurity is evidence of the complexity inherent in cultural integration (Fig.97).

In a word, the splendid Dunhuang murals are a complete system with distinctive features showing the integration of many cultures and civilizations. They are more than a record documenting the Chinese people's spirit of acceptance, or a presentation manifesting deeply-rooted Chinese dance traditions; indeed, they are living proof of the indelible contributions made by overseas cultures that left a lasting influence on Chinese civilization.

图 97 持琵琶的伎乐天(新疆克孜尔千佛洞第 8 窟)
Fig.97 Heavenly Musician Playing a *Pipa* (Cave 8, Kizil Thousand Buddha Caves, Xinjiang)

继承与创新
敦煌乐舞的发扬光大

***Inheritance and Innovation*:**
Development of Dunhuang Music and Dance

我们今天鉴赏与研究敦煌壁画里的乐舞形象，并不仅仅是为了发思古之幽情，更重要的是要在正确理解优秀传统文化的基础上，继承发扬光大，开拓创新，使之为现实服务。

Today, we appreciate and study the images of dancers in Dunhuang art not only to honor the past, but more importantly to have a profound understanding of Chinese culture, and to inherit, continue, and further develop the rich traditions of the past for modern purposes.

《丝路花雨》等舞剧的创作演出

"Rain of Flowers on the Silk Road" and Other Dance Performances Created for the Modern Stage

珍贵而丰富的敦煌壁画乐舞形象,为艺术家的文艺创作提供了可资借鉴的形象资料,也激发了他们的创作灵感。早在20世纪中期,著名的戏剧大师梅兰芳与舞蹈家戴爱莲就根据相关资料创作了《天女散花》《飞天》等令人耳目一新的京剧、舞蹈。改革开放以来,随着敦煌历史文化知识的普及与敦煌学的发展,运用敦煌壁画里的舞蹈形象创作的新舞剧也一一呈现在广大观众面前。1978年创作排演的大型民族舞剧《丝路花雨》就是其中的佼佼者。

舞剧《丝路花雨》以丝绸之路上的商贸大会及敦煌莫高窟的壁画创作为历史背景,用舞蹈语汇演述了老画工神笔张和爱女英娘悲欢离合的动人故事,反映了唐代西部地区的多民族与各国的经济和文化交流盛况,突出宣扬正义、热爱和平、加强各族人民友谊的主题。舞剧主人公英娘的高超舞技艺术地再现了敦煌壁画中的优美舞

The abundance of invaluable historical images of musical dance at Dunhuang serve as graphic reference for artists, giving them literary and artistic inspiration. As early as the mid-20th century, Mei Lanfang, the legendary Beijing opera performer, and Dai Ailian, a famous dancer, composed "Heavenly Ladies Scattering Flowers", "Flying *Apsaras*", and other unconventional operas and dances. Since the 1980s, there has been an increased awareness of Dunhuang history and culture among Chinese people, which has contributed to the development of Dunhuang studies; as a result, more and more new dance pieces and musicals have been created based on dance figures found in the Dunhuang murals. One of the most highly acclaimed of these is "Rain of Flowers on the Silk Road", which was first created and performed onstage in 1978.

Set in the Tang Dynasty among the Silk Road and the Mogao Caves, the dance drama "Rain of Flowers on the Silk Road" tells the story of master cave temple painter Zhang and his beloved

姿，尤其是将著名的反弹琵琶舞姿复原并丰富、演化为一套完整的舞蹈，给广大观众留下了深刻的印象。剧中还表演了一批群舞、队舞，如百戏杂耍中的舞蹈，波斯花园中的刺绣舞、马铃舞、黑巾舞，梦幻中的柘枝舞、凭栏仙女舞、香音鸟舞，以及二十七国大会上的盘中舞、印度舞、土耳其舞、霓裳羽衣舞、新疆舞等，场面热烈而辉煌，色彩绚丽夺目，令人目不暇接又回味无穷。该舞剧在演出当年，就获得了文化部庆祝中华人民共和国建国三十周年创作与演出的一等奖。

《丝路花雨》在北京人民大会堂公演后，又到全国各地巡回演出，获得盛誉。从 1981 年 6 月起，先后到朝鲜、法国、意大利、日本、泰国、西班牙、土耳其、德国、南斯拉夫等四十多个国家和我国港澳台地区巡演，引起巨大反响，被誉为“中国民族舞剧的典范”“中国民族舞剧的新成果”，也为宣传敦煌艺术与促进文化交流做出了积极贡献。1994 年，该舞剧在中华民族 20 世纪舞

daughter Ying Niang. With the themes of justice, peace, and friendship among peoples, the dance gives a picture of the economic and cultural exchange between various nationalities and kingdoms in the Western Regions. The main character Ying Niang impresses the audience with her outstanding dance skills, bringing the breath-taking dance movements as seen in Dunhuang murals to life. In particular, the legendary dancing with the *pipa* behind the back is recreated, enhanced, and beautifully arranged into a complete dance routine. Group choreography is also presented in the production, including acrobatics, the ribbon dance, a bird dance performed in a Persian garden, as well as the plate dance, Indian dance, Turkish dance, Rainbow and Feather dance, and Xinjiang folk dance. The magnificent spectacle and dazzling colors are a visual feast for the eyes. When it debuted in 1978 it was awarded first prize for composition and performance by the Ministry of Culture at the celebrations commemorating the 30th anniversary of the founding of the People's Republic of China.

After its successful performance in Beijing's Great Hall of the People, "Rain of Flowers on the Silk Road" went on tour in China and earned acclaim nationwide. Since June of 1981, this drama has been produced in more than 40 countries and regions, including France, Germany, Italy, Spain, the former Yugoslavia, Turkey, North Korea, Japan, Thailand, as well as China's Taiwan, Hong

蹈经典评比中荣获“经典作品金像奖”,被誉为“中国舞剧的里程碑”。二十多年来,《丝路花雨》也为敦煌艺术的创新与现代化提供了实践经验。其后,甘肃艺术家创作、演出的《飞天》《天姿馨曲》《唐韵胡旋》《千手观音》《大梦敦煌》《敦煌古乐》《天马萧萧》《敦煌情韵》等大型舞剧、舞蹈,以及北京、陕西、湖北艺术家创作的《敦煌彩塑》《大唐乐舞》《编钟乐舞》等,乃至日本、韩国舞蹈家在这方面的创作与教学,都得益于《丝路花雨》的启示。尤其是中国残疾人艺术团编演的造型乐舞《千手观音》(图 98),于 2005 年在中央电视台春节联欢晚会上演播后,身患残疾的姑娘们的出色表演,深深打动了亿万观众,在国内外引起了新的轰动和新一轮的敦煌乐舞热。

《千手观音》舞蹈的最早雏形是《丝路花雨》中的“六臂神舞”,后由甘肃省艺术学校的高金荣女士根据敦煌莫高窟第 3 窟的千手千眼观音壁画,重新创作为《敦煌手姿》舞。1998 年在北京演出时,根据笔者的建议又更名为《千手观音》。佛教发源地——印度的观音造像,本是男性,面部留有胡

Kong, and Macao. It contributed to the promotion of Dunhuang cultural exchange between countries, and was declared a model Chinese drama. In 1994, the drama won first place in Chinese National 20th Century Choreography Classics Appraisal and was recognized as "A Significant Milestone in Chinese Drama." Over the past twenty years, "Rain of Flowers on the Silk Road" has remained a pioneer in new ways of bringing Dunhuang art to the modern stage. After its overwhelming success, artists from Gansu Province have gone on to create more large-scale musical dance spectacles, such as "Flying *Apsaras*," "Sweet Melody of Heavenly Beauty," "Rhymes of Tang and Whirling of Hu," "Thousand-Armed Avalokitesvara," "Dunhuang, My Dreamland," "Ancient Dunhuang Music," "Neighing Heavenly Horses," "Romantic Music of Dunhuang" and others. Artists from Beijing, Shaanxi Province, and Hubei Province have also created works with Dunhuang related themes. The influence of "Rain of Flowers on the Silk Road" has also gone beyond the domestic arts, inspiring Korean and Japanese dancers in their teaching and practice. A fantastic version of the "Thousand-Armed Avalokitesvara" was created and performed by the China Disabled People's Performing Arts Troupe, inspired millions of viewers when it was performed as part of the line-up on

子(笔者在阿旃陀石窟所见),在传入中国后,我国民众尊信观音是大慈大悲、救苦救难的女性菩萨。她有千眼可洞察人间的是非善恶,有千手能救援身陷苦难的人们。“千手千眼观音”形象,是千百年来我国古代画家、雕塑家的集体创造,且代代传承,世世创新,也是无数能工巧匠的智慧结晶。当代的舞蹈家编创的《千手观音》,则是用舞蹈艺术继承与发扬了祖先的创造。中国残疾人艺术团的艺术指导、杰出的舞蹈编导张继刚于继承中有发展,特别是在表演人数、队列、服饰、舞蹈动作等方面又有新的创造,尤其是聋哑姑娘们在艰苦的排练中克服了常人难以想象的困难,表演臻善臻美,使金碧辉煌的乐舞场面散发出感人的高尚精神与青春活力,使舞蹈的审美及德育作用发挥到了极致。

CCTV's Spring Festival Gala in 2005 (Fig.98). It was a big hit and created intense interest in Dunhuang dance both at home and abroad.

The prototype for the "Thousand-Armed Avalokitesvara" was the "Six-armed Goddess Dance" performed in "Rain of Flowers on the Silk Road". Later, based on the image of the bodhisattva painted on Mogao Cave 3, Gao Jinrong from Gansu Art School converted it into Dunhuang Mudra Dance. When performed in Beijing in 1998, the dance was renamed the "Thousand-Armed Avalokitesvara" under the writer's recommendation. In India—the birthplace of Buddhism—Avalokitesvara Bodhisattva was presented as a male figure with a mustache. However, when Buddhism was introduced to China, this bodhisattva of compassion, named *Guanyin* in Chinese, was gradually feminized and changed into the manifestation of a merciful mother figure who relieves suffering and offers sanctuary for those in need. As depicted in art, the "Thousand-Armed Avalokitesvara" is a brilliant figure created and improved by generations of painters and sculptors. The "Thousand-Armed Avalokitesvara" developed by modern artists not only honors the creation of our ancestors, but also adds novelty by making adjustments in the number of dancers, formations, costumes and dance movements. Director Zhang Jigang from the China Disabled People's Performing Art Troupe led a group of deaf and hearing-impaired young girls to successfully overcome many challenges. Their flawless performance and gorgeous visuals left an impression of idealistic youth and energy, which contributed to the aesthetic appreciation by the audience.

图 98　中国残疾人艺术团的《千手观音》剧照
Fig.98　Stage Photo of "Thousand-Armed Avalokitesvara" Performed by the China Disabled People's Performing Arts Troupe

敦煌舞的教学实践

Teaching and Research of Dunhuang Dance

为了在学习继承的基础上做好传承、创新敦煌舞蹈的工作，尤其是在教学实践中培养年轻一代的敦煌舞蹈演员与编导人员，自 1979 年秋起，任甘肃省艺术学校校长的高金荣女士五次深入敦煌莫高窟，面壁潜心研究敦煌舞姿的复原与再创作。为了将看似静止的壁画形象变化为动态的舞蹈程式，她从最为关键的舞伎眼神、S 形“三道弯”体态及呼吸着手，提炼与分析手姿手势与肋、胯、膝的动作，丰富肢体曲线，确定多种步法与旋转、跳跃，把握好节奏变化，再配以乐器、长绸等舞具，编著了《敦煌舞基本训练教材》，并付诸教学实践。从 1981 年起，高金荣在艺校开设了相应的课程，先后培养出三届善习敦煌舞的学生，同时创作或修改排演了《长沙女引》《莫高女神》《妙音反弹》《六

Gao Jinrong, head of the Gansu Art School, is dedicated to researching, developing, and teaching Dunhuang dance to the next generation of dancers and directors. To this end, she has visited the Mogao Caves five times since the autumn of 1979, to research Dunhuang choreography in order to recreate ancient dances as well as create new ones. To translate stationary two-dimensional images into dynamic dance movements, she studied facial expressions, angles of poses, hand gestures and *mudras*, as well as positions of legs, hips, and knees. She also researched musical instruments and dance props such as the broad sashes used in the ribbon dances. Through this research she has determined a variety of dance steps, spins, and jumps. She published her findings in *A Textbook on the Fundamentals of Dunhuang Dance* and applied it to her teaching practice. Since 1981, a curriculum based on her research has been taught in her school, which has graduated three classes of students specializing in Dunhuang dance. She has also consulted on dozens of dance education projects including "Changsha Girl Prelude," "Goddesses of the Mogao Caves," "Echoes of Sublime Music," "Six-Armed Musician," "Colored Silk of Dunhuang," and "Bodhisattva in Meditation."

臂伎乐》《敦煌彩绸》《思维菩萨》等十余个教学汇报节目。

1983年8月,中国敦煌吐鲁番学会在兰州举行成立大会及学术讨论会,高女士率领参加敦煌舞训练的学员在会上做了汇报演出,引起热烈反响。敦煌学家与舞蹈界高度赞扬这一开拓创新的工作。季羡林先生撰写专文肯定敦煌舞的训练与演出,他在文章中指出:"舞蹈基本训练和一些舞蹈小品,虽然目前还只限于兰州,但我同其他看过的人确信,它一定能走出兰州,走向全国,走向世界;同样推陈出新,发扬祖国艺术,为祖国争光。"(见《舞蹈论丛》1983年第4期)事实证明了季老的预言,"敦煌舞基本训练"于1986年夏晋京演出多场,大获成功。其后多次应邀赴海外演出,为弘扬中华民族优秀的文化艺术和增进各国人民对敦煌艺术的了解起到了积极的作用。

At the inaugural meeting of the China Institute of Dunhuang and Turfan Studies held in Lanzhou in August, 1983, Gao Jinrong directed her students in a performance which received wide recognition. Dunhuang experts along with people from the art community spokc highly of her unprecedented and innovative work. Professor Ji Xianlin also wrote an article especially dedicated to the training and performance of Dunhuang dance, in which he pointed out that "though the basic training and small dance pieces are practiced only in Lanzhou, those of us who have seen this dance are convinced it has the potential to win over a much broader audience, possibly nationwide or even worldwide. We should push for new achievements based on past success and carry forward the national art to honor our country." Ji Xianlin's predictions soon came true. The summer of 1986 witnessed success as the dance production "Fundamentals of Dunhuang Dance" was performed a dozen times in Beijing. It then went overseas after receiving several invitations to perform abroad. This show played an active role in promoting Chinese culture and raising international awareness of Dunhuang art.

敦煌乐器的仿制研究

Reconstructing Dunhuang Instruments

乐曲(曲谱)与乐器是敦煌乐舞中不可或缺的组成部分,尤其是林林总总的乐器,既为舞蹈伴奏之用,又常常作为舞蹈者本身所持的舞具而包含在具体的舞蹈程式之中。对敦煌伎乐与乐器的研究,敦煌研究院的郑汝中研究员做出了非常出色的研究,这方面他有几本专著问世,具体成果可参看其代表作《敦煌壁画乐舞研究》(见甘肃教育出版社出版 2000 年版),兹不赘述。这里只是简要介绍他在敦煌乐器仿制研究上的成绩。

郑汝中对敦煌乐器的仿制研究,建立在他多年对敦煌壁画中所绘乐器图像的调查、分类、考究的扎实基础之上。他统计的敦煌石窟壁画乐器有 44 种、6000 多件,通过摄制相关照片,建立详细的档案,进行全面的分类考察,参照有关文献与存世的

Music notation and musical instruments are an indispensable part of Dunhuang art. Musical instruments functioned both as accompaniment and dance prop. In the study of Dunhuang performers and instruments, Zheng Ruzhong, a researcher at the Dunhuang Academy, has done outstanding research in this area. In 2000, he published *Music and Dance in Dunhuang Mural Art* (Gansu Educational Publishing House, 2000). Here we can not go into elaborate detail, but briefly introduce his research on reconstructing Dunhuang instruments.

Zheng's study on recreating Dunhuang instruments is based on his research, classification, and investigation of the musical instruments depicted in Dunhuang cave murals. According to his statistics, there are more than 6,000 instruments classified into 44 types. After taking photographs, creating detailed profiles, doing classification research, and referring to relevant documents, he set up a research project called "Study on the Reconstruction of Musical Instruments in Dunhuang Murals." Beginning in 1989, it took him three years to finish the project. The main features of instruments depicted in the Dunhuang murals can be summarized as follows: 1) their time span of development was

实物资料，经过反复论证，设立“敦煌壁画乐器仿制研究”课题，从1989年起，花费三年时间，付诸实践。敦煌壁画所绘乐器的特点是时间跨越千年，发展脉络清晰，形制变化多样，造型丰富复杂。虽然其中许多乐器至今还在民间流传使用，但已有不少变异；有一部分乐器古代文献虽有记载，今天已经泯灭失传；尤其还有几种乐器则仅见于壁画，未见古今流传，为敦煌特有造型。这就使得仿制工作带有极大的挑战性。郑汝中经过艰苦研究与精心设计，确定了“依据古代乐器形制，运用现代科技与先进材料”的原则，在敦煌研究院、北京昭明万邦敦煌文化发展公司与北京乐器厂的共同努力下，于1991年仿制成吹、拉、弹、打四大类60余件乐器。同年10月，文化部艺术研究院音乐研究所乐声学实验室对这批仿制乐器做了频谱测量报告，得出了它们的谐波成分清晰、稳定的结论。1992年，又在中国音乐

over 1,000 years; 2) their development can be clearly traced; 3) there was considerable change in shape and structure over time; and 4) there are a great variety of shapes and forms. Although some of the instruments are still in use today, there has been considerable evolution. Some of the instruments have been recorded in documents, but they no longer exist; several instruments can only be seen in the murals but apparently never existed in real life and therefore are seen as unique to Dunhuang. These factors altogether make reconstructing the instruments challenging work. After laborious research, Zheng applied modern science and materials to recreating the shape and structure of these ancient instruments. With the joint efforts of the Dunhuang Academy, the Beijing Zhaoming Wanbang Dunhuang Cultural Development Company, and the Beijing Instruments Factory, in 1991 they finally managed to recreate more than 60 musical instruments in four categories: wind instruments, string instruments, plucked string instruments and percussion instruments. In October of the same year, the music laboratory at the Institute of Music of the Academy of Arts (now known as the Chinese National Academy of Arts), made a spectrum measuring report on these instruments and came to the conclusion that their harmonic sound waves were clear and stable in frequency. In 1992, an appraisal meeting and concert using the reconstructed instruments was held at the China Conservatory of Music and

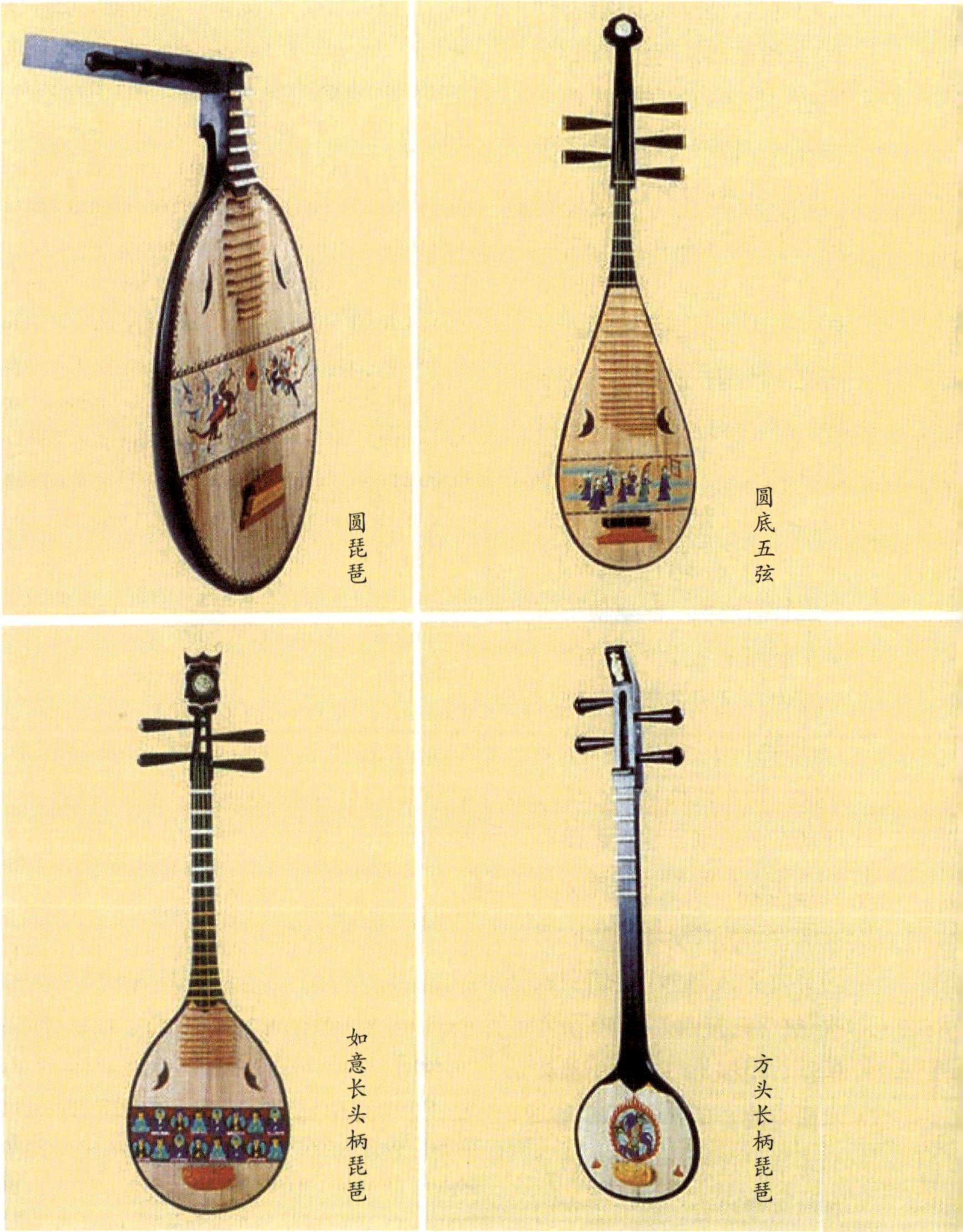

图 99　敦煌乐器仿制品图片之一

Fig.99　Replica of Dunhuang Musical Instruments, 1

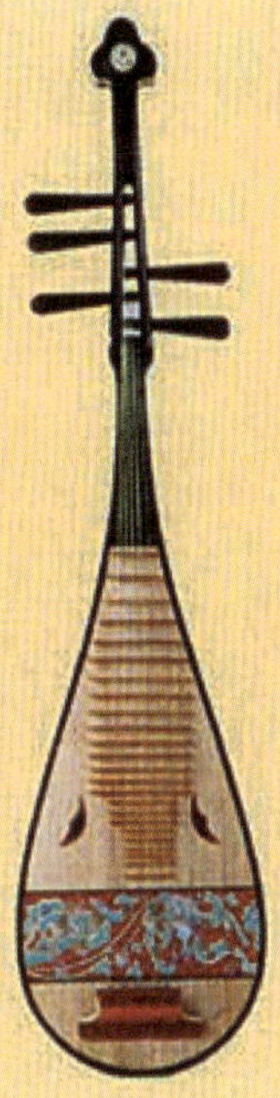

圆底五弦

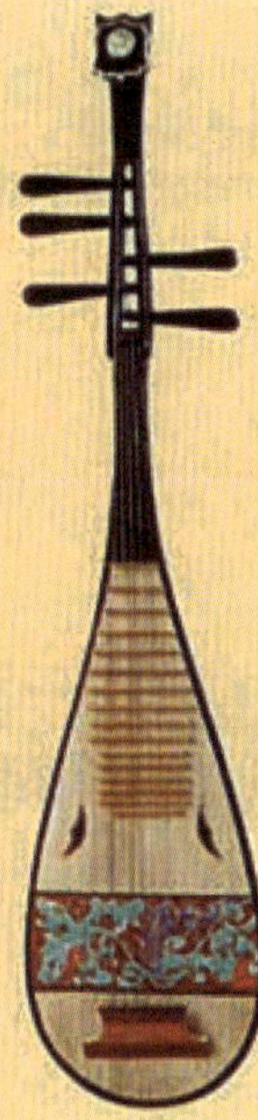

平底五弦

大棒形琵琶

小棒形琵琶

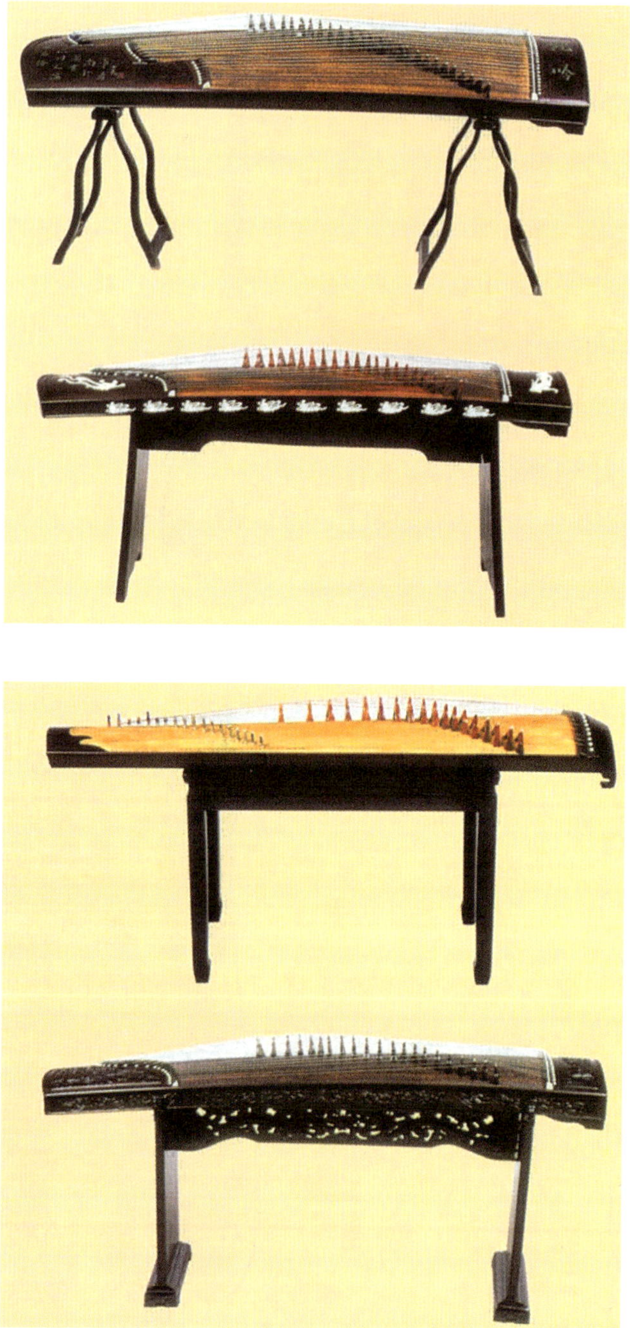

图 100　敦煌乐器仿制品图片之二

Fig.100　Replica of Dunhuang Musical Instruments, 2

图 101　敦煌乐器仿制品图片之三
Fig.101　Replica of Dunhuang Musical Instruments, 3

图 102　敦煌乐器仿制品图片之四
Fig.102　Replica of Dunhuang Musical Instruments, 4

学院小礼堂举行的鉴定会及演奏会上获得与会专家的一致肯定;同年荣获文化部科技进步二等奖(图 99~ 图 103)。可以说,敦煌乐器的仿制研究,既是推动敦煌乐舞研究深入发展的需要,也为敦煌学研究如何更好地为现实生活服务开拓了一个全新的领域。

was well-received from the experts present. In the same year, the Ministry of Culture awarded Zheng Ruzhong Second Prize in the National Scientific and Technological Progress Awards. In conclusion, this research on reconstructing Dunhuang instruments not only represents a breakthrough in people's understanding of music history, but also the establishment of a new field in its own right (Fig.99–Fig.103).

图 103 敦煌乐器仿制品图片之五

Fig.103 Replica of Dunhuang Musical Instruments, 5

敦煌舞伎服饰的研究与复原

Researching and Reconstructing Dunhuang Dance Costumes

敦煌乐舞研究近年来还有新的成果，这就是上海东华大学研究生贾一亮女士对敦煌舞伎服饰的研究与复原工作。这里只是就这项成果的意义谈谈认识。

历来学者专家对敦煌乐舞的研究，着重在舞蹈的源流及以动作、神态为中心的舞容以及舞具，而对舞者服饰的描述一般比较简单。尤其是衣裙的各种样式、名称，它们所使用的材质、图案、色彩与染织及缝制工艺，因为壁画褪色与剥蚀的原因，又涉及论者并不熟悉的科技知识，故大都语焉不详，甚至多有误解。这就成为乐舞研究中的薄弱环节，影响了研究的深入。鉴于此，贾一亮在敦煌美术史专家赵声良研究员的具体指导下，在逐一细细观摩与分析敦煌壁画里一百余身舞伎的基础上，从服装科学的角度，对他们的头饰及衣、领、裙、裤等加以归类区别，并做了色彩分析、纹样整理与衣式搭配的初步探索，最后尝试复原了敦煌唐代经变画中舞伎的九种服饰。这一成

Some recent discoveries have been made in the field of Dunhuang performing arts by Jia Yiliang, a postgraduate at Donghua University in Shanghai. She works on the research and recreation of Dunhuang dance costume. Here we will only touch briefly on a few of her significant findings.

In Dunhuang music and dance research, previous scholars and experts have concentrated on its historical origins, the physical appearance of dancers, and the musical instruments, while giving minimal attention to their costumes. The fabric, patterns, colors, dyeing processes, and weaving methods they used have rarely been explained in detail or even understood. This is both due to the deterioration of the artwork as well as lack of textile expertise on the part of scholars in the field of Dunhuang research. Considering this, under the guidance of Zhao Shengliang, a Dunhuang art and history expert, Ms. Jia has studied the styles and textile composition of dance costume as seen in Dunhuang mural art. She has analyzed approximately 100 dancers and their costumes, including clothing and hair

果的意义，首先在于使我们对敦煌壁画舞伎形象服饰的判定有了比较科学的界定标准，而这种标准是研究古代舞蹈种类、风格、特色所必不可少的。同时，研究者利用自己的专业特长，将样式（包括纹样）、色彩、材质纳入服装设计的视野来观察服饰，无疑会对其他研究者带来有益的启示。至于作者在复原古代服饰款式、色彩上所做的努力，更是充分显示了敦煌研究的无限魅力与生命力，也为我们今天进一步探索如何让敦煌文化艺术走进现代社会，走近千家万户，实现古为今用，提供了宝贵的经验。

accessories, making preliminary explorations of textile composition, color analysis, and fabric design classification. Then she reconstructed nine types of dance costumes as seen in the cave murals. This represents the first time that modern textile science has been applied in the field of Dunhuang research. Ms. Jia has made use of her expertise in clothing styles and textile design, including knowledge of dye processes and weaving methods, to study these costumes, shedding light on a previously obscure subject. Her research also demonstrates the infinite fascination and vitality of Dunhuang studies, giving us yet more opportunities to introduce Dunhuang culture to modern society and showing its relevance to the world at large.

参考文献(原文)
Works Cited

[1] 隋书·音乐志. 点校缩印本[M]. 北京：中华书局，1997.

[2] 新唐书·礼乐志. 点校缩印本[M]. 北京：中华书局. 1997.

[3] 中国舞蹈艺术研究会舞蹈史研究组. 全唐诗中的乐舞资料[G]. 北京:人民音乐出版社，1958.

[4] 王克芬. 中国舞蹈史（隋唐五代部分)[M]. 北京. 文化艺术出版社，1987.

[5] 王克芬. 中国舞蹈发展史[M]. 上海：上海人民出版社，1989.

[6] 王克芬. 敦煌石窟全集·舞蹈画卷[M]. 香港：商务印书馆，2001.

[7] 郑汝中. 敦煌壁画乐舞研究[M]. 兰州：甘肃教育出版社，2002.

[8] 高金荣. 敦煌石窟舞乐艺术[M]. 兰州：甘肃人民出版社，2000.

参考文献(译文)
Translation References

[1] 姜秋霞主编. 敦煌文化关键词 [M]. 北京：外语教学与研究出版社，2019.

[2] 俞平伯等著. 唐诗鉴赏辞典[M]. 上海:上海辞书出版社,2013.

[3] 中国社会科学院语言研究所词典编辑室编. 现代汉语辞典(第7版)[M]. 北京：商务印书馆，2016.

[4] 周啸天主编. 唐诗鉴赏辞典 [M]. 北京：商务印书馆国际有限公司，2012.